THEORIES AND METHODS
OF GROUP COUNSELING
IN THE SCHOOLS

THEORIES AND METHODS
OF GROUP COUNSELING
IN THE SCHOOLS

Second Edition

Edited by

GEORGE M. GAZDA

Professor of Education
University of Georgia
Athens, Georgia
and
Consulting Professor of Psychiatry
Medical College of Georgia
Augusta, Georgia

CHARLES C THOMAS · PUBLISHER
Springfield · *Illinois* · *U.S.A.*

Published and Distributed Throughout the World by
CHARLES C THOMAS • PUBLISHER
301-327 East Lawrence Avenue, Springfield, Illinois, U.S.A.

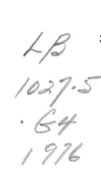

© *1976, by* CHARLES C THOMAS • PUBLISHER

ISBN 0-398-03547-4

Library of Congress Catalog Card Number: 76-1916

With THOMAS BOOKS careful attention is given to all details of manufacturing and design. It is the Publisher's desire to present books that are satisfactory as to their physical qualities and artistic possibilities and appropriate for their particular use. THOMAS BOOKS will be true to those laws of quality that assure a good name and good will.

Library of Congress Cataloging in Publication Data

Gazda, George Michael, 1931-
    Theories and methods of group counseling in the schools.

    Includes bibliographies and indexes.
    1. Personnel service in education. 2. Group counseling. I. Title. [DNLM: 1. Counseling. 2. Group processes. 3. Schools. LB1027.5 T396]
LB1027.5.G4 1976   371.4'044   76-1916
ISBN 0-398-03547-4

Printed in the United States of America
C-11

CONTRIBUTORS

ELIZABETH ACHESON, ED.D., *Associate Professor of Reading/ Language Arts, Rider College, Lawrenceville, New Jersey.*

WARREN C. BONNEY, PH.D., *Professor of Education, Department of Counseling and Human Development Services, University of Georgia, Athens, Georgia.*

DANIEL W. FULLMER, PH.D., *Professor of Educational Psychology, University of Hawaii, Honolulu, Hawaii.*

GEORGE M. GAZDA, ED.D., *Professor of Education, Department of Counseling and Human Development Services, University of Georgia, Athens, Georgia and Consulting Professor of Psychiatry, Department of Psychiatry, Medical College of Georgia, Augusta, Georgia.*

RICHARD A. GRANUM, ED.D., *Director of Adult Counseling, Center for Continuing Education, University of Georgia, Athens, Georgia.*

PRENTISS M. HOSFORD, ED.D., *Consultant, Atlanta Public Schools, Instructional Services Center, and Private Practice Metro-Atlanta Psychological Services, Atlanta, Georgia.*

WALTER M. LIFTON, PH.D., *Professor of Education, Department of Counseling and Personnel Services, School of Education, State University of New York at Albany.*

MERLE M. OHLSEN, PH.D., *Holmstedt Distinguished Professor of Guidance and Psychological Services, Department of Education, Indiana State University, Terre Haute, Indiana.*

BARBARA B. VARENHORST, PH.D., *Consulting Psychologist, Palo Alto Unified School District, Palo Alto, California.*

v

to my brothers
Thomas, Andrew, Lawrence, and Charles

PREFACE

THIS BOOK IS DESIGNED for the school counselor. It is designed to provide a rationale and method for using group counseling at all grade levels in education, and in addition, two chapters are included emphasizing the use of group counseling with families. The editor takes the position that the methods and, to some extent, the rationale for group counseling must vary with the age level and maturity of the counselee. For the preschool and early school child, play and action techniques with mixed sex groups are emphasized; for the preadolescent, a different level of play, more appropriate to the age level, is involved and homogenous grouping with regard to sex is recommended; and for the adolescent and adult, interview group counseling is the treatment of choice. Variations of this "developmental approach" to group counseling also are described, especially for those counselees that are on the borderline of various age groups.

The basic purpose of this book is to give the student of group counseling and the practicing group counselor a theoretically sound and comprehensive method of group counseling for the school setting. The book is intended as a textbook for courses in group counseling theory and procedures, and as such all authors were asked, and for the most part complied, to address themselves to the following areas: theoretical foundations of the position, including a description of how the process produces change (supported with research whenever possible); goals of the treatment; uniqueness of the treatment; counselors' roles; client roles; qualifications of the counselor; composition of the group, including ages, problem types, and preferred number; limitations of the treatment; sample protocols, where they would add clarity; ethical considerations; and suggested readings.

Chapter contributors were selected because of their expertise with a particular approach to group counseling, and because of their current work with school counselors and group counseling in the schools. The positions described in this text are, of course, also appropriate for use by others than school counselors who work in the helping professions within the school setting. School psychologists, psychiatric social workers, clinical psychologists, and others with appropriate training and experience should find this text a useful guide.

Chapter I was included to show the history and development of group counseling and to illustrate the contributions to it by related disciplines. Significant contributors to group counseling and their contributions are also cited in this chapter. An "Historical Time Line" was included to give a perspective to the total group movement and group counseling's position in it. A general framework for group counseling in the schools was established in Chapter I.

Chapter II represents the editor's attempt to summarize the special ethical considerations accompanying group counseling and group work in general. This chapter was intended to represent *guidelines* for consideration and not *rules* to be followed. For the school counselor, the revised Ethical Standards (1974) of the American Personnel and Guidance Association contain the Association's ethical requirements for group workers.

Chapter III contains a summary of the editor's Developmental Group Counseling model. It provides an overview of a model appropriate to all age levels. A more comprehensive description can be found in the editor's text, *Group Counseling: A Developmental Approach.*

Chapter IV by Drs. Prentiss Hosford and Elizabeth Acheson represents an exciting new application of psychodramatic principles to group counseling and group guidance. The rationale of this chapter can be applied to group guidance and counseling; this the authors very ably do. Combining principles from drama and therapy, they have adapted Dorothy Heathcote's Child Drama for use in the less intensive classroom group guidance and the more intensive small counseling groups. This model represents a very significant contribution to group work, especially with children. In addition, it also has demonstrated applications to certain adolescents and adults.

Chapter V represents an eclectic approach to group counseling with adolescents by Dr. Merle Ohlsen. Dr. Ohlsen provided significant leadership to the group counseling field in its beginning, and he continues to make significant contributions through his research, writing, and professional involvement.

In Chapter VI, Dr. Walter Lifton provides an excellent overview of the client-centered approach to group counseling. Dr. Lifton, along with Dr. Ohlsen, was one of the significant early leaders and contributors to the group counseling field, and he continues to exert a major influence on the direction in which the field is moving.

In Chapter VII, Dr. Barbara Varenhorst has presented the viewpoint of a behavioral approach to group counseling. She has been instrumental in the development and implementation of this model in group counseling.

In Chapters VIII and IX the emphasis shifts to group counseling with the family. Dr. Richard Granum has ably presented an Adlerian approach in Chapter VIII, which extends to other groups in addition to the family, whereas Dr. Daniel Fullmer has outlined the basic components of his Family Group Consultation model. With the increasing application of group counseling to the family setting, the editor felt the need to present at least two well-accepted models of this medium.

Although Chapter X represents Dr. Warren Bonney's group counseling model with his emphasis on group dynamics, it also provides the reader with a more detailed discussion of the group process in general. The editor believes that the process summarized by Dr. Bonney applies equally to all the other positions detailed in this text and, therefore, it is included at the end to allow the reader the opportunity to make this mental application to the preceding chapters.

Theories and Methods of Group Counseling in the Schools was developed to improve the counselor's understanding and practice of group counseling in educational settings. It is my wish, as editor, that the efforts of each contributor to this text will improve group counseling services for the ultimate benefit of our youth.

I shall take this opportunity as editor to thank the chapter contributors to this text. Without their cooperation a text such as this could only be approximated, since it would be dependent upon one or more individual *interpretations* of the positions of others. In addition to the contributors I also express my sincere appreciation to my secretary, Mary Rylee, who helped immensely with the correspondence, typing of portions of the manuscript, and assembling the final manuscript. And, as always, my wife Barbara typed much of the manuscript, and my son David was very understanding while I spent many hours working on it. For their many contributions to me, I am most grateful. I wish to recognize my brothers, to whom I have dedicated this book, for the significant influence they had on my life through the numerous ways that they, along with my parents, helped me to appreciate the constructive forces of the small group—the family.

G. M. GAZDA

CONTENTS

THEORIES AND METHODS
OF GROUP COUNSELING
IN THE SCHOOLS

I

GROUP COUNSELING

Origin, Definition, and Contributing
Disciplines and Individuals

GEORGE M. GAZDA

ORIGIN

THE ORIGIN OF the term *group counseling* is somewhat obscure. Its historical antecedent was most liktly group guidance or case conference. In other words, much like its counterpart, group psychotherapy, group counseling in its inception was very likely a class method similar to what is referred to today as *group guidance*. The earliest use in print in the United States of the term *group counseling* appears to have been in 1931. Dr. Richard D. Allen (1931), in an article entitled "A Group Guidance Curriculum in the Senior High School" published in *Education,* used group counseling in the following context:

> *Group thinking and the case-conference method* usually take the place of the recitation. . . . Problems of educational and vocational guidance require teachers who are specially selected and trained for the work, who understand problems of individual differences and are continually studying them. These teachers require continuous contacts with the same pupils for several years, a knowledge of occupations and occupational problems, and special training in methods of individual and group counseling.
>
> All of these considerations draw attention to the class counselor as the logical teacher of the new unit. There is much similarity between the techniques of individual guidance and group guidance. When the counselor finds by individual interviews that certain problems are common to most of the pupils, such problems become units in the group guidance course. The class discussions of these problems should reduce the length and number of individual interviews with a saving of considerable time and expense. In fact, the separation of group counseling from individual counseling would seem very short-sighted.
>
> If the above principle prevails, the next serious problem concerns its practical application in the time schedule of the school. Ideally,

such a course should be *extensive* rather than *intensive* in its nature, in order to accomplish its objectives effectively. Its purpose is to arouse interests in current educational, vocational and social problems, to develop social attitudes, and to build up a background of occupational information. Such objectives require considerable *time extended over several years* (p. 190).

This lengthy quotation is included to show that what Allen described as *group counseling* in 1931 today is generally referred to as *group guidance*. Also, it should be noted that Allen used the terms *case-conference*, *group guidance*, and *group counseling* interchangeably.

Although Allen's use of *group counseling* appeared in print in 1931, it is very likely that he had used the expression before 1931. For example, John M. Brewer, writing the Introduction to Allen's *Organization and Supervision of Guidance in Public Education*, published in 1937, wrote, "For more than a decade his colleagues in the Harvard Summer School have urged Dr. Allen to put his ideas into permanent form" (xxi).

Jones, as early as 1934, in his second edition of *Principles of Guidance*, states, "It [group guidance] is a term that has come into use chiefly through the excellent work of Richard D. Allen in Providence, Rhode Island. It includes all those forms of guidance activities that are undertaken in groups or in classes" (p. 284). Jones (1934, p. 291) also refers to the "Boston Plan for Group Counseling in Intermediate Schools" and cites the source as two circulars[1] developed by the Committee on Guidance of the Boston Public Schools. Although group counseling is used in the title of the Boston publication, the description of the nature of the process described by Jones places it squarely in the realm of group guidance and not group counseling as it is defined today.

In his fifth edition of *Principles of Guidance*, published in 1963, Jones had this to say about Allen's case conference procedures: "A technique that combined the techniques of 'counsel-

---

1. Boston Public Schools: *Guidance—Educational and Vocational, A Tentative Plan for Group Counseling,* Board of Superintendents' Circular No. 2, 1928-1929, and Board of Superintendents' Circular No. 17, 1928-1929, First Supplement to Board of Superintendents' Circular No. 2. Boston, Printing Department, 1929.

ing in groups' and 'group counseling' was used by Allen and practiced in the public schools of Providence, Rhode Island more than twenty-five years ago" (pp. 218-219). Jones contends that the purpose of the case conference was to provide the counselor with a means for students to discuss their personal and social relationships. Common problems of group members were used as the basis for discussion. A case was presented to the group to illustrate the problem, and all students were expected to compare their own experiences with those revealed through the case. The leader encouraged the group to seek the more permanent values exposed rather than the more immediate temporary ones, and the leader also encouraged the participants to consider the effect upon others of their proposed action before performing it. Conclusions were summarized to formulate generalizations for other situations. Jones stated that Allen believed his method worked best when "each case represented a common, usual, or typical situation that concerned most of the group. The case should involve persons and personal or social relations" (1963, p. 219).

According to Jones, Allen characterized the case conference leader as one who never expressed approval or disapproval of any opinion or attitude and never stated opinions of his or her own. In addition, the leader was impartial and open-minded and encouraged the expression of all points of view; the leader would occasionally restate and summarize the group's thinking and organize the group so that it was large enough to guarantee a diversity of opinions, but not so large as to prevent each member the opportunity to enter into discussion.

The goals and procedures of Allen's case conference approach described by Jones are similar to those of contemporary group counselors. Most contemporary group counselors, however, do not structure their groups around specific cases.

DEFINITION[2]

Although group counesling is very likely here to stay—witness its inclusion in the *Review of Educational Research, Psycholog-*

---

2. For additional treatment of this topic, see Chapter III "Group Counseling: A Developmental Approach" in this text.

ical Abstracts, Education Index, and similar indexes and references—it was not without substantial opposition. A brief tracing
of the resistance to its acceptance is outlined below through the
use of selected quotations. In his second edition of *Principles of
Guidance,* Jones (1934) wrote, "Counseling has such an intimate
sound that it would seem advisable to limit it to that intimate,
heart-to-heart talk between teacher and pupil. It is frankly admitted that it is difficult to draw the line sharply between the essence of what is done in the personal interview and what is done
in small groups. But it is even more difficult to make any distinction between group counseling and the more modern forms
of class work . . ." (p. 274).

Almost twenty years later, in his fifth edition of the same text,
Jones (1963) wrote, "The values of group guidance are generally accepted, but the term 'group counseling' is still rejected by
many guidance authorities. Some believe that group counseling
is an 'anomaly' and say that it is as silly to speak of 'group counseling 'as 'group courtship' " (pp. 217-218).

In the thirty-seventh yearbook of the National Society for the
Study of Education, Part I, "Guidance in Educational Institutions," Gilbert Wrenn (1938) wrote, "First of all, counseling is
personal. It cannot be performed with a group. 'Group counseling' is a tautology; counseling is always personal" (p. 119). And
in 1942, Brewer, also a highly respected guidance authority,
wrote, " 'Group guidance' was invented, apparently, as a term to
mean classroom study, recitation, or discussion; is it any longer
needed? 'Group counseling' is a similar term, but might it not be
best to confine the word counseling to work with individuals?"
(p. 294).

Slavson (1964), too, resists the use of the term group counseling. He stated, "Counseling should be done on a one-to-one relation" (p. 102). He also believes that there are different treat-
ments for different levels of the person's psyche. On the continuum from least to most in terms of depth and intensity of
treatment and level of psyche reached, Slavson places group
counseling at the level of least depth and intensity and most superficial level of psyche dealt with and group psychotherapy at

the level of greatest depth and intensity and deepest level of psyche reached. Group guidance lies in the middle of this continuum. In terms of duration of treatment, the order from shortest to longest is group counseling, group guidance, and group psychotherapy. Slavson's conception of group counseling and his placement of it on the above continuum is not in accord with the majority of group counselors.

Gazda, Duncan, and Sisson (1971) surveyed one thousand members of the American Personnel and Guidance Association's Interest Group on Group Procedures to determine distinctions among various group procedures, among other purposes. (The majority of the 164 respondents held doctorate degrees and were members of the American Personnel and Guidance Association and/or the American Psychological Association.)

The respondents were asked to indicate distinctions that they would make among group guidance, group counseling, T-groups, sensitivity groups, encounter groups, and psychotherapy groups on each of the following criteria: (1) purposes of each, (2) clientele best served, and (3) "essential" professional preparation requirements. Group guidance was viewed as essentially different (on all three criteria) from the other group procedures. Likewise, group therapy was viewed as distinctly different from group counseling, sensitivity, and T-groups on the same dimensions. However, the respondents did not distinguish between group counseling, T-groups, and sensitivity groups on the three criteria. (In other words, they viewed these three group procedures as similar on the criteria.) In the author's chapter of this text: "Group Counseling: A Developmental Approach," Figure III-1 illustrates the relationships among group procedures. Group guidance and certain human potential-type groups are described as primarily preventive in purpose; group counseling, T-groups, sensitivity groups, encounter groups, and organizational development (OD) groups are described as partially preventive, growth-engendering, and remedial in purpose; group psychotherapy is described as remedial in purpose. The clientele served, degree of disturbance of the clientele, setting of the treatment, goals of treatment, size of group, and length and duration of treatment are, accordingly, reflected in the emphasis or purpose of each of these three distinctly different groupings. Although the lines between group procedures, especially group counseling, encounter groups and therapy groups are becoming more and more blurred because of each borrowing from the other, there is still need to make certain distinctions based on the criteria described in the author's *Group Counseling: A Developmental Approach* (1971) and summarized in this text in a chapter by the same title.

Lifton (1966) also has dealt with the confusion of "group" terminology (including group counseling) and concluded "that although some nine years have passed since the earlier edition of this text [his first edition] was written, confusion and disagreement over the meaning of terms still exist" (p. 13). A "group procedures" interest group of some thirty members of the American Personnel and Guidance Association met at the Association's 1966 Convention in Washington, D. C., and appeared to confirm Lifton's conclusion when they had difficulty differentiating between group guidance and group counseling.[3]

To muddy the waters still more, the term *multiple counseling* was introduced by Froehlich (n.d.). Froehlich's use of multiple counseling is consistent with the generally accepted use of *group counseling;* however, Helen Driver (1958) introduced multiple counseling to mean the conjunctive use of individual counseling with group counseling. Still others frequently use multiple counseling when they are referring to the use of more than one counselor.

Granted the confusion over the definition of group counseling, there is evidence that it is abating. A survey of fifty-four of the more prominent contributors to the field of group counseling for the period 1960 to 1965 revealed that 80 percent preferred the term *group counseling* to *group guidance, multiple counseling, group therapy, psychodrama,* and *sociodrama* when they were asked to select the term that they preferred to use to describe "counseling with more than one individual simultaneously" (Gazda, Duncan, and Meadows, 1967). This appears con-

---

3. Personal communication.

sistent with a conclusion reached by Bennett as early as 1963. She states, "The term group counseling has become very popular, and practices under this name have been introduced rather widely in school systems. One might almost call it an epidemic" (p. 136).

Forty-three of the respondents to the survey by Gazda, et al. (1967), who preferred the term group counseling were asked to define it. From their definitions, a composite definition was generated.

Group counseling is a dynamic interpersonal process focusing on conscious thought and behavior and involving the therapy functions of permissiveness, orientation to reality, catharsis, and mutual trust, caring, understanding, acceptance, and support. The therapy functions are created and nurtured in a small group through the sharing of personal concerns with one's peers and the counselor(s). The group counselees are basically normal individuals with various concerns which are not debilitating to the extent requiring extensive personality change. The group counselees may utilize the group interaction to increase understanding and acceptance of values and goals and to learn and/or unlearn certain attitudes and behaviors (Gazda, Duncan, and Meadows, 1967, p. 305).

DISCIPLINES CONTRIBUTING TO GROUP COUNSELING

The previous reference to R. D. Allen's use of the term group counseling suggests that Allen may have coined the expression; however, the author does not contend that he has discovered the missing link. More likely than not, several individuals were using the term in Allen's era. Several movements have contributed to the group counseling movement. The most significant of these contributing movements were group psychotherapy, child guidance, vocational guidance, social casework, group work, group dynamics, and the human potential movement.

Group Psychotherapy

Corsini (1957) has referred to group psychotherapy as "a conglomerate of methods and theories having diverse multiple origins in the past, resulting inevitably from social demands, and developed in various forms by many persons" (p. 9). J. L. Moreno (1966) contends that group psychotherapy has its roots in medicine, sociology, and religion. If one accepts July 1, 1905 (Hadden, 1955), the date that J. H. Pratt introduced his "class method," as the beginning of group psychotherapy, rather than some ancient ritual such as Mesmer's group treatment through suggestion, the history of group psychotherapy covers approximately a mere seventy years.

The term *group therapy* was introduced by J. L. Moreno in 1931 (Z. Moreno, 1966), and *group psychotherapy* was introduced, also by J. L. Moreno in 1932 (Corsini, 1957). For the most part, group therapy and group psychotherapy are used synonymously in current discourse; group therapy has become the shortened or colloquial version of group psychotherapy.

Even though the term group psychotherapy was not coined until 1932 by J. L. Moreno, an emigrant to America, there is considerable evidence that group psychotherapy is an American invention and that various forms were being practiced in the United States, mostly by psychiatrists and ministers, long before Moreno labeled the practice. Group therapy was coined by Moreno about the same time as the expression *group counseling* was used in the literature by R. D. Allen; however, there is every reason to believe that Allen's use of group counseling was more closely related to group instruction than was the meaning that Moreno intended when he coined group therapy and group psychotherapy.

Numerous systems of group psychotherapy were described in the professional literature well in advance of the group counseling professional literature. It is recognized, therefore, that group psychotherapy, as practiced and as described in the literature, provided much of the theoretical rationale for the emergence of group counseling. Just how much credit the group psychotherapy movement should receive for the emergence and development of group counseling is uncertain, but the writer believes it to be considerable, probably the most significant of the several disciplines or movements contributing to the emergence and growth of group counseling.

Child Guidance

There exists the possibility that group counseling originated in Europe. Dreikurs and Corsini (1954) contend that between 1900 and 1930 major steps were being made in Europe toward a systematic use of the group method called "collective counceling *(sic)*." They believe that Alfred Adler, in his child guidance clinics in Vienna, was likely the first psychiatrist to use *collective counseling* formally and systematically.

Ansbacher and Ansbacher (1956) translated many of Adler's works, and in their commentary on his writing they stated, "Although Adler himself never practiced group therapy he suggested its use for the treatment of criminals" (p. 347). It is not because of his suggestion for using group therapy with criminals that Adler is considered by some to be the father of the group counseling movement, but rather because of his application of group techniques in his child guidance clinics. According to the Ansbachers, Adler was conducting group procedures—perhaps collective counseling—as early as 1922.

The rationale and methods employed by Adler and his followers are described by Ansbacher and Ansbacher (1956). However, the Ansbachers, because they were unable to find "more than a mere mention" of Adler's rationale and methods in his own writings, were forced to turn to secondary sources, i.e. the writings of Seidler and Zilat, and Rayner and Holub. Seidler and Zilat described the "public" character of Adlerian child guidance clinics; for example, the child was interviewed in the presence of an adult audience. Doris Rayner defends this form of treatment by stating that the child benefits because the child comes to view his or her difficulty as a "community problem" and the audience (parents) receives an education in parent-child behavior. Martha Holub agreed with Rayner's position of the mutual therapeutic benefits to the child and adult through participation in this Adlerian "open-door" treatment procedure.

In 1942 Brewer described the child guidance movement "as yet largely dissociated from the work of the schools . . ." (p. 263).

Nevertheless, because of its many similarities, the child guidance movement has influenced, directly or indirectly, the group counseling movement. Currently, Adlerian-oriented counselors are making a very significant contribution in elementary school guidance programs and parent and child guidance clinics not too unlike those originated by Adler in Vienna.

Vocational Guidance

Frank Parsons has been recognized as the father of the vocational guidance movement because of his founding of the Vocational Bureau of Boston in 1908 (Brewer, 1942). Just when, where, and by whom the word *group* was added to the word *guidance* is not known; however, according to Brewer (1942), Charles L. Jacobs of San Jose was one of the first to suggest a wider use of the term *guidance* when, in the October 1915 issue of *Manual Training and Vocational Education,* he stated that his work included three departments—educational guidance, vocational guidance, and avocational guidance.

Classes in Occupational Information. As early as 1908 William A. Wheatley was instrumental in introducing a course in occupational information for freshman boys at Westport, Connecticut High School. Similar courses were offered in Boston and New York City soon after Wheatley's (Brewer, 1942).

Homeroom. McKown authored a text, *Home Room Guidance,* as early as 1934. The content of the text and the fact that McKown proposed the director of guidance as the director of homeroom guidance suggests its close association to group guidance and counseling. In fact, some schools referred to the homeroom as "the 'guidance hour,' or 'guidance room'" (McKown, 1934, p. 53). In a publication of approximately the same vintage of McKown's, Strang (1935) cited the contribution of the homeroom teacher as being fourfold: "to establish friendly relationships, to discover the abilities and needs, and to develop right attitudes toward school, home, and community" (p. 116). Once more the group guidance and counseling "flavor" was expressed in the work of the homeroom teacher.

EXTRACURRICULAR ACTIVITIES. C. R. Foster authored a book,

Extra Curricular Activities, in 1925, in which he recognized guidance as an extracurricular activity. In the same text, Foster also urged the counselor to "hold many group conferences with the students on the subject of future educational or vocational plans" (p. 182). Pittsburgh was cited by Foster as including instructional guidance taking "the form of tenth-grade group conferences which were held for the purpose of discussing Pittsburgh's industrial life and the opportunities it affords the young people" (p. 183).

The vocational guidance movement was instrumental in the introduction of homeroom guidance, classes in occupational information, and certain extracurricular activities that were forerunners of current group guidance and group counseling.

Social Casework

In reviewing the history of the Marriage Council of Philadelphia, Gaskill and Mudd (1950) stated that group counseling and family life education had been part of the "Marriage Council's service from the agency's inception in 1932" (p. 194). Whether or not the term *group counseling* itself was actually used by the Council as early as 1932 and whether or not the treatment was similar to current group counseling is not indicated. However, Gaskill and Mudd gave the following definition of group counseling for which they express their indebtedness to Hazel Froscher, Margery Klein, and Helen Phillips:

> . . . a dynamic relationship between a counselor and the members of a group, involving presentation and discussion of subjects about which the counselor has special knowledge, which is of general or specific concern to the group, and around which emotions may be brought out and attitudes developed or changed. The relationship between the group members themselves and the counselor's use of this is essentially important in the total process (1950, p. 195).

The definition implies that the counselor gives a presentation and encourages discussion of it. Gaskill and Mudd (1950), in their description of the group counseling sessions, indicate that the group ranged between thirty-five and fifty persons in size, and they further described the group sessions as a *course* including speakers other than the group counselor. This approach to group counseling seems more closely related to group guidance or a family living class rather than the typical small, eight- to ten-member counseling groups where leader-imposed content is absent or minimal.

Group Work

Sullivan (1952) described a group in this manner:

> The group must be a small stable one which feels itself as an entity and which the individual can feel close identification. Membership . . . is voluntary. There is a group leader, who is consciously making constructive use of the process of personality interaction among the members. The leader utilizes the desire of a normal person to be accepted by his fellows. He establishes the dignity of the individual and teaches acceptance of differences in race, creed, and nationality. Group work stresses programs evolved by the group itself, in consultation with the leader who guides toward socially desirable ends. Creative activities are encouraged to provide legitimate channels of self-expressions and to relieve emotional stress. Competition for its own sake is minimized and group members learn from situations where cooperation brings rich satisfaction. The trained leader arranges for leadership practice by group members; individual responsibility and group responsibility grow as the group takes on new functions. The atmosphere is friendly, informal, and democratic (p. 189).

This description of group work contains many of the ingredients that are present in definitions of group counseling, and the possible influence on group counseling of the group work specialists becomes readily apparent.

Group Dynamics

The group dynamics movement, according to Bonner (1959), had its beginning in the late 1800's, notably in Europe. Contribution to the group dynamics discipline came from sociology, psychology, philosophy, and education, but primarily from sociology and psychology.

Bonner is careful not to give major credit to a single individual or discipline; however, he cites Kurt Lewin and J. L. Moreno for making significant, but dissimilar contributions during the contemporary phase of development—1930's to the present.

The National Training Laboratories (NTL) was established in Bethel, Maine in 1947, however, "it was not until the middle to late 1950's before the tools and techniques of group dynamics really found their way into education and more specifically, into guidance" (Glanz and Hayes, 1967, p. 4). In 1964, Durkin, after a careful survey of group dynamicists and group therapists wrote:

> In spite of the general impression to the contrary, there was almost no therapy actually being conducted on solely group dynamics principles by group dynamicists. From private correspondence with some of the leading social scientists, I learned that they did not acknowledge group dynamics therapy as an identifiable approach and that they were meticulous in distinguishing between their work and group therapy (p. 4).

One can conclude from the Glanz and Hayes statement above that group dynamics principles and concepts only very recently have begun to affect the field of *group guidance*. Also, Durkin emphasized that, although group dynamics had begun to influence the field of group therapy, as late as 1964 there was still no complete application of group therapy based primarily on group dynamics principles.

The application of group dynamics principles to *group counseling* has a rather recent history. The explication of these applications can be found in the writings of Bonney (1969), Gazda (1971), Fullmer (1971), and Mahler (1969).

Human Potential Movement

The human potential emphasis began to be felt in the early and middle 1960's. Its origin is multiple and diverse. The disciplines of psychology, education, and management have made significant contributions. Some of the more influential contributors have been Carl Rogers, Abraham Maslow, Herbert Otto, Jack Gibb, and William Schutz. The more practical elements of the movement are being applied to classroom instruction and, in that sense, are *group guidance* oriented. In the highly experimental and perhaps even ethically questionable forms of group application, it is affecting *group counseling* by introducing more body contact and more structured game playing.

SIGNIFICANT CONTRIBUTORS

For one to attempt to appraise and record some of the most significant contributors to the speciality of *group counseling* while living in the era of the beginning of the movement is to court professional suicide; nevertheless, an attempt will be made to sketch briefly the author's perception of those who have been and, in most instances, are still making significant contributions to the group counseling movement. The author concluded that the leaders of the group counseling movement are citizens of the United States, and this assumption seems supported by Brewer (1942). If this conclusion is erroneous, it might at least stimulate others to investigate and challenge it.

The credit for coining the term group counseling may be attributed to Richard D. Allen, although there is no absolute proof of this. Others who were among the first to publish and teach in the field of group counseling were Margaret Bennett, Ruth Strang, and Jane Warters. Evelyn Gaskill and Emily Mudd should be cited for their early use of group counseling in social casework and Hanna Grunwald for the current application of group counseling in case work agencies.

Clifford Froehlich and Helen Driver have influenced the group counseling movement with their introduction of multiple counseling, and E. Wayne Wright, upon the death of Froehlich, continued the multiple counseling emphasis. However, multiple counseling is now only rarely accepted as the preferred term for group counseling (Gazda, Duncan, and Meadows, 1967).

Merle Ohlsen, Fred Proff, and several of their colleagues and students at the University of Illinois, the author among them, are known for their early attempt to research group counseling. Ohlsen has also contributed two significant texts to the field. Ben Cohn (who was influenced by Ohlsen) and his associates of the Board of Cooperative Educational Services of Bedford Hills,

New York, researched the effects of group counseling on acting-out adolescents. Stanley Capalan did research with similar groups. Clarence Mahler and Edson Caldwell co-authored one of the first texts on group counseling in the school, and Mahler has since produced his own very useful text.

Among those representing the various schools of group counseling, Walter Lifton has been the most prominent proponent of the client-centered approach to group counseling. Rudolf Dreikurs, Manford Sonstegard, Oscar Christensen, Donald Dinkmeyer, James Muro, G. Edward Stormer, and Richard Granum are among the most significant Adlerian-oriented contributors to the field of group counseling. John Krumboltz, Barbara Varenhorst, Carl E. Thoresen, and Beverly Potter are making their contributions with a behavior-oriented application of group counseling.

Dan Fullmer and Harold Bernard have introduced to the field *family group consultation*, whereas Joseph Knowles has been instrumental in the successful application of the group approach to *pastoral counseling*.

Robert Carkhuff has influenced the direction that group counseling and counseling in general is taking with his research and writings regarding the "core dimensions" of a helping relationship and his over-all model—Systematic Human Resources Development (HRD).

There are many others[4] who have contributed significantly to the development of group counseling through their training procedures, professional involvement, research, and/or writing. Al-

---

4. Norman Kagan, John Vriend, Wayne Dyer, Joseph Lechowicz, James Lee, Vincent Calia, Jack Duncan, Kevin Geoffroy, Fannie Cooley, Richard Granum, Larry Hornsby, Robert Kaltenbach, Jonell Kirby, Roger Peters, Charles Truax, Ken Matheney, Sherman Day, Jack Blakeman, Ronald Ruble, William Mermis, Gratton Kemp, Thomas J. Long, Gary Landreth, Sharon Anderson, Richard Malnati, Marilyn Bates, C. E. Johnson, Richard Caple, Al Dye, Richard Diedrich, David Zimpfer, C. E. Smith, Merville Shaw, Wesley Schmidt, Frank Noble, Cal Daane, Sheldon Glass, William Lewis, W. F. Hill, M. E. Meadows, Al Roark, Betty Bosdell, Earl Koile, Robert Myrick, Robert Berg, S. Dietz, Pete Havens, Oscar Mink, Robert Griffin, Burl Gilliand, Alicia Tilley, Thomas Hennessy, Robert Naun, and Marion Belka.

Figure I-1

Group Procedures Historical Time Line

Group Psychotherapy

J. H. Pratt ("class method") (1905) Boston, Mass.

J. L. Moreno (1910) Vienna – – – – – – – – – – – – – –|

                                              Group Guidance

                    G. Boyden (1912) – – – –|
                    Beaufort, Connecticut

A. Adler (1921) Vienna – – – – – – – – – – – – – – – – –|
L. C. Marsh & E. W. Lazell (1921) U.S.A.– – – – – – – – –|
T. Burrow (1925) U.S.A. – – – – – – – – – – – – – – – –| – A. Adler
L. Wender (1929) U.S.A. – – – – – – – – – – – – – – – –| (1921)
P. Schilder (1930's) U.S.A.– – – – – – – – – – – – – – – –| Vienna
S. R. Slavson (1930's) U.S.A.

                                            Group Counseling

      J. L. Moreno coined term – – – – – – – – – – – – – –| R. D. Allen (1931) – – –|
      "group therapy" (1931)   Providence, R. I.
      J. L. Moreno coined term – – – – – – – – – – – – – –|
      "group psychotherapy" (1932)
      J. L. Moreno founded the – – – – – – – – – – – – – –|
      American Society of Group Psycho-
      therapy and Psychodrama (ASGPP-
      1941-42)
      S. R. Slavson founded the – – – – – – – – – – – – –| First Annual Meeting of
      American Group Psychotherapy   ASGPP at the Sociometric
      Association (AGPA) (1942)   —Institute, New York City,
                                              1943
      First Annual Conference of – – – – – – – – – – – –|
      AGPA held at Russell Sage Foundation
      Jan. 14 & 15, 1944.

              T-Groups

K. Lewin, L. Bradford, R. Lip-
pitt, & K. Benne (Connecticut
Laboratory, 1946)
  |

L. Bradford, R. Lippitt, & K.   *Sociatry (Group Psycho-* – –|
Benne (Gould Academy, Beth- *therapy and Psychodrama)*
el Maine "Basic Skill Training founded by J. L. Moreno,
Groups," 1947)   1947
  |

"T-group" name change from *International Journal of* – –|
BST Group, 1949   *Group Psychotherapy*
  | founded by S. R. Slavson
National Training Laboratory (1949-51)
in Group Development of the
National Education Associa-
tion with Leland Bradford 1st
Exec. Dir. 1950
  |

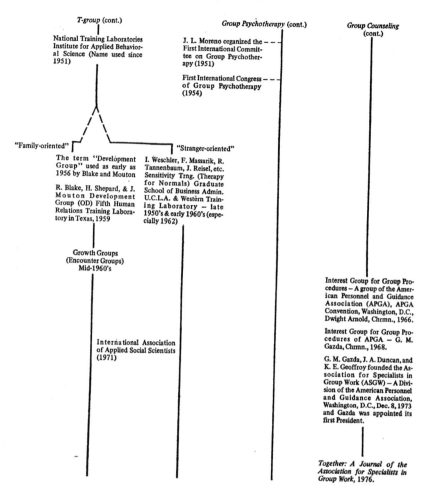

T-group (cont.)

National Training Laboratories Institute for Applied Behavioral Science (Name used since 1951)

"Family-oriented"

The term "Development Group" used as early as 1956 by Blake and Mouton

R. Blake, H. Shepard, & J. Mouton Development Group (OD) Fifth Human Relations Training Laboratory in Texas, 1959

Growth Groups (Encounter Groups) Mid-1960's

International Association of Applied Social Scientists (1971)

Group Psychotherapy (cont.)

J. L. Moreno organized the First International Committee on Group Psychotherapy (1951)

First International Congress of Group Psychotherapy (1954)

"Stranger-oriented"

I. Weschler, F. Massarik, R. Tannenbaum, J. Reisel, etc. Sensitivity Trng. (Therapy for Normals) Graduate School of Business Admin. U.C.L.A. & Western Training Laboratory — late 1950's & early 1960's (especially 1962)

Group Counseling (cont.)

Interest Group for Group Procedures — A group of the American Personnel and Guidance Association (APGA), APGA Convention, Washington, D.C., Dwight Arnold, Chrmn., 1966.

Interest Group for Group Procedures of APGA — G. M. Gazda, Chrmn., 1968.

G. M. Gazda, J. A. Duncan, and K. E. Geoffroy founded the Association for Specialists in Group Work (ASGW) — A Division of the American Personnel and Guidance Association, Washington, D.C., Dec. 8, 1973 and Gazda was appointed its first President.

Together: A Journal of the Association for Specialists in Group Work, 1976.

though the list of contributors is lengthy, it is by no means inclusive. For example, Lechowicz (1973) identified over 229 "experts" in group counseling. His criteria for defining an expert included:

1. The author must have published in the area of group counseling, group guidance, group psychotherapy, or multiple counseling.
2. At least two different publications of each author have been cited by other authors.
3. The cited publications were dated between 1950 and 1972 (p. 41).

In 1966, Dwight Arnold assumed a leadership role in develop ing an "interest group" among the American Personnel and Guidance Association members for the purpose of defining the field, sharing information on training programs, and establishing communication among practitioners to provide some form of organization to the loose-knit group counseling movement. The author assumed Dr. Arnold's coordinator role in 1968 and developed this interest group from approximately one hundred to over one thousand five hundred. On December 8, 1973, the author, along with Jack Duncan and Kevin Geoffroy, succeeded in establishing the Association for Specialists in Group Work (ASGW) as the eleventh division of the American Personnel and Guidance Association (the parent organization of over 40,000 members). He served as the new division's first president, followed by Jack Duncan and Clarence Mahler. At the time of the writing of this chapter ASGW has grown to an association of over one thousand members. With the establishment of this new division for group work, of which group counseling is the core, the continued growth and impact of group counseling seems likely.

Although this chapter focused primarily on the historical development of group psychotherapy and group counseling, many other related group procedures were developing and influencing these two group specialities. In the 1960's especially, clear differentiations among the many group procedures and disciplines became difficult. Figure I-1—Group Procedures Historical Time Line—is included (1) to illustrate the concurrent development of several group disciplines, (2) to illustrate the possible mutual influence of the disciplines/procedures on each other, and (3) to serve as a brief summary of several significant group developments which, for the most part, were cited in this chapter.

SUMMARY

This chapter traces the history and development of group counseling and defines it. Significant contributors and a brief summary of their contributions are included. The contributions of related disciplines to the development of group counseling are outlined. A historical time line is developed to illustrate the interrelationship in the development of the small group field.

REFERENCES

Allen, R. D.: A group guidance curriculum in the senior high school. *Education, 52:*189, 1931.

Ansbacher, H. L., and Ansbacher, R. R. (Eds.): *The Individual Psychology of Alfred Adler.* New York, Basic, 1956.

Bennett, M. E.: *Guidance and Counseling in Groups,* 2nd ed. New York, McGraw, 1963.

Bonner, H.: *Group Dynamics.* New York, Ronald, 1959.

Bonney, W. C.: Group counseling and developmental processes. In Gazda, G. M. (Ed.): *Theories and Methods of Group Counseling in the Schools.* Springfield, Thomas, 1969.

Brewer, J. M.: Introduction. In Allen, R. D. (Ed.): *Organization and Supervision of Guidance in Public Education.* New York, Inor, 1937.

Brewer, J. M.: *History of Vocational Guidance.* New York, Har-Row, 1942.

Corsini, R. J.: *Methods of Group Psychotherapy.* Chicago, William James, 1957.

Dreikurs, R., and Corsini, R. J.: Twenty years of group psychotherapy. *American Journal of Psychiatry, 110:*567, 1954.

Driver, H. I.: *Counseling and Learning in Small-group Discussion.* Madison, Monona, 1958.

Durkin, H., et al. (AGPA Committee on History): A brief history of the American Group Psychotherapy Association. *International Journal of Group Psychotherapy, 21(4):*406, 1971.

Foster, C. R.: *Extra-curricular Activities in the High School.* Richmond, Johnson, 1925.

Froehlich, C. P.: *Multiple Counseling—A Research Proposal.* Berkeley, University of California Department of Education, n.d.

Fullmer, D. W.: *Counseling: Group Theory and System.* Scranton, Intl Textbook, 1971.

Gaskill, E. R., and Mudd, E. H.: A decade of group counseling. *Social Casework, 31:*194, 1950.

Gazda, G. M.: *Group Counseling: A Developmental Approach.* Boston, Allyn, 1971.

Gazda, G. M., Duncan, J. A., and Meadows, M. E.: Counseling and group procedures—report of a survey. *Counselor Education and Supervision, 6:*305, 1967.

Gazda, G. M., Duncan, J. A., and Sisson, P. J.: Professional issues in group work. *Personnel and Guidance Journal, 49(8):*637, 1971.

Glanz, E. C., and Hayes, R. W.: *Groups in Guidance,* 2nd ed. Boston, Allyn, 1968.

Hadden, S. B.: Historic background of group psychotherapy. *International Journal of Group Psychotherapy,* 5:62, 1955.

Jones, A. J.: *Principles of Guidance,* 2nd ed. New York, McGraw, 1934.

Jones, A. J.: *Principles of Guidance,* 5th ed. New York, McGraw, 1963.

Lechowicz, J. S.: *Group Counseling Instruction: A Model Based on Behavioral Objectives Developed Via the Delphi Technique.* Unpublished doctoral dissertation, University of Georgia, Athens, Georgia, 1973.

Lifton, W. M.: *Working with Groups,* 2nd ed. New York, Wiley, 1966.

Mahler, C. A.: *Group Counseling in the Schools.* Boston, HM, 1969.

McKowan, H. C.: *Home Room Guidance.* New York, McGraw, 1934.

Moreno, J. L., et al. (Eds.): *The International Handbook of Group Psychotherapy.* New York, Philos Lib, 1966.

Moreno, Z. T.: Evolution and dynamics of the groups psychotherapy movement. In Moreno, J. L., et al. (Eds.): *The International Handbook of Group Psychotherapy.* New York, Philos Lib, 1966.

Slavson, S. R.: *A Textbook in Analytic Group Psychotherapy.* New York, Intl Univs Pr, 1964.

Strang, R.: *The Role of the Teacher in Personnel Work.* New York, Bureau of Publications, Teachers College, Columbia Univ., 1935.

Sullivan, D. F. (Ed.): *Readings in Group Work.* New York, Assn Pr, 1952.

Wrenn, C. G.: Counseling with students. In Whipple, G. M. (Ed.): *Guidance in Educational Institutions, Part I. National Society for the Study of Education.* Bloomington, Public School Pub, 1938.

II

GUIDELINES FOR ETHICAL PRACTICE IN GROUP COUNSELING AND RELATED GROUP WORK[1]

GEORGE M. GAZDA

INTRODUCTION

THE TITLE OF THIS CHAPTER was carefully considered, because no single author can hope to do more than present some tentative guidelines based on a search and evaluation of the numerous positions taken by a wide range of professionals engaged in group work, especially counseling, therapy and quasitherapy groups. (The reader is reminded at this point that the author does not intend to deal directly with the training of group leaders since wide variations will be dictated by the potential group leader's discipline.)

A survey (Gazda et al., 1973) of twenty-six professional associations, societies and/or individuals representing these associations in which group procedures were a part of the functions employed by the membership, produced twenty responses. The twenty respondents represented all of the basic professional associations wherein the membership would use group work in their practice. The "codes of ethics," "ethical guidelines/standards," and similar documents were obtained from each of these associations. In addition, draft documents and published articles on the subject of ethical practices in group work were carefully studied in an attempt to provide this overview of the recommendations that are being espoused by concerned professionals and associations. The Suggested Readings at the end of this chapter indicates the extent of Gazda's review.

---

1. The basic part of this chapter has been reproduced from G. M. Gazda's chap. III: "Some Tentative Guidelines for Ethical Practice by Group Work Practitioners." In G. M. Gazda (Ed.): *Basic Approaches to Group Psychotherapy and Group Counseling*, 2nd ed. Springfield, Thomas, 1975. Courtesy of Charles C Thomas, Publisher.

For this author, the most interesting outcome of his review was the fact that the literature is beginning to reflect a fair degree of agreement on a number of basic issues or topics that are especially relevant to group work. In other words, a certain consensus is being achieved on what constitutes the basic ethical issues that cut across many and varied group procedures and related disciplines in the "helping professions."

Although the emphasis in this text is group counseling, the increasing similarity of other forms of group work to this form is blurring the distinctions and therefore suggests a look at the total group work discipline. Chapter III of this text illustrates how the author differentiates among the various kinds of group work by classifying them along a prevention-remediation continuum, i.e. whether the goals or purposes are primarily preventative or remedial/rehabilitative, including combinations of the two ends of the continuum. For purposes of this discussion only group work will be defined, with an emphasis on small group work for personal growth rather than task accomplishment; but special types of group work may be the focus with respect to particular guidelines. *Group work refers to the dynamic interaction between collections of individuals for prevention or remediation of difficulties or for the enhancement of personal growth/enrichment through the interaction of those who meet together for a commonly agreed upon purpose and at prearranged times.* A number of people meeting in this purposeful way have the potential to become a group if they succeed in clarifying their goals, agreeing on ways to accomplish them, and maintaining the committed participation of all involved.

Lakin (1972, p. 7) has identified what he considers to be the "conditions for membership" in "experiential" groups. His definition of experiential groups includes interpersonal encounter, psychotherapy, and sensitivity groups. His conditions for membership (what one might call "functional" membership) include the following:[2]

---

2. Martin Lakin: *Experimental Groups: The Uses of Interpersonal Encounter, Psychotherapy Groups, and Sensitivity Training,* 1972. General Learning Corporation. Reprinted by permission.

1. Contribute to the shaping and coherence of the group;
2. Invest in it emotionally;
3. Help move it toward a goal [metagoal];
4. Help establish its norms, and obey them;
5. Take on some specific role or function;
6. Help establish a viable level of open communication;
7. Help establish a desired level of intimacy;
8. Make contributions relevant to others;
9. Make a place for each person;
10. Acknowledge the group's significance.

Some exposition of what is meant by ethical guidelines or "ethics" also seems apropos. *Ethics of group work are those agreed upon practices consistent with broader ethical commitments (political, moral, and religious) that are thought reasonable and which responsible practitioners and clients will generally support at a given point in time.*

By their very nature ethics are not absolutes. They inevitably change as the culture and scientific evidence dictates. Otherwise they would become prejudicial barriers that restrict rather than guidelines within which professional and client growth can proceed with some measure of order, confidence, and security. Because there are few unchanging, universal absolutes in the field of human relations, codes or guidelines for ethical practices are seldom equally acceptable to all responsible practitioners at the same time. At the present time, commonalities of beliefs are emerging in group work, and these commonalities will be the emphasis of most of the remaining portions of this chapter.

GROUP LEADERSHIP

As stated earlier in this chapter, the writer does not intend to focus on group leadership *training* since training standards must reflect the purpose of the professional discipline with which the leader identifies. Currently there are very few disciplines that have clear-cut, proven guidelines for training group practitioners. More specifically there is a serious lack of well-defined standards for training group practitioners to function at various levels of expertise in varying settings and with differing clientele. But, there are some leader-related elements for which guidelines are indicated; and assuming leader competency, these can be useful guidelines for all or most group leaders. They are as follows:

1. The group leader should have a generally accepted code of ethics.
2. The group leader should have evidence that he/she has received training commensurate with his/her group practice.
3. The group leader should have evidence that his/her leadership is effective; i.e. posttreatment and follow-up data of group members illustrates that they have benefited from membership in the leader's group.
4. The group leader should have a well-conceptualized model for explaining behavioral change.
5. The group leader should possess the necessary certification licensure or similar evidence of qualifications generally accepted by his/her discipline.
6. The group leader who does not possess professional credentials must function under the supervision of a professionally qualified person.
7. The group leader should attend refresher courses, workshops, et cetera, to upgrade his/her skills and obtain evaluation of others regarding his/her skills and/or level of functioning.
8. The group leader should have a clear set of ground rules that guide him/her in the leadership of his group.

RECRUITMENT OF GROUP PARTICIPANTS

Professional standards as detailed by the group leader's discipline should be adhered to at all times in the recruitment of group members. Often these guidelines are more explicit for those in private practice, but are vague when it comes to policies governing recruitment within an institutional setting such as schools, business, and industrial organizations. Some guidelines that apply to one or both of the above settings are as follows:

1. Announcements should include an explicit statement of the group's:
   a. purpose,

    b. length and duration of group sessions,

    c. number of group participants.

2. Announcements should include an explicit statement regarding the leader's qualifications for leading the proposed group.

3. Announcements should include an explicit statement regarding the leader's fee which specifies:

    a. the amount for professional service,

    b. the amount for any meals, lodging, materials, et cetera,

    c. the amount for follow-up services.

4. Group members should not be coerced to join a group by superiors or the group leader.

5. Claims that cannot be substantiated by *scientific* evidence should not be made.

SCREENING OF GROUP PARTICIPANTS

Since there is evidence that not just anyone can benefit from a group experience, some form of screening procedure should be instituted by the leader to ensure that prospective group members understand what will be expected of them and to select only those members where there is likelihood that they will benefit themselves and other group participants. Some general guidelines to ensure that these conditions prevail are as follows:

1. Prospective group members should be appraised as to their ability to achieve specific benefits from the experience. High risk members should ordinarily be excluded from group treatment. The American Medical Association's Council on Mental Health cited the following who "run a risk of adverse reaction from sensitivity training": "(a) persons who are frankly psychotic and those with an impaired sense of reality; (b) persons with a significant degree of psychoneurosis; (c) those with a history of marked emotional lability; (d) those who react to stress with psychological decompensation or psychosomatic illness; and (e) persons in a crisis situation" (1971, p. 1854). (Except for "b" these individuals would also be poor risks for counseling and therapy groups and quasitherapy groups.)

2. Prospective group members should be informed that their participation must be voluntary. (Rare exceptions are perhaps defensible; if they are made they must be fully documented.)

3. Prospective group members should be told candidly what will be expected of them, the risks that they will incur, and what techniques will be employed by the leader.

4. Prospective group members should be told that they have "freedom of exit" from the group.

5. Prospective group members should be told that they have the freedom to resist following suggestions or prescriptions of the group members and/or leader.

6. Prospective group members should be informed whether or not confidentiality is a requirement for group membership. (It is expected that it would be in therapy, counseling, and other experiential groups, although it must be pointed out that complete confidentiality cannot be guaranteed.)

7. Prospective group members should be informed explicitly of areas or instances that the group leader may be required to break confidence, e.g. imminent harm to the group member or others.

8. Prospective group members should be informed of any research that might be carried out on the group and their permission must be secured in writing.

9. Prospective group members must be informed regarding recording of group sessions and their consent must be obtained. Furthermore, they should be told that they can stop the recorder at any point that they choose if they find that it is restricting their participation.

10. Prospective group members should be queried to determine whether or not they are in similar treatment with others. Clearance with the other professional who is treating the potential group member must be obtained.

11. Prospective group members should be informed that the leader may need to remove them from the group if it is

determined that they are being harmed or are harmful to others.

Ordinarily, superiors should not be placed in groups with subordinates unless they are fully aware of the risks involved and choose such an arrangement. Likewise, students/trainees should not be required to be in therapy/counseling with their teachers or others who may have evaluative control over them.

CONFIDENTIALITY

There is general acceptance among group leaders that confidentiality is necessary as a prerequisite for the development of group trust, cohesion, and productive work in counseling, therapy, and quasitherapy groups. The importance of this concept should be discussed fully with a prospective group participant in the screening process (see Screening of Group Participants). It is discussed separately here to specify other dimensions of confidentiality in group work. Some general guidelines regarding confidentiality are as follows:

1. The group leader shall refrain from revealing unnecessary identifying data of group members when seeking professional consultation. He/she should discuss the group or individuals within it for professional purposes only.
2. All data collected from group participants for research purposes must be obtained only after group members have given their written permission.
3. The group leader must disguise all data that identifies group members if it is used in publications and/or instruction.
4. The group leader periodically should remind group members of the importance of strict confidentiality in counseling, therapy, and quasitherapy groups.

TERMINATION AND FOLLOW-UP

The major criticism of counseling, therapy, and quasitherapy group leaders' handling of termination and follow-up is the abrupt termination of short-term, week-end types of group encounters with no follow-up provided. This condition frequently occurs when an out-of-town group leader provides a training-therapy combination workshop. Since the leader is present only for the workshop, he or she is unfamiliar with the local professional resources and is not in a position to make a satisfactory referral when it is needed. And since the leader often does not plan a return or follow-up session, the participants are left on their own to secure follow-up assistance if needed. The guidelines are thus directed to this type of situation. Suggested guidelines are as follows:

1. The group leader should plan a follow-up for short-term, time-limited groups.
2. The group leader should be acquainted with and have a commitment from a qualified professional to whom group participants can be referred when the leader cannot continue professional involvement.
3. Group participants should be informed of competent referral sources to whom they will have access provided that such assistance is needed.

"LEADERLESS" GROUPS

Until such time as greater supportive research evidence is available, therapy and quasitherapy groups without the presence of some kind of professional leader should be discouraged. In particular, groups that are directed by audiotaped instruction should not be permitted unless a professionally trained leader is monitoring the group. As more evidence such as that obtained in the Lieberman, Yalom, and Miles (1973) study is obtained—evidence that supported the effectiveness of "leaderless" groups—these restrictions will be less necessary. (These suggestions may seem to limit the use of self-help groups such as AA and Synanon. This is true only if there is no previously established body of knowledge or evidence to support the use of self-help, and in the case of AA and Synanon such supportive evidence is available.)

GENERAL PROCEDURES FOR HANDLING UNETHICAL PRACTICE/BEHAVIOR

There are generally accepted procedures established by most professional associations for policing their membership. The code of ethics or ethical standards is not only the professional instrument, but often the legal criterion against which an accused person may be held accountable. Therefore it behooves professionals to know their ethical responsibilities and practice accordingly. Most ethical codes also indicate the procedure that one is to follow when he/she has evidence of unethical practice/behavior.

In general, one should first protect the clients affected by the unethical practice/behavior. Assuming that the client is in no immediate danger, the "accused" should be informed of his or her unethical practice/behavior and asked to correct the situation. If the "accused" refuses to correct the situation, the professional is bound by his/her ethics to report (with proper regard to accuracy of details, fairness, and discretion) the incident to the appropriate professional association's "ethical practices committee" and/or the "accused's" superior or institutional representative. A professional person who ignores unethical practice/behavior of others is equally guilty in the view of the associations within the helping professions.

Recently the American Psychological Association amended its bylaws (Article II Section 18) to specify the manner in which the Ethics Committee will proceed to bring charges against one of its members. The bylaws also describe the nature of the hearing available to an accused member, the right to counsel, opportunity to cross-examine witnesses, present his/her own witnesses and documents, and right of appeal. The essence of the procedure is that the Ethics Committee shall have the burden of responsibility to establish the charges by supportive evidence.

SUMMARY

This chapter contains some tentative guidelines for the ethical practice of group workers, especially for those leading therapy or quasitherapy groups. The guidelines are based on a careful review of the literature and also upon a questionnaire survey sent to appropriate professional associations/societies within the "helping professions."

A review of the literature revealed that the various professional associations whose membership is engaged in some form of group work are beginning to reach a consensus on a number of guidelines—especially for counseling, therapy, and quasitherapy groups.

This chapter begins with the definition of "group work" and "ethics of group work," and includes a listing of Lakin's "conditions for membership" in "experiential" groups. Next, tentative guidelines for ethical practice are outlined under the following specific topics: Group Leadership, Recruitment of Group Participants, Screening of Group Participants, Confidentiality, Termination and Follow-up, "Leaderless" Groups, and General Procedures for Handling Unethical Practice/Behavior.

SUGGESTED READINGS

American College Personnel Association Task Force on Group Procedures: A proposed statement for ACPA regarding the use of group procedures in higher education. *Journal of College Student Personnel, 13(1):*90, 1972.

American College Personnel Association Task Force on Group Procedures: Guidelines for Group Facilitators in Higher Education (mimeographed) Author, n.d.

American Group Psychotherapy Association: *Guidelines for the Training of Group Psychotherapists.* New York, Author, n.d.

American Medical Association's Council on Mental Health: Sensitivity training. *Journal of the American Medical Association, 217(13):*1853, 1971.

American Personnel and Guidance Association: *Ethical Standards Casebook.* Washington, D. C., Author, 1965.

American Personnel and Guidance Association: *Ethical Standards: American Personnel and Guidance Association.* Washington, D. C., Author, 1974.

American Psychiatric Association: *Task Force Report 1: Encounter Groups and Psychiatry.* Washington, D. C., Author, 1970.

American Psychological Association: *Casebook on Ethical Standards of Psychologists.* Washington, D. C., Author, 1967.

American Psychological Association: *Ethical Principles in the Conduct of Research with Human Participants.* Washington, D. C., Author, 1973.

American Psychological Association: Guidelines for psychologists conducting growth groups. *American Psychologist, 28(10):*933, 1973.

Berzon, B., and Solomon, L.: The self-directed therapeutic group: three studies. *Journal of Counseling Psychology, 13:*491, 1966.

Birnbaum, M.: Sense about sensitivity training. *Saturday Review,* 82, Nov. 15, 1969.

Carkhuff, R., and Truax, C.: Lay mental health counseling: the effects of lay group counseling. *Journal of Consulting Psychology, 29:*426, 1965.

Gazda, G. M.: *Group Counseling: A Developmental Approach* (Ch. 8 Ethics and Professional Issues). Boston, Allyn, 1971.

Gazda, G. M.: *Group Procedures in Education.* Washington, D. C., Am Personnel, 1971.

Gazda, G. M., Duncan, J. A., and Meadows, M. E.: Group counseling and group procedures—report of a survey. *Counselor Education and Supervision, 6:*305, 1967.

Gazda, G. M., Duncan, J. A., and Sisson, P. J.: Professional issues in group work. *Personnel and Guidance Journal, 49(8):*637, 1971.

Gazda, G. M., et al.: Recommended changes and additions to APGA Code of Ethics to accommodate group workers. *Counselor Education and Supervision, 13(2):*155, 1973.

Golan, S. E.: Emerging areas of ethical concern. *American Psychologist, 24:*454, 1969.

Jenkins, D.: Ethics and responsibility in human relations training. In I. Weschler and E. Schein (Eds.): *Issues in Training.* Washington, D. C., National Training Laboratories, National Education Association, 1962.

Kelman, H. S.: *A Time to Speak—On Human Values and Social Research.* San Francisco, Josey-Bass, 1968.

Lakin, M.: Some ethical issues in sensitivity training. *American Psychologist, 24:*923, 1969.

Lakin, M.: *Experiential Groups: The Uses of Interpersonal Encounter, Psychotherapy Groups, and Sensitivity Training.* Morristown, General Learning Pr, 1972.

Moreno, J. L.: Code of ethics of group psychotherapists. *Group Psychotherapy, 10:*143, 1957.

Moreno, J. L.: Code of ethics for group psychotherapy and psychodrama: relationship to the Hippocratic Oath. *Psychodrama and Group Psychotherapy Monograph* No. 31. Beacon, Beacon Hse, 1962.

National Training Laboratory Institute: *Standards for the Use of Laboratory Method,* Washington, D. C., Author, 1969.

Olsen, L. C.: Ethical standards for group leaders. *Personnel and Guidance Journal, 50(4):*288, 1971.

Patterson, C. H.: Ethical standards for groups. *Counseling Psychologist, 3:*93, 1972.

Shostrom, E. L.: Group therapy: Let the buyer beware. *Psychology Today, 2(12):*37, 1969.

Zimpfer, D.: Needed: professional ethics for working with groups. *Personnel and Guidance Journal, 50(4):*280, 1971.

Zytowski, D.: Obligatory counseling with college underachievers. *Group Psychotherapy, 16*:8, 1963.

REFERENCES

American Medical Association's Council on Mental Health: sensitivity training. *Journal of the American Medical Association, 217(13)*:1853, 1971.

Gazda, G. M., et al.: Recommended changes and additions to APGA Code of Ethics to accommodate group workers. *Counselor Education and Supervision, 13(2)*:155, 1973.

Lakin, M.: *Experiential Groups: The Uses of Interpersonal Encounter, Psychotherapy Groups, and Sensitivity Training*. Morristown, General Learning Pr, 1972.

Lieberman, M. A., Yalom, I. D., and Miles, M. D.: *Encounter Groups: First Facts*. New York, Basic, 1973.

III

GROUP COUNSELING: A DEVELOPMENTAL APPROACH[1]

George M. Gazda

Figure III-1 (p. 36) illustrates the relationship among various group procedures. These relationships have also been supported by means of a survey of group experts (Gazda, Duncan, and Sisson, 1971). Group experts who responded to a questionnaire did not make clear differentiations among group counseling, encounter groups, T-groups, and sensitivity groups. That is, they defined them similarly based on such criteria as type of clientele served, degree of disturbance of clientele, setting of the treatment, goals of treatment, size of group, and length and duration of treatment. These groups, however, were viewed as distinctly different from guidance groups and therapy groups. More specifically, they were in the middle of the continuum shown in Figure III-1, i.e. they were viewed as partially remedial, partially growth engendering and partially preventive. Guidance groups were viewed as preventive and therapy groups as remedial.

Group counseling has been defined as follows:

> Group counseling is a dynamic interpersonal process focusing on conscious thought and behavior and involving the therapy functions of permissiveness, orientation to reality, catharsis, and mutual trust, caring, understanding, acceptance, and support. The therapy functions are created and nurtured in a small group through the sharing of personal concerns with one's peers and the counselor(s). The group counselees are basically normal individuals with various concerns which are not debilitating to the extent requiring extensive

---

1. Parts of this chapter are reproduced from Gazda, G. M. *Group Counseling: A Developmental Approach*, 1971. Courtesy of Allyn and Bacon, Inc., Boston, Massachusetts, and from Gazda, G. M. *Basic Approaches to Group Psychotherapy and Group Counseling* (2nd ed., 1975). Courtesy Charles C Thomas, Springfield, Illinois.

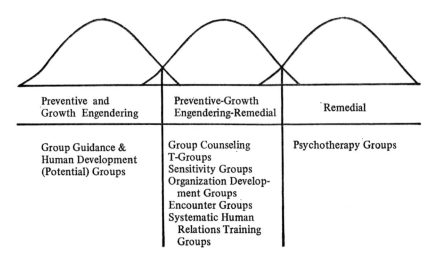

Preventive and Growth Engendering	Preventive-Growth Engendering-Remedial	Remedial
Group Guidance & Human Development (Potential) Groups	Group Counseling T-Groups Sensitivity Groups Organization Development Groups Encounter Groups Systematic Human Relations Training Groups	Psychotherapy Groups

FIGURE III-1

personality change. The group counselees may utilize the group interaction to increase understanding and acceptance of values and goals and to learn and/or unlearn certain attitudes and behaviors (Gazda, Duncan, and Meadows, 1967, p. 305).

Group counseling is perhaps best differentiated from group therapy at the same time that both are defined by Brammer and Shostrom's (1960) use of a series of adjectives in which counseling is described as

> educational, supportive, situational, problem-solving, conscious awareness, emphasis on "normals," and short-term. Psychotherapy is characterized by supportive (in a more particular sense), reconstructive, depth analysis, analytical, focus on the unconscious, emphasis on "neurotics" or other severe emotional problems, and long-term (1960, p. 6).

Although these differentiations were applied to individual counseling and psychotherapy, they are equally applicable to group counseling and group psychotherapy.

A DEVELOPMENTAL APPROACH

Prior to *Group Counseling: A Developmental Approach* (Gazda, 1971), no systematic attempt had been made to provide an approach to *group counseling* that was applicable to all age levels. Previous attempts have "singled out" methods of group counseling with children, with adolescents, or with adults. Slavson (1945), however, long ago recognized the need for differential treatment for different age groups in *group therapy*. "Group therapy," he said, "is practiced on different levels, and in discussing its functions in therapy, it is necessary that these levels be kept in mind" (p. 201).

The author's experience also has demonstrated the need for a position that allows for and accommodates a different emphasis with different age groups in group counseling. The developmental approach to group counseling, therefore, utilizes the developmental task concept (Havighurst, 1948, 1952, 1953) with subsequent coping behaviors, to serve as broad guidelines for the group counselor. Havighurst defines developmental task as follows:

> A developmental task is a task which arises at or about a certain period in the life of the individual, successful achievement of which leads to his happiness and to success with later tasks, while failure leads to unhappiness in the individual, disapproval by society, and difficulty with later tasks (1952, p. 2).

Havighurst (1952) also cites two reasons why the concept of developmental task is useful to educators. His reasons seem equally applicable to counselors and counseling: "First, it helps in discovering and stating the purpose of education [group counseling] efforts" (p. 5). He describes timing to mean *teachable moment* (1952, p. 5). Readiness for group counseling is determined by the dissonance between the developmental task and its subsequent coping behavior.

Zaccaria (1965) gives a more comprehensive interpretation of developmental tasks than does Havighurst. His interpretation includes Havighurst's (1952) "bio-socio-psychological" emphasis, the "vocational developmental" emphasis of Super et al. (1957, 1963), and Erikson's (1950, 1959, 1963) "psychosocial crises." Since Zaccaria's description of the developmental tasks concept is more inclusive than Havighurst's the author has utilized all three approaches plus the developmental phases in the cognitive domain, *a la,* Piaget, the physical-sexual domain, *a la,* Gesell, Ilg, and Ames, and the moral domain, *a la,* Kohlberg, in developing the guidelines for use by the counselor in assessing individuals' progress along their developmental pathways. Difficulty with the mastery of a developmental stage signals to the parent, teacher, counselor, and significant others that assistance or corrective action is necessary. Group counseling through the approach outlined in this chapter should help to provide this assistance.

Western society and much of western culture is organized on the basis of an expected progressive development in the biological, sociological, cognitive, moral, and psychological realms of its citizens and, as such, the concept of developmental task has general applicability. For example, our schools are organized on a preschool and kindergarten, early elementary school, middle school, and high school basis; state laws govern marriageable ages of its citizens; federal laws govern legal retirement age; and so forth (Muuss, 1962).

Although there are wide ranges in the biological, social, and psychological development of individuals, there are classifiable periods between and within age groups. Several individuals (Blocher, 1966; Brammer and Shostrom, 1960; Erikson, 1950; Gesell, et al., 1946; Gesell, et al., 1956; Havighurst, 1952; Kohlberg, 1973; Piaget, see Flavell, 1963; Super et al., 1957, 1963) have developed various classification schemes for the developmental phases. For group counseling purposes, the phases can be divided into (1) early childhood or preschool and early school, ages five to nine; (2) preadolescent, ages nine to thirteen; (3) adolescent, ages thirteen to twenty; and (4) adult. That there is sometimes considerable overlap between age groups is well documented. There is also a special discrepancy between the sexes at the end of the latency period and beginning of pubescence, beginning between ages eight to thirteen for girls and ten to fifteen for boys. The group counselor, therefore, must be alert to individual differences and organize groups to accommodate them. Since "Little is known as to what the values of a group to a child of three or four may be" (Slavson, 1945, p. 203), the emphasis of my approach begins with the kindergarten child of age five.

Systematic Human Relations Training, *a la* Carkhuff (1969 ab), provides a theoretically and empirically sound method for training those professionals, e.g. teachers, who are not technically included among the "helping" professionals. When combined with the rationale and methodology of Developmental Group Counseling, it makes possible the training of "functional professionals" (Carkhuff, 1970). Now this combined application of Carkhuff's Systematic Human Relations Training with Developmental Group Counseling is of vital importance because it makes possible the extension of Developmental Group Counseling through *functional professionals* (i.e. persons who do not have the paper credentials—certificates, degrees, or licenses—but who are in fact capable of serving as facilitators or helpers) to the culturally different, the educationally deficient and even the mentally retarded.

The typical group counselor today is a middle-class WASP. This counselor will be unable in many instances to transcend the racial, cultural, ethnic, economic, etc., barriers between himself or herself and many who desperately need counseling assistance. Thus he/she must extend the role of group counselor to group trainer also. In the role of trainer, he/she can be guided by the basic tenets of Developmental Group Counseling (Gazda, 1971) and Systematic Human Relations Training (Gazda et al., 1973; Gazda, Walters, and Childers, 1975). For example, the prospective counselor will very often be alien, if not alienated, to the black community as a whole. Nevertheless, there will be those within the black community (indigenous personnel) who could serve as functional professionals to reach those beyond the reach of a middle-class WASP. Somewhat analogous to AA and Synanon, volunteers from within a given cultural or problem area (e.g. the black community, alienated youth, etc.), must be given training to function as facilitators or helpers.

The expressed effort to go through others who are capable of reaching and assisting the culturally different, etc., is an example of "reaching" them by moving through media (persons, in this case) that are most "natural" to them whether or not their problem or potential problem is the result of inadequate coping behavior for a given developmental task or an alienated feeling towards those of different color, age group, or economic condition.

In addition to stressing the necessity of reaching others through "functional professionals," the Developmental model described herein focuses on the need to utilize activities and media that are most natural to a given group—especially age group, but also ethnic, socioeconomic, etc., group. Therefore, the potential group leader must be flexible enough and skilled enough to substitute an active sport or game such as basketball for a chess game for ghetto youth if he expects to approach or "reach" them through *activities* that are natural and comfortable for them.

DYNAMICS OF GROUPS

Leadership

Counselor's Ability to Help

Truax (1969) reported that one third of trained professionals functioning in roles purported to be "helping" such as psychiatrists, counselors, social workers, etc., did in fact help their clients or persons seeking help from them; one third actually harmed their clients; and one third had no measurable positive or negative effect. And he concluded that the more helpers are trained with old methods the farther behind the professions are getting. Further evidence to corroborate Truax's conclusion is presented in Truax and Carkhuff (1967), Carkhuff and Berenson (1967), and Carkhuff (1969ab).

Essentially, the conclusion has been reached that traditional methods of preparing professionals in the field of human relations have not been at all effective and that considerably more care should be shown in certifying professional helpers. Carkhuff (1969a) has outlined the most comprehensive method to date for the selection and training of both lay and professional helpers. His conclusion, based on a vast amount of research (Berenson and Carkhuff, 1967; Carkhuff, 1969a, 1969b, 1971;

Carkhuff and Berenson, 1967; Truax and Carkhuff, 1967; Rogers, Gendlin, Kiesler, and Truax, 1967) suggests that the effective counselor or helper must offer high levels of the facilitative or "core" conditions of *empathy, warmth,* and *respect* as well as the more action- and activity-oriented conditions of *concreteness, genuineness,* appropriate *self-disclosure, confrontation,* and *immediacy* (Carkhuff, 1969a, p. 21).

Truax and Carkhuff (1967, p. 1) described the effective counselor as integrated, nondefensive, and authenic or *genuine* in the therapeutic encounter. They also described him or her as one who provides a nonthreatening, safe, trusting, or secure atmosphere by his or her acceptance, unconditional positive regard, love or *nonpossessive warmth* for the client. And finally, the effective counselor is able to "be with," "grasp the meaning of," or *accurately* and *empathically* understand the client on a moment-by-moment basis.

The qualities of the most effective encounter group leaders obtained in a study of encounter groups and their leaders by Lieberman, Yalom, and Miles (1973) included moderate use of stimulation and executive behavior, high levels of caring, and utilization of meaning attribution (leader's role in giving meaning to group members' experiences). The strongest association with positive outcome was meaning attribution.

Perhaps most important in the several reports of research cited above is the concurrence that the counselor must first demonstrate the qualities of a healthy human being, which are qualities described by Truax and Carkhuff (1967) and Carkhuff (1969a). Furthermore, the counselees or "helpees" *a la* Carkhuff (1969a) of the counselor do in fact improve their behavior as a result of the help the counselor provides them. Details for determining one's level as a helper are described in Carkhuff (1969a), in Gazda, et al. (1973), and in Gazda, Walters, and Childers (1975). It behooves all prospective helpers to determine their level of functioning and, if it is not at a facilitative level, to raise it or discontinue the role of helper.

Goldstein, Heller, and Sechrest (1966, Chapter 8) reviewed the research pertaining to the orientation of group psychotherapists and its effect on clients. They concluded that there was a major need to research the group therapist's orientation from a perspective which also considered the *interacting* influence of stage of therapy, patient and therapist personality and behavioral characteristics, therapist and patient goals, and other related variables.

Leader Orientation

The qualities of a group counselor who is likely to be helpful were outlined above. At this point emphasis will be placed on relating the effects of his or her interaction to what happens in a counseling group. Once more one must turn to the group dynamics research for direction. Goldstein et al. (1966), following a review of research in both group psychotherapy and group dynamics, concluded that the research

> . . . pointedly provides basic evidence for the prediction of more favorable patient response to a leader-centered versus a group-centered therapist orientation in the early stages of group psychotherapy. . . . However, in spite of its less favorable early effects, there is a considerable body of group dynamics research suggesting that the group-centered approach is very likely to result in patient behavior much more highly related to a favorable therapeutic outcome than would be the case if an essentially leader-centered approach persisted beyond the first 10 to 20 therapy sessions (p. 377).

The findings reported by Goldstein et al., are based to a considerable extent on patient expectancies of group leadership. In this regard they found:

> In sum, these diverse studies focusing on leadership expectancies in psychotherapy and other settings appear to converge in the general conclusion that the more discrepant the expectancies, the less the attraction to the group, the less the satisfaction of group members, and the more the strain or negative affect between leader and led or therapist on patient (p. 375).

If one can conclude that patients seeking group psychotherapy or, similarly, counselees seeking group counseling will approach the experience expecting direction and assistance from the leader, a rule of thumb to follow would be for the group counselor to be more active in the early group sessions and to move gradually from a leader-centered approach to a group-centered approach as counseling proceeds. This practice should reduce counselee initial hostility, increase receptiveness, and provide the best overall plan for building a therapeutic climate.

This rule-of-thumb procedure is congruent with the model described by Carkhuff (1969a), the model which seems to have the greatest support for application to group counseling. Carkhuff, in describing guidelines for the communication of empathy (a prerequisite for developing a facilitative base), stated that especially at the beginning of helping the helper would find that by increasing his or her verbal responsiveness, he/she would not only provide a model for an increasingly active helpee but would also serve to increase the probability of accuracy in communication.

In the beginning of a counseling group, the counselor is actively trying to build the facilitative base of mutual trust and caring through the utilization of interchangeable responses that incorporate the core conditions of empathy, respect, and warmth. As the counselees develop this base, they will provide cues that indicate they wish to explore their problems beyond the initial depth to a greater depth. The group counselor assists the counselees to move toward a greater depth of exploration which, in turn, leads to greater understanding and eventual positive action through the application of the more action-oriented core conditions of concreteness, genuineness, appropriate self-disclosure, confrontation, and immediacy (Carkhuff, 1969a).

STRUCTURING. Structuring refers to the counselor's orientation of group members. Research results support the use of the following procedures:

> (1) Be positive in building expectancy states. Group members should be told that (a) they most likely will like and be liked by other members of the group (Schachter, Ellertson, McBride, and Gregory, 1960); and (b) the group was set up to consist of individuals who share similar opinions and values (Festinger, Schachter, and Back, 1950).
>
> (2) Stress the hard work that will be involved in the group counseling process. This should increase the effort expended by counselees (Cohen, 1959; Yaryan and Festinger, 1961; Zimbardo, 1960).

(3) Stress the careful screening that went into selection of the group members. (This procedure should increase the attractiveness of the group to the counselees—see research reviewed by Goldstein et al., 1966, pp. 344-348.)

(4) Define the norm of the group as different from the usual social norm; that is, that it is appropriate and beneficial to discuss one's personal concerns in the counseling group. Reinforcement of this new norm should make the transition to self-disclosure and revelation of one's problems more acceptable to group members (Bonney and Foley, 1963).

GOAL SETTING. Several studies have shown that clarity of group goals and means of achieving them increase the group's attraction for members, generate greater group cohesiveness, and reduce intragroup hostility. Is group cohesiveness, however, desired in group counseling? Truax (1961) studied the effects of cohesiveness in therapy groups and made the following observation:

> These results indicate that cohesion, long a central concept in the analysis of small group behavior, is also of importance in the analysis of group psychotherapy; successful group psychotherapy groups are cohesive. . . . These findings . . . point to a variable unique to the group setting and one which is susceptible to external manipulation (p. 16).

A counselee's purpose for seeking help or goal setting should be verbalized in initial interviews before he or she enters a group; however, he/she is encouraged to repeat these in the first session of the group. Therefore, to increase the possibility of goal achievement through group counseling, the counselor should encourage the counselees to verbalize their goals as specifically and concretely as they can in the beginning and to increase their specificity as clarity occurs through the counseling experience.

Berne (1966) has referred to goal setting as the therapist-patient contract. He considers the contract to exist between the therapist and the institution which employs him or her and between the therapist and patient. Therefore, the patient should know the therapist's institutional obligations which may impinge on the patient's goals. For example, if the counselor has an obligation to report use of drugs by counselees, the counselee should know this and thus not be placed in jeopardy. Berne (1966) also cautions that the contract between therapist and patient may need to be amended from time to time as determinants underlying symptoms or responses are made more explicit. The same opportunity for goal modification should be applied to group counselees.

Occasions arise wherein subgroups develop within a counseling group and frequently they begin to compete with each other to the point of creating severe friction within the total group. This situation usually calls for reconstituting the group or instituting a superordinate goal such as the counselor's introducing a legitimate threat to the total group that is sufficient to bring together the warring factions in a total group effort to counteract the outside threat. The threat might be impending loss of a meeting place, the revocation of institutional time for group counseling, or some other administrative threat to the group's existence.

NORM SETTING. The concept of norm setting has particular relevance to group counseling in that it is equivalent to what is expected and/or allowable in the group. The norm may be either explicit or implicit, but in either case the group members know what they are permitted to do with its subsequent rewards and what they are forbidden to do with its subsequent punishments.

Included in the setting of group norms, of course, is the group counselor. He or she is active both in assisting the group develop the norms and is himself/herself being influenced by the group with respect to the role or roles the group will expect him or her to follow. The counselor's actions are especially significant in determining group norms in the first few sessions. His or her own modeling such as responding empathically and showing warmth and respect to all members, supporting shy members, etc., can go a long way toward setting the climate for the group. That is, when the group is most in need of leadership early in its Exploratory Stage, the counselor has perhaps the greatest opportunity to influence its direction. Bonney (1969) contends that the leader

should assume an active though not highly directive part in the formation of the group's norms. Ideally the setting of norms should emanate from the group itself. . . . The eventual acceptance of a group norm should . . . be left to the consensus of the group and not forced by the leader, particularly in the early stages of the group's development (p. 167).

Stages of Group Development

A number of group therapists and group counselors (Bach, 1954; Bonney, 1969; Gendlin and Beebe, 1968; Mahler, 1969) have identified stages or phases through which counseling and therapy groups purportedly pass, ranging from three phases (Gendlin and Beebe, 1968) to seven (Bach, 1954). The stages through which counseling groups progress are most clearly visible in closed groups, i.e. groups that retain the same membership throughout the duration of the group's existence. In open groups or groups that add new members as old members terminate and especially when the influx of new members is frequent, the stage development is affected and, as Gendlin and Beebe (1968) have noted, the old members reach a Tired Phase because of the constant necessity of the old members assisting the new members through the Breaking Through Phase—the phase during which the member experiences an explosive freeing and growth process. With open groups, then, it is incumbent upon the counselor to know the potential effect of too rapid a turnover in an ongoing group. It is necessary to protect the Sustaining Phase (Gendlin and Beebe, 1968) or work phase of the core members of a group and to prevent them from reaching the Tired Phase.

Hill (1961, 1963, 1965) has developed an Interaction Matrix based on a hypothesis that therapy groups proceed along two dimentions of *content* and *work* and through approximately sixteen to twenty cells or levels of interaction. The Hill model has many of the same elements that were included in the model developed by Carkhuff (1969a). The Carkhuff model adapted to the author's phases of group development is shown in Table III-I. This model emphasizes the necessity of building a facilitative base through high level expressions of empathy, respect, and warmth in the early phases of developing sound relationships.

TABLE III-1

COUNSELOR OFFERED CONDITIONS FOR THERAPEUTIC CHANGE (PART A)*	Phase I (Downward or Inward Phase of Self-Exploration)		Phase II Upward or Outward Phase of Emergent Directionality and Action)
	Initial Stage of Individual Dimensions	*Intermediary Stages of Individual Dimensions*	*Final Stage of Individual Dimensions*
EMPATHY	Level 3 (interchangeability)	Levels 4 and 5 (additive responses)	Levels 4 and 5 (emphasizing periodic feedback only)
RESPECT	Level 3 (unconditionality)	Level 4 (positive regard)	Levels 4 and 5 (regard and conditionality)
CONCRETENESS	Levels 3 and above (specificity of exploration)	Deemphasized (abstract exploration)	Levels 4 and 5 (specificity of direction)
GENUINENESS	Level 3 (absence of ingenuineness)	Levels 4 and 5 (self-disclosure and spontaneity)	Levels 4 and 5 (spontaneity)
CONFRONTATION		Levels 3 (general and open)	Levels 4 and 5 (directionful)
IMMEDIACY		Levels 3 (general and open)	Levels 4 and 5 (directionful)
GROUP (COUNSELEE) STAGES IN THERAPEUTIC CHANGE (PART B)†	Stage 1 Exploratory	Stage 2 Transition Stage 3 Action	Stage 4 Termination

* From Chapter 7 of *Helping and Human Relations: A Primer for Lay and Professional Helpers. Vol. 2. Practice and Research*, by Robert R. Carkhuff. Copyright © 1969 by Holt, Rinehart and Winston, Inc. Reprinted by permission of Holt, Rinehart and Winston, Inc., New York.
† From Chapter 5 of *Group Counseling: A Developmental Approach*, by George M. Gazda. Copyright © 1971 by Allyn and Bacon, Inc. Reprinted by permission of Allyn and Bacon, Inc., Boston.

Building a facilitative base is prerequisite to the implementation of the action-oriented dimensions at later stages in helping relationships. The action-oriented dimensions are geared to changing behavior. The facilitative-action-oriented dimensions include genuineness, specificity or concreteness of expression, and appropriate self-disclosure by the leader, whereas the action-oriented dimensions include the leader behavior just cited plus *appropriate* confrontation and immediacy or "telling it like it is" between leader and helpees in the here-and-now.

The amount, the kind, and the timing of counselor intervention in groups, therefore, is related to the stage or phase of a group's development. It cannot be independent of the stage, however, since the group is influenced by counselor behavior and vice versa. It has been the author's experience that counseling groups go through four rather definite stages. These stages usually occur in the given group session and across sessions. They are (1) Exploratory Stage, (2) Transition Stage, (3) Action Stage, and (4) Termination Stage. These four stages are named similarly by others. For example, Bonney (1969) refers to the Exploratory Stage as the Establishment Stage, and Mahler (1969) calls it the Involvement Stage. Both Bonney and Mahler have a second or Transition Stage. The Action Stage can be equated to Mahler's Working Stage. The fourth or Termination Stage is equivalent to Mahler's Ending Stage.

Exploratory Stage

During this stage the group members introduce themselves and describe the goals that each hopes to achieve. They also agree on some basic ground rules. Following the initial session the counselees usually engage in social and superficial discussions about themselves, each parrying with the other to present him or herself in an acceptable fashion. This is the kind of activity in which members assign to each other what Hollander (1964) has called "idiosyncratic credits." Bonney (1969) has referred to this as the "process by which the group consciously and unconsciously, assigns power and influence, in varying degrees to each member of the group" (p. 166). It is also a means of establishing various roles that each person will first assume in the group. Hidden agendas begin to emerge and the group begins to establish norms that will eventually become the unofficial but controlling ground rules.

It is especially important that the group counselor be actively helpful during the Exploratory Stage. He/she shows his/her helpfulness by clarifying goals for the group and the group means for achieving them, by telling the group something about himself or herself and, most importantly, by modeling the facilitative dimensions of empathy, respect, warmth, and genuineness. In the Carkhuff (1969a) sense, the counselor gives consistently minimally facilitative or better responses, i.e. he/she consistently gives responses to each counselee that are *interchangeable* with those of the counselee—interchangeable especially with respect to the affect expressed by the counselee and also to the content or message expressed. It is during this initial or Exploratory Stage that a facilitative base of mutual trust and caring is built. Without this, the group fails to reach the next stage in its development.

Transition Stage

The Transition Stage occurs at a point when one or more counselees begin to self-disclose at a level significantly deeper than the "historical" type of disclosures heretofore given in the group. At this point the group members experience a feeling of threat since the typical social group does not usually function in this manner. The members may attempt to block the self-disclosures with overly supportive responses or by attempts to change the subject—more precisely to revert to the superficial conversation of a historical nature found in the Exploratory Stage.

To move the group as a whole through the Transition Stage to the Action Stage, or work stage, requires high levels of *perception* or sensitivity and accuracy in *timing* of counselor responses. The counselor must be able to encourage volunteers to self-disclose at a level that gives them a feeling of involvement and simultaneously he or she must be able to hold the anxiety level of the more threatened group members to a level that will not force their defense systems to over-react. Following the Carkhuff model for moving from counselee exploration to understanding to action, the counselor must be able to give responses that are at least minimally action-oriented, i.e. he/she must begin to add the facilitative action-oriented dimensions of genuineness, concreteness and appropriate self-disclosure to those of empathy, respect, and warmth. The counselor should also be willing to self-disclose, when appropriate. Thus, the counselor models for the counselees who are beginning to involve themselves in the action-oriented dimensions of problem resolution. Counselor self-disclosure early in the life of the group is usually discouraged, because it tends to place the focus on the counselor rather than the counselees.

Action Stage

The Action Stage is synonymous with the work or productive stage of a counseling group. Also, it involves the implementation of the action-oriented dimensions, *a la* Carkhuff's model, of confrontation and immediacy plus the facilitative-action dimensions of genuineness, concreteness, and appropriate self-disclosures.

The group counselor must orient the counselees toward a belief that their condition will not change until they take definite steps (action) to modify it. Insofar as the counselees' goals can be achieved by modifying their behavior in the group itself, they should be encouraged to do so and rewarded when they do. In this regard talking about how one is planning to change is no longer defensible; the counselee must demonstrate it in the here-and-now of the group experience. The counselor utilizes appropriate confrontations and shares with the counselee here-and-now feelings about the counselee's in-group behavior. (Berenson and Mitchell (1975) concluded that confrontation is never necessary, but that it may be used effectively by very high functioning helpers.) The counselor also encourages other group members to do likewise.

Each counselee should have a program or plan of action developed so that all possible variables can be brought to bear on the resolution of the counselee deficits. One way to involve the total counselee is to evaluate the counselee's assets and deficits based on five well-defined areas of developmental stages: psychosocial, physical-sexual, cognitive, vocational, and moral. Not only is the totality of the counselee considered, but external variables are also important considerations in problem resolutions. These variables involve the physical environment and the significant others in the counselee's life space. Therefore, all significant others should be involved in developing and assisting in implementing the plan or program that will best aid the counselee in problem resolution. Expertise must be present in this group so that appropriate intervention strategies (Catterall and Gazda, in press) can be utilized.

In the final analysis, counselee action is goal related and dependent upon behavioral modifications to be employed outside of the group settings. It is encouraged in the form of homework to be done and then reported back to the group at the next session. Attempts that fail to achieve the desired goal can be appraised and modified, even role-played in the group, until counselee satisfaction is achieved.

If the group counselor has involved all group members in the action phase of group counseling, the counselor will seldom need to confront group members. Rather the group members will confront each other and the group counselor will be more of a gatekeeper of group safety. The counselor will be one of the most expert timing devices in the group—the one who can best predict when a given counselee is ready to move to decision making and/or action.

Termination Stage

The Termination Stage begins with a tapering off of counselee self-disclosures, especially in new areas of concern. In a closed group with a preset termination date, the tapering off usually begins naturally two to three sessions before this date and frequently includes half-hearted attempts by the counselees to continue the sessions beyond the preset deadline. Not unusual during the last three or four sessions is the initiation of a "going around" procedure wherein each member solicits frank feedback from every other member. Also common during the Termination Stage is a general and spontaneous need of counselees to tell how much the group members and the group experience have meant to them. They are reluctant to see the group experience terminate and they usually make plans for a group reunion at some specific date in the future.

The group counselor's responsibility at termination is to reinforce the growth made by group members and to make sure that all group counselees have had the opportunity to work out their differences with the counselor and other group members before leave taking. If any member of the group, for whatever reason, continues to require counseling, the counselor must assume this responsibility or assist the counselee in a mutually satisfactory referral.

COUNSELEE SELECTION AND GROUP COMPOSITION
General Guidelines

Frank (1952), Slavson (1953), and Hulse (1954) have pointed to the lack of knowledge in arriving at optimum composition for therapy groups. A similar observation can be made for group counseling. Research has not clearly demonstrated ideal combinations of members for maximum growth through group counseling. Nevertheless, certain guidelines have been utilized and are presented here for consideration, possible application, and research. The author's experience leads him to concur with Lowrey and Slavson (1943) *that the most essential element in a therapy group is the skill and insight in grouping, and the second most important factor is the personality of the therapist.*

Lieberman, Yalom, and Miles' (1973) comprehensive study of encounter groups showed that the leader's theoretical rationale was not related to positive changes or growth of group members. Rather, leader characteristics/behaviors were significantly related to group members' changes.

Previous citations in this chapter of the finding of Carkhuff and Truax regarding leader/counselor characteristics point to the important relationship of the counselor's characteristics and counselee outcome. These researchers have established the fact that effective helpers must function at high levels on the core dimensions. What has not yet been adequately established is the relationship between effective leaders and group composition. Can effective leadership alone lead a poorly composed counseling group to growth, or must the group itself possess at least minimal conditions before even effective leaders can produce growth? The author's convictions lie with the latter part of this question.

Based on a rather thorough review of the literature, Truax and Carkhuff (1967) concluded that supportive research on the question of what type of client, patient, or counselee would benefit most from counseling or psychotherapy has not been done; however, those counselees who are likely to improve or deteriorate can sometimes be predicted. Even then this may be more a factor of the leader's ability to provide a therapeutic relationship than a true picture of what the counselee is like. Nevertheless, they did find research data to support some *tentative conclusions* related to counselee selection for individual and/or group counseling. Their findings (Truax and Carkhuff, 1967, Chapter 5) are summarized as follows:

1. Matching of counselee and counselor types is critical where the counselor is quite restricted in his or her ability to show understanding, warmth, or genuineness to all but a narrow range of individuals.
2. Counselee readiness is a moderately good predictor of the degree of positive change. In this regard, counselees who have high expectations and high regard for the counselor tend to show the greatest immediate change while those who differ on the aims and methods of counselor help tend to terminate treatment quickly.
3. The research evidence is unclear regarding the characteristics of counselees likely to benefit most from counseling or therapy. In general, the counselees with the greatest felt disturbance and the least overt disturbance show the greatest improvement at posttreatment.
4. The greater the initial psychological disturbance but the lesser the initial behavioral disturbance, the greater the predicted improvement *during* treatment.
5. Counselor liking or disliking for the counselee will affect outcome. Higher therapeutic conditions are offered to counselees who are liked by the counselor.

6. Social class variables (e.g. occupational and educational level, and intelligence) regarding type and duration of counseling offered, reflect general prejudices of the profession but do not neccessarily reflect counselee response to counseling.

7. Counselee hope or initial expectations of help through counseling is a major factor contributing to the likelihood of its actually occurring.

8. Degree of counselee change is independently influenced *both* by the level of therapeutic conditions offered by the counselor and the initial degree and type of personal disturbance of the counselee.

9. Accurate empathic understanding seems to be more critical for outcome with nonverbal counselees while nonpossessive warmth and genuineness tend to be equally effective in producing preferred outcome with both verbal and nonverbal counselees.

10. The therapeutic conditions of accurate empathy, nonpossesive warmth, and genuineness are of equal importance in producing personality change in the most disturbed and least disturbed counselees.

11. Level of self-exploration by the counselee is a crude predictor of counselee outcome, i.e. the greater the degree of counselee self-exploration, the more likely the outcome will be positive. (The Truax Depth of Self-Explorations Scale in Truax and Carkhuff, 1967, Chapter 5, can be used to obtain a measure of counselee level of self-exploration.)

The guidelines which have been cited above for rule-of-thumb selection of counselees come from both the individual and group counseling research literature and include characteristics of the counselee and counselor. However, the group setting is unique and creates greater problems for predicting possible counselee reaction(s). McGrath and Altman (1966), in their extensive review of small group research concluded: "Actually very few data are available about the role of personality characteristics of members on various group phenomena. Rather, such properties should be studied with respect to the composition of the group" (p. 57). They further concluded ". . . there is very little research on group composition, and what there is gives an unclear picture" (p. 60).

The Lieberman, Yalom, and Miles (1973) study has added some new information of relevance to the problem. In their study they found that the nature of the group as a social system is important. More specifically, they found that

> . . . Groups with norms that favor moderate emotional intensity and confrontation, supportive peer control, and those with looser boundaries of what could be legitimately discussed showed higher learning. Groups that were more cohesive, more involving, and more harminous during the latter part of their life were better as learning environments.
>
> . . . group members who liked their groups, who participated actively, and who were valued by other group members learned more; marginal or deviant members tended to have negative outcomes (p. 76).

With respect to the group counseling research, Anderson (1969) made this observation in his three-year review of the literature:

> Group counseling research reflects little interest in client selection or client preparation as a major independent variable. The available data suggest that people who are affectively oriented, flexible, highly motivated to change, and sufficiently well adjusted to interact rationally with others function well in counseling groups (p. 212).

Following a comprehensive review of group dynamics and group psychotherapy research, Goldstein et al. (1966) developed the following hypothesis concerning group composition: "On a variety of interactive, communicative and compatibility criteria, prediction of subsequent within-group behavior will be more accurate when based on direct behavioral measurement than on interview or psychometric measurement" (p. 329). In order to apply the above principle, they proposed three criteria as guidelines: (1) consistency or typical performance, (2) relation to task success, and (3) objective observation (1966, p. 333). To determine consistency of counselee behavior in a group, two means were suggested: (a) trial groups (see also Bell and French, 1955; Blake, Mouton, and Fruchter, 1954; Borgatta and Bales, 1955; and Gazda, 1968), and (b) simulated groups.

Trial or preliminary grouping is possible where there is a relatively large pool of potential counselees, such as in schools or other institutional settings. Potential counselees are placed in a large temporary group, observed for three or four sessions, and then placed in a permanent group based on their needs and contributions and the needs of the permanent group to which they are added (in the case of open-ended groups) or a new group (closed) when a new group is being organized.

The simulated method for screening consists of a prospective member's listening, via audiotape, to a simulated group experience and responding as if he or she were a member. This method allows the prospective group counselee to be observed regarding his or her reaction to type of group leadership and group members. Blake and Brehm (1954) and Bass (1960) describe this method in more detail.

To relate task or group success (therapeutic outcome) to group composition, Goldstein et al. (1966) suggested the study and application of findings of characteristic rate of group member interaction, leadership behavior, the effects of group cohesiveness on outcome, and related therapy group dimensions.

Group cohesiveness was found by Truax (1961) to be one of three group conditions significantly related to intrapersonal exploration by counselees in groups. Most of the research in support of group cohesiveness as a powerful agent in affecting behavior is in the field of group dynamics or from nontherapy-oriented groups (see Goldstein et al., Chapter 9). Bach, a group therapist with a group dynamics orientation, had this to say about group cohesiveness in therapy groups:

> This principle of cohesiveness is most relevant to the therapy group, for much of the therapeutic process is mediated by all members. The most unique feature of group therapy is the cotherapeutic influence of peers, not of the doctor alone. Traditionally, the doctor is thought of as having the most influence, but in group therapy this is actually not necessarily so, because the relatively low degree of cohesiveness between doctor and patient as compared with the often very deeply involved peer relationships between the patients gives the copatient a greater power of effective influence (1954, p. 348).

After a careful consideration of the research relevant to group composition for therapy, Yalom (1970) made the following statement:

On the basis of our present state of knowledge, therefore, I propose that cohesiveness be our primary guideline in the composition of therapy groups. The hoped-for dissonance will unfold in the group, provided the therapist functions effectively in the pretherapy orientation of patients and during the early group meetings. . . .

A cohesive frame of reference for group composition is by no means inconsistent with the notion of demographic heterogeneity; however, it does set limits for the degree of heterogeneity. . . . It makes eminently good sense to suppose that the greater the range of interpersonal relationships clarified within the group, the more universal the carryover will be. . . . However, the demographic variation must be conceived within the general rubric of cohesiveness; too extreme a variation breeds deviancy and undermines cohesiveness (p. 204).

After surveying individual therapy research, group therapy research, and group dynamics research Goldstein et al. (1966) generated the following *hypotheses* relative to the means of achieving cohesiveness in therapy groups:

1. Therapy group cohesiveness may be increased by intergroup competition (p. 407).
2. Therapy group cohesiveness may be increased by the temporary inclusion, within the therapy group of a "deviant plant" (p. 411).
3. Therapy group cohesiveness may be increased by dissolving or reorienting diverging subgroups. The creation of a series of groupwide tasks characterized by superordinate goals with inherent task appeal and demanding interdependent linking across all group members for task completion will result in such subgroup dissolution or reorientation (p. 417).
4. Therapy group cohesiveness may be increased by differential reinforcement by the therapist or patient group-oriented verbalizations versus individual-oriented verbalizations (p. 421).

Although the Goldstein et al. review of the literature which led to the generation of the above hypotheses did not include *group counseling* literature per se, there is little or no reason to doubt that the findings apply equally to group counseling. In order to achieve objective observations of group behavior for predicting outcome a number of interaction process scales were suggested by Goldstein et al. (1966), such as those by Bales, Carter,

Heyns, Steinzer, Benne and Sheats, and Fouriezos, et al. A significant omission in their list is the Hill Interaction Matrix, HIM-A and HIM-B (Hill, 1961, 1963, 1965, 1967). Hill (1967) has stated that "With the HIM-B or HIM-A the pattern of preferences for a group leader or group member can be determined and, by extension, the composition of the group can also be determined and the compatibility of the members with each other and the leader can be measured" (p. 12). There is considerable evidence now building in the related literature to suggest that the Hill instruments, including HIM-G, can also be used to predict outcome of a counseling group as a whole—though perhaps not for each individual participant.

The Multidimensional Evaluation Structure Analysis (Stone, Coles, and Lindem, 1970) represents an addition to the scales for evaluating group interaction that shows great promise for use in selecting members for groups based on the use of paired-comparison ratings. This carefully designed, computer-programmed instrument has great potential for composing groups, giving members feedback, and monitoring group process (Gazda, Evans, and Kaltenbach, 1975).

Still another category for predicting an individual's behavior in a group consists of personal interviews and other measures of psychological appraisal. Research data (Goldstein et al., 1966) do not support this means as effective in predicting within-group behavior of members. However, Schutz's (1966) FIRO-B or three dimensional theory of interpersonal behavior, with his several questionnaires, holds considerable promise as do the indexes of Discrimination and Communication developed by Carkhuff (1969ab), the indexes of Perceiving and Communicating developed by Gazda et al. (1973), and Gazda, Walters, and Childers (1975). The use of biographical data such as used by Dr. Owens of the University of Georgia's Department of Psychology for predicting group interaction has not even been attempted and leaves an entire area open to research. Other techniques which already have been employed with limited success are Bach's (1954) use of MAPS Figure Grouping, the Life

Space Drawings and a number of situational and psychodramatic tests described by Goldstein et al. (1966, p. 326).

Both Ginott (1961) and Slavson (1964) believe that a person's capacity for "social hunger" is a primary prerequisite for placement in a therapy group. Ginott, in particular, applies this criterion in the selection of children for therapy groups. According to Slavson (1964), "Social hunger has the same relation to group psychotherapy as transference does to individual psychotherapy." Slavson defines social hunger as ". . . the desire to be with people and belong with others" (p. 492).

Social hunger provides the group counselor with a good rule-of-thumb procedure for selecting group counselees; however, it is insufficient in itself since it is difficult to appraise. Insofar as they are related to counselee readiness or hope, the previous guidelines, based on research cited by Truax and Carkhuff (1967), lend credence and specificity to their application in counselee selection.

Screening Interview

A diagnostic interview is held with each prospective group counselee to give the counselor an opportunity to describe the ground rules for and responsibilities of the group and to enable the counselor to ascertain the counselee's readiness and acceptability for a group counseling experience. The diagnosis is often useful for effective empathic understanding on the counselor's part and it is essential for him or her also to know the degree of seriousness of the counselee's problem (Truax and Carkhuff, 1967), since prospective counselees who are experiencing a serious crisis in their lives should be seen individually. They tend to dominate a group with their immediate needs and prevent others from getting help. This often turns the group against them because they monopolize the time.

Not all counselors can help all counselees; therefore the group counselor must know himself/herself and his or her limitations in this regard. The diagnostic interview permits the counselor to determine whether or not a prospective group counselee has a problem similar to one that the counselor has been unsuccessful in solving in his or her own life. The counselee should be referred to someone else if he or she has a problem which the counselor has proven inadequate in solving. Carkhuff (1969a) makes this point very succinctly:

> If the helper cannot establish himself as a person who is himself living at more effective levels than the distressed person, if the helper cannot establish that given the same circumstances be could bring about a more effective resolution, there is no meaningful basis for helping (p. 45).

The screening interview provides the counselor the opportunity to go over the ground rules of the proposed group with the candidate. The rules are carefully explained in this interview, and are reviewed again at the beginning of the group during the first session and at other times throughout the counseling session as often as is necessary for their communication and clarification. The screening interview also serves as a hurdle to group membership which makes it more appealing upon admission—providing the initiation is not too severe (Goldstein et al., 1966).

To heighten the candidate's appeal for the counseling group, he or she is told (after being accepted by the counselor) that he/she will very likely find the other group members to be congenial and helpful. A review of research by Goldstein et al. (1966), suggests that this type of positive premembership structuring leads to increased acceptance of members for each other and resultant group cohesiveness.

Ground Rules[2]

Following the counselor's hopeful and positive introduction in the screening interview, the counselor reviews for the candidate the following ground rules that the candidate will be expected to follow as a member of the group.

1. Set a goal or goals for yourself before you enter the group, or at the very latest, as early as you can isolate and define your direc-

---

2. The following ground rules are written at a level used with adolescent and adult groups. They are modified and abbreviated for children's groups—especially as the ground rules are related to voluntary participation of the counselees.

tion of change. Revise these goals as clarification and/or experience dictates.

2. Discuss as honestly and concretely as you can the nature of your troubles, including the successful and unsuccessful coping behaviors you have employed.

3. When you are not discussing your own difficulties, listen *intently* to the other group members and try to help them say what they are trying to say. Communicate your understanding, caring, and empathy for them.

4. You are to maintain the confidentiality of all that is discussed in the group. (There are no exceptions to this rule other than those things that pertain to you only.)

5. You will be on time and attend regularly until termination of the group (if a closed group) and until you have met your goals (if the group is open-ended).

6. You will give to the counselor the privilege of removing you from the group if the counselor deems it necessary for your health and/or for the overall benefit of the group.

7. You will concur that all decisions affecting the group as a whole will be made by consensus only.

8. You should inform the group counselor in private, before the group is constituted, of individuals who would, for various reasons, constitute a serious impediment to your group participation. The "cards should be stacked in the counselee's favor" as much as possible; therefore those individuals who could inhibit the counselee should be excluded from the group if at all possible.)

9. You may request individual counseling interviews, but what is discussed in these interviews should be shared with the group at the appropriate time and at the discretion of the counselor and yourself.

VALUES AND UNIQUENESS OF GROUP COUNSELING

There are certain features and values of group counseling and psychotherapy in general that should be recognized. These values and unique features are cited below with full awareness that they are not limited to Developmental Group Counseling and that all have not been experimentally validated. Lacking experimental validation, the value and unique features of group counseling (therapy) are supported by reference to agreement among experts.

Respondents to a national survey (Gazda, Duncan, and Meadows, 1967) cited the following advantages—values and uniqueness:

1. Approximates a real life situation, or small community of peers, through which each member can test reality, practice identification, obtain feedback and support, share ideas, feelings, and concerns, leading to personal growth and improved interpersonal relations;
2. Provides for more economical and better use of counselor's time;
3. Facilitates an effective use of peer group pressure;
4. Makes certain individuals (e.g., the defensive, shy, dependent, and school behavior problem) more amenable to individual counseling;
5. Enables counselees to serve as cocounselors;
6. Provides a method for counselor training; and
7. Implements subsequent individual counseling.

The limitations and disadvantages of Developmental Group Counseling are not believed to be any different from those of any other form of group counseling or psychotherapy. For example, when authors were asked to list the limitations and disadvantages of group counseling as a part of a survey questionnaire, their responses in order of frequency included the following:

. . . inappropriate treatment for certain problem types, e.g., sociopathic or psychopathic children, and the severely disturbed; difficult to control confidentiality, depth of involvement, collusion of unhealthy effects, and anxiety level; requires a more skillful counselor, including a greater sensitivity and expertness in group dynamics; is difficult to select appropriate combinations of group members; permits certain participants, e.g., the shy and withdrawn, to refrain from participation; does not provide for adequate individual attention for some counselees; can be difficult, especially in the school setting, to arrange a convenient time for a group meeting; does not represent an economical use of counselor's time; may lead to acceptance of the group milieu which may become artificial; and it is difficult to train adequate practitioners (Gazda, et al., 1967, p. 307).

Still other limitations of group counseling and therapy are cited. Beck (1958) calls attention to the unsuitability of group therapy for those lacking communication skills; the lessened control of the group therapist, the unpredictability of group process, intragroup jealousies, and lack of opportunity for depth treatment at critical moments. Prados (1953) cites as a weakness the tendency of members to act out unconscious infantile impulses, and Spotnitz (1961) cites the tendency of some participants, because of group comfort and a decrease in the urgency to tackle their problems, to drop out of therapy prematurely.

Therapists who practice psychoanalytic psychotherapy on an individual basis frequently contend that the use of a group interferes with or makes impossible the development of a transference relationship and hence is not effective therapy. Some psychoanalytically oriented group therapists feel that the transference relationship between counselees and therapist is sometimes interfered with by the presence of other counselees.

In summary, it seems possible that the same elements that make for a potent therapeutic climate and force are those that also add greater risks to the treatment, e.g. the presence of several counselees in a group decreases the counselor's control and thus subjects the counselees to greater risks of the group's ostracism, pressure, rivalry, breaking of confidence and the like, with the possible resultant harmful effects. Still other limitations or weaknesses of group counseling lie in the difficulty to bring together regularly a number of counselees at the same time and the reduced ability of the counselor to focus on nonverbal behavior.

Attention will now be focused on the application of Developmental Group Counseling to the various age groups and illustrate the application with a protocol.

APPLICATION OF A DEVELOPMENTAL APPROACH TO GROUP COUNSELING FOR CHILDREN FIVE TO NINE YEARS OF AGE[3]

One of the developmental tasks for children from five to nine is "achieving an appropriate dependence-independence pattern" (Tryon and Lilienthal, 1950). Using this task with its appropriate coping behaviors as an early warning system for detecting potential trouble for given children, a teacher has referred three children who are having difficulty performing appropriate cop-

---

3. From Gazda, G. M.: *Group Counseling: A Developmental Approach,* 1971. Courtesy of Allyn and Bacon, Inc., Boston, Massachusetts.

ing behavior to accomplish successfully this task. The children are two boys and a girl. The girl is an eight-year-old, shy, overly dependent child. One boy is aggressive and too independent for his own safety. He is seven years old. The other boy is nine years old, and, prior to the recent birth of a male sibling, appeared to be making good progress in his dependence-independence functioning. With the arrival of a new baby brother, this nine-year-old boy became very dependent on his teacher (a female) and his parents, and stayed very close to his teacher and his mother. The group counselor is a young woman in her mid-twenties.

A group has been carefully selected to provide potential models for each child and also to contain some built-in controls—namely an older boy whose age and size alone can assist the counselor in controlling the one younger but aggressive boy. The counselor also has obtained extensive case data on each child and has decided in interviews with the teacher and parents that the common problem for each child is a need to develop appropriate behavior to cope with the task of achieving a proper balance between dependence and independence.

The counselor uses a free-play setting for the first three or four sessions. She meets the group for forty-five minutes and holds the sessions in a playroom. During this time the children can play with a variety of toys and materials. The counselor shows an interest in each child and makes every effort to establish rapport or build the base of mutual trust and liking for one another. After rapport has been established, the counselor begins to structure the last half of each play session. At first she does this through story reading and telling and through the use of puppets. She introduces vicarious models in this way and verbally rewards appropriate dependence-independence behavior. Moving from puppets to dolls, she structures situations and asks the children to use the dolls to work out solutions. She rewards appropriate solutions verbally and asks for replays of inappropriate solutions until they approach appropriate coping behavior for dealing with the dependence-independence task.

As the children show progress with vicarious modeling, the

counselor also sets up sociodramas and psychodramas revolving around school and family situations for the group to use in modifying their behavior. Finally, the counselor moves into the realm of the here-and-now relationships between herself and each child and those between each child. She models for the child by encouraging their appropriate independence from her and by rewarding appropriate dependence also.

The media selected for their play and action qualities are used to promote relationship development and problem resolution and are not therefore in themselves a primary focus of the treatment. The counselor is always conscious of the *timing* of her moves and of the purpose of her techniques. She moves from the least threatening situations in the beginning to the more threatening but more relevant procedures as the children show signs of growth. The above procedure or model provides ample opportunity for vicarious and real-life modeling and numerous opportunities for implementing other learning principles of desensitization, shaping, operant conditioning, discriminate and assertive training, and reciprocal inhibition. The deliberate use of these principles represents the science of play group counseling, whereas the when and how of implementing them represent the art of this form of treatment.

The maximum size of a play group for counseling should be five. If a cocounselor is utilized, one might include six or seven children. The size is determined by the degree to which the counselor is able to maintain adequate control over the group. Since young children have few social controls, the counselor must limit the size to retain the control.

GROUP COUNSELING FOR PREADOLESCENTS
(AGES NINE TO THIRTEEN)

Since preadolescents prefer to associate with members of the same sex group, this is the only age group where the preferred method is to segregate by sex for counseling. Because the preadolescent has greater self-control, the group size can range from five to seven or even larger if cocounselors are used. The composition of the group is balanced to provide adequate models for everyone in the group. Sessions should run at least one hour twice a week or perhaps one and one-half to two hours once a week if twice-a-week meetings are not possible.

English and Higgins (1971) used a client-centered group counseling approach with preadolescents from the fourth and fifth grades and, failing to get significant results, concluded: "Logically, it appears that the client-centered approach places unrealistic demands on preadolescents to assume responsibility and initiative, especially for verbalizing" (p. 509).

Alper and Kranzler (1970) and Kranzler (1968) have suggested that all conventional approaches to group counseling are inappropriate with preadolescents. The author concurs with this position and therefore recommends the activity-interview model because of the natural inclinations of this age group toward games and activities.

ACTIVITY-INTERVIEW GROUP COUNSELING
(AGES NINE TO THIRTEEN)[4]

Activity-interview group counseling is a composite of activity group therapy, *a la* Slavson, and interview group counseling. In essence an activity, such as checkers, is used to involve the group and to lower the inhibitions and defenses of the group members. The activity itself may provide an opportunity for physical catharsis or a nonsystematized desensitization. It serves the same purpose as systematic desensitization practiced by behaviorally-oriented counselors and therapists. In addition to providing a means for tension reduction through physical catharsis, the activity also provides an opportunity for interpersonal interactions which are the concern of the counselor and members in the group "interview" period following the game or activity. Activity-interview group counseling is a combination of prevention and remediation; thus it is intended for preadolescents, in particular, but also for adolescents and some adults, who are not suffering from debilitating emotional problems.

The activities may be many and varied. They should be chosen

---

4. From Gazda, G. M.: *Group Counseling: A Developmental Approach*, 1971. Courtesy of Allyn and Bacon, Inc., Boston, Massachusetts.

by the group counselor according to the needs of the group members. Care should be taken to vary the games or activities in order to provide some success experiences for all members of the group. The athletic-type preadolescent should have the opportunity to demonstrate his talents in team sports like basketball, touch football, and volleyball. In like fashion, the less athletic preadolescent should have an opportunity to experience success in table games such as electric bowling, ping-pong, chess, checkers, and the like. Still other activities such as dancing and swimming and arts and crafts should be used for those who may have talents apart from the physical or intellective.

Simulation and gaming constitutes a new and promising medium for use in group counseling with the preadolescent in particular. Games such as the Life Career Game (Varenhorst, 1968) can be adapted for small counseling groups and would provide the less physically competitive preadolescent with a substitute means for showing ability or excellence, such as in problem solving. It would also appeal to the group counselor who has less interest and enthusiasm for the more physically active team sports.

Simulating problem-resolution can serve as a means of vicariously conditioning preadolescents by rewarding choices or decisions that lead the hypothetical person to success experiences and not rewarding or vicariously punishing the hypothetical person's inappropriate choices, decisions, et cetera. Thus, this medium could serve much like role playing, to protect the real counselee, but go beyond it in complexity of problems, external factors affecting decisions, and so forth. The use of action mazes using two or three members as a team could be arranged and when warranted competition between or among teams could be encouraged. To facilitate total group understanding of appropriate and inappropriate moves through the maze, group discussions could follow the completion of the maze.

Since the activity itself in activity-interview group counseling represents only part of the treatment, those activities that involve simultaneously several, if not all the group members, should be most utilized. The discussion phase (interview group counseling session) usually following the game or activity, constitutes the second part of the treatment. During this period the counselor helps the group members focus on the nature of the interactions that occurred during the activity phase of the treatment. The behavior that occurred during the activity is related to the life style of a given group member.

The counselor builds a strong facilitative base with high levels of empathy, respect, and warmth. Only after having established a feeling of mutual trust and caring does the counselor move the group member into the planning and action phase of the treatment through appropriate self-disclosure, genuineness, concreteness, confrontation, and immediacy, *a la* Carkhuff (1969 ab).

The interview or discussion phase need not be held in a formal setting such as a conference room, although such a room should be available when movement from an activity setting is required. The conference room can also be set up as a dual-purpose room including equipment and materials for group activities as well as chairs for the interview phase.

Day (1967) studied the use of activity group counseling with culturally disadvantaged, behavioral-problem boys referred for counseling by classroom teachers. The subjects were twenty-five culturally disadvantaged Negro boys, ranging in age from eleven to fourteen. They were initially selected through the use of behavior ratings by classroom teachers.

The experimental group met in activity counseling three times a week for five weeks. During this time, the control group received no counseling or guidance activities. Immediately after termination of the experimental groups, activity group counseling was provided for the control group. These students served as their own control for the purpose of statistical evaluation.

A criterion instrument used in measuring the change of classroom behavior was the Haggerty-Olson-Wickman Behavior Rating Schedule B (HOW). The criterion instrument used in measuring change in peer acceptance was a sociometric instrument designed by the investigator. Differences in mean gains for classroom social behavior, classroom emotional behavior, and total classroom behavior were calculated for the experimental versus the control group and for the control group during the control phase versus the control group during the counseling phase.

The results indicate that those students receiving activity group counseling showed favorable gains in classroom social behavior and total classroom behavior ($p. < .05$). Day concluded:

1. Activity group counseling has an effect on classroom behavior of culturally disadvantaged, behavioral problem students. Social behaviors were particularly affected by the experience of activity group counseling. Emotional behavior was also affected by activity group counseling, although nonsignificantly.
2. Written evaluation by teachers confirmed that twenty-three of the twenty-five subjects were seen as significantly improved in classroom behavior.
3. Activity group counseling was seen by the participants as a very positive experience. All of the subjects in this study expressed a desire to continue counseling in groups. Each student rated the experience as being both helpful and pleasant.
4. Activity group counseling can be conducted within the confines of the typical school setting using facilities in the school (1967, p. 103).

Blakeman (1967) investigated the effects of activity group counseling on the classroom behavior of seventh- and eighth-grade problem boys of Caucasian origin who ranged in age from eleven to fourteen. Forty-nine boys were recommended by teachers and then interviewed as possible participants for the study. From this group forty boys volunteered to participate. This investigation included group activity meetings that were held weekly after school for one hour over a period of six weeks. The activities included touch football, golf, table tennis, swimming, and visits to a nearby confectionary. Criterion instruments for behavioral improvement were the Self-Evaluation Picture Tests (SEPT) and the Haggerty-Olson-Wickman Behavioral Ratings Schedule (HOW). An independent examination of the experimental group indicated that activity group treatment had a positive effect upon the self-evaluation and classroom behavior of these behavioral problem boys. Evaluation of the data further indicated that experimental students changed in the desired direction, and no regression was noted over a four and one half month period. Blakeman concluded:

1. It can be stated with reasonable sureness that activity-group treatment effects desirable changes in boys' self-evaluation to significant degrees.
2. Graduate training programs can easily incorporate activity group counseling experiences and practicum courses for trainees. A variety of activities seem appropriate as a setting for activity group treatment. All of these are available within the school confines (pp. 69-70).

The following protocol illustrates the dual-purpose setting used with a group of black preadolescent "problem students," ranging in age from eleven to fourteen in the Day study previously described. The protocol includes portions taken from the sixth group session. The setting is a dual-purpose room in which six black boys are milling around the room. Some are reading; others are drawing; one is throwing darts. J. (the subject of discussion) is very active. The counselor is a white male.

Protocol

J.: I'm not gonna' tell anything in the meeting today because everything I do, R. tells Mr. A.

R.: I did not tell!

Co.: Let's hear about this.

J.: I am not going to say anything.

R.: He went and shot off his big mouth, and because I told Mr. A. now he is mad at me.

J.: Ah Peanut, that isn't either what happened. That isn't the first time you've done this, Peanut. I've been playing with you all day and you've been doing it all along. Every time you touch him he gets mad. Just touch him a little bit and he gets mad; he's a baby.

Co.: How about that, Group? How would you handle that?

W.: J. is to blame; he is always to blame. He's a great big bully.

J.: I didn't touch him. I know what I'm gonna' do about it! I'm just not gonna' associate with anybody in this group anymore.

R.: Don't worry; it will pass over.

J.: No, it won't pass over, R. I'm the only one around this school that even likes you a little bit, and I don't see how I can like you now. You're gonna' be so lonely. I'm the best friend you got and you did me dirty and that's all I'm gonna' have to do with you.

Co.: It sounds like J. is pretty mad this time.

M.: I think they are both at fault. I think they are both babies.

Co.: Let's talk about the basketball game we played yesterday.

J.: I'm not going to talk. Every time I talk, somebody tells on me, I've been in the office more than anybody this year, more than any of you punks.

Co.: J., it sounds like maybe you are blaming R. for some of your problems.

J.: This is part of the office and every time I may do something wrong, R. goes to Mr. A. and tells him all about it.

Co.: Do you consider this part of the office? Is this like the principal's office?

J.: It was before you came. I don't mind if he tells you, but I don't want him telling Mr. A., and I don't want him telling the principal.

R.: J., you think I am the cause of all your problems.

J.: The way I feel about it, if I weren't around you everything would be all right. That's what I'm gonna' do; stay away from you.

Co.: It sounds like R. is responsible for everything you had had to go wrong this year, J.

J.: Most all of 'em, anyway.

Co.: Most all of them?

J.: Yes, all of them. Everything I've been in trouble is 'cause of him.

Co.: It sounds like J. and R. have had everything to say, so far. What do some of the rest of you think? I wonder if some of the other boys might not be able to help you out.

J.: Every time I see two or three boys beat up on him, fight him, jump on him, I help him. Now, first time things go wrong, he runs in and tells Mr. A. I'm through with him.

Co.: We don't seem to be getting very far with this argument; why don't we try something. Why don't we try J. and R. just being quiet for a minute and let some of the other boys give some of their opinions of how they might handle a situation like this.

J.: No, I'm not through yet. I want to talk some more. I don't like Peanut, and I'm not having any more to do with him.

R.: I think Mr. Counselor has a good idea; let's try that.

T.: I think they both got problems. I think they both need to work on 'em.

M.: I think we ought to put them together and let them fight it out.

Co.: It seems to be a lot of buzzing, but no one wants to say things directly to J. or R. about the situation. I get the idea that all of you would like to, but you're kinda' frightened of what they might say back.

J.: I think the way to settle this whole thing is if I don't associate with R. anymore. When he gets tired of not associating with me, he'll come around and say, "Let's make friends again," and then we'll be friends.

Co.: I'm still puzzled about your saying R. is responsible for all your problems.

J.: Yes, he is. And even though you want me to say something, I'm not gonna' say nothing different. He is responsible for all my problems. Let's do something different; I'm tired of this. I don't want to be talking all day long. I'm mad at this group.

Co.: It seems like J. doesn't feel like the group is satisfying him any more. How do the rest of you feel?

Group: It's great; it's what we want. Let's do it.

W.: Let's get J. out of the group if he doesn't like it.

H.: If he wants out, let's get him out.

L.: Yeah, let's get him out, if he doesn't want to be in the group; let's get him out.

Co.: I guess the boys are saying, J., that the door is open.

J.: Well, one thing about this group is that when we do play basketball or football, we got a sorry bunch of players. None of them really want to play ball. They're just a bunch of goofoffs. We got a sorry bunch of players.

M.: That's what you say. You shoot all the time anyway, how would you know? You never pass it to anyone. Why don't you try to teach some of the boys how to play rather than chewing at them all the time?

R.: Well, I'd like to say something. I tell you this. When J. has the ball, even if you're wide open, he won't pass it to you. He won't pass it to any little boys. All he wants to do is shoot or pass it to one of the big boys. He keeps on dribbling like he don't know or even hear. All he does is shoot.

M.: I think J. and I are the best basketball players in here and I think we play harder than any of the other boys. I think J. doesn't like the other boys. He never passes. I try at least to be good to them.

J.: Yeah, W., L., and T., they're no good. They won't even play. They lose interest in the game, and if you don't keep on them all the time, they won't even play. No sense to pass to them, anyway. They just dribble and lose it. They're no good anyway.

L.: The group wasn't formed just for basketball. There is other reasons, too. Someone else might be good in football. You just want to be the big hog in everything you do, J.

Co.: It seems like some of you boys felt like being good in basketball was the main purpose in the group, while others seem to think that there are other purposes in the group.

T.: Yeah, keep us out of trouble.

J.: I'd like to talk now. Now, you say I don't pass the ball, but who in here does pass the ball? Every time I pass to T. or W., they lose the ball. Every time. So why pass to them? Just lose it if I pass it to them.

W.: What are you talking about, boy? You don't even know what you are talking about.

J.: Now you answer that, W. Why would I pass it to you? Now . . . if you see somebody that ain't gonna' do no good with something that is given to them, why give to them? Why do it? Why give it to them?

Co.: It seems like J. sees a different purpose for the group. He wants to be a good basketball player and have a basketball team. Some of the rest of you don't feel that way.

M.: Well, I think anybody that don't know how to play ought to learn, and I think this is a good place to learn to do things. I think J. is wrong. I think we ought to be teaching boys to learn.

J.: The time to learn is not while you're playing the game. The time to learn is on your own in your own yard. Besides that, you can't teach boys that don't want to learn. Some of these boys would rather play dodge, so go let them play dodge, but when they come on a basketball floor, they ought to play basketball and they ought to try to be good. If they don't show a lot of interest, they shouldn't ought to be out there.

W.: I'm no good at basketball, but I think that I'd have a lot of fun playing basketball if J. weren't there.

R.: J. always shoots the ball so when we get back to this meeting, he can just talk about what he did during the game.

Co.: Let's take a look now, boys, at what we are doing. It seems as though everybody is ganging up against J., and it seems like we're trying to tell him that he's not a very good sport when it comes to playing basketball. I think maybe we're being a little hard on him.

J.: Don't worry about me. I don't feel bad.

M.: I think this is good because I think J. needs help. I think he needs help badly not only in basketball but all over.

J.: I don't think I need no help.

M.: Yes, you do need some help. You need lots of help.

J.: You can't help me.

Co.: M., what do you see he needs help in?

M.: He needs to learn how to keep his mouth shut, and he needs to learn how to act.

J.: I don't need no help from none of you. I don't want any help from anybody.

Co.: You don't want any help, from any of us?

R.: That's his main problem. When somebody tries to help him, he won't let them. It is the same thing he was saying. If he won't help himself, how can we help?

J.: Be quiet. Oh, shut up, Peanut. Peanut, will you shut up! I'm leaving this group. I'm through with this group. This group can't help me. I don't like this group, any of you, and I'm not gonna' be in the group. I am through with you, and I don't want anything to do with you or anybody in this group.

Co.: Sorry you feel this way, J. It sounds like we have been a little hard on you today. It seems like the boys had a lot on their minds.

R.: Yet, it is true.

J.: I'm quitting. I don't want anything to do with you. I don't want to come to any more of the group meetings. Count me out.

Co.: We'll leave it up to you, J. Whatever you decide is all right with us. I think, though, that we should leave it open if you would like to come back.

J.: I won't come back, and I won't have any more to do with it.

M.: I hope you do come back, J. I like you. I just think there are some things you need to work on.

W.: Yeah, we like you, J. I'm sorry that you are so mad.

R.: I like you too, J., even if you are mad at me. And if you don't want to be in the group, I don't think you should have to be.

(Session Ends)

J. says that he is quitting and is very angry. J. comes back to the counselor during the week, however, and apologizes for getting angry. He comes back to the group and is a model group member.

The protocol illustrates a very action-oriented approach on the part of the counselor. He assumed that he had a good relationship built with J. and the group. The counselor and the group members showed empathy, warmth, respect, self-disclosure, genuineness, concreteness, immediacy, and confrontation—with a rather heavy emphasis on confrontation. If J. had not previously experienced the counselor and group members as helpful individuals, the result of this session would not have been so positive.

GROUP COUNSELING FOR HIGH SCHOOL-AGE PERSONS

Group counseling has been described earlier as being preventive, growth-engendering, and remedial. It is preventive to the extent that one has access to accurate information that can be used to make wise decisions. It is growth-engendering to the degree that the person's potential may be released through greater self-understanding and self-acceptance. It is remedial to the degree that a person's inappropriate habits and attitudes are modified.

The most natural and efficient medium through which the typical adolescent and adult communicate is the spoken word; therefore interview group counseling is the preferred mode of treatment for adolescents and adults. The preferred size is eight to ten; the preferred composition is heterogeneous without a wide age range and without extreme differences in intelligence, seriousness of problems, culture, and the like. High school freshmen and sophomores can be combined by age group as can juniors and seniors. Sophomores and juniors can also usually be combined; however, mixing freshmen with juniors and seniors is generally contraindicated. There are a variety of possible meeting schedules including one and one-half to two hours one day a week, one and one-half hours to two hours twice a week, and perhaps a twelve to twenty-four-hour marathon added to either of the above procedures as a part of the overall program. The duration of the treatment should be a minimum of eight to ten weeks and preferably twelve weeks or longer, depending upon the needs of the students. Video feedback can be adapted to a typical interview counseling group. The setting for an interview group should be a room capable of seating comfortably eight to ten people in a circular fashion with no table or other obstacle within the circle's center.

The following interview group counseling protocol consists of excerpts taken from the first session of a counseling group composed of high school juniors and seniors. The group consisted of four girls and two boys. Their common concern or interest was planning for college. The protocol begins following the introductions. The author was serving as the counselor.

Protocol

Cathy: I've been in classes at ——— High School where we are phased. We have Phase 1, Phase 2, and Phase 3. If you are in Phase 1, you are supposed to have advanced ability and you are supposed to be able to learn easily; therefore lots of times people say, "Well you should be able to do this because you have your ability already." I think that I am often on my own. In some cases this is good; but when you've been in this type of class all your life, you get sort of tired of hearing it and sometimes you *can't* do it by yourself. I'd just like to express that people who *can* do things need encouragement, also. You can't just say, "Here, do it." You've got to give them some attention, too.

Sue: Well, yeah, I agree with that, about the phases and all. You do get tired of it when you are in it all the time. I think a lot of kids that aren't in the top phases are hurt by thinking they are stupid and they don't put out what they could.

Jean: The teacher doesn't realize that when she has a class she's dealing with different types of students that have different interests and backgrounds. Instead of relating to the kids themselves, she's saying, "Okay, this is what we've got to learn," not "This is what will help you." This is where they are at fault. The teachers may take the easy way out and don't go to the trouble of relating to the kids and giving them something meaningful. This applies to all kids, not just to the elite.

Counselor (Co.): I heard Cathy saying that even though she's involved in accelerated classes, she gets to a point at times where she'd like to be encouraged too, noticed by the teacher, and not told, "You're on your own because after all you are an accelerated student."

Cathy: That's it exactly. Of course you have some teachers that are different. Like I say, when you have been in these classes for years, you get it all over and over. You know, that you're in a phasing class and that you can do this or that without any trouble but you would still like to be encouraged and know that the teachers care not only about what you're learning, but they care also about you.

Jean: Another thing is wrong with phasing. I think the slower phase groups could get a lot more, because I think these kids have a lot to offer, but they don't get a chance. Sometimes, too, the top phase kids think they're real smart, and they think the other kids are stupid.

Co.: Jean, you think its bad, then, for some kids to get the idea that there are other kids that are stupid and they got all the brains and they get kind of conceited.

James: I see myself thinking that way sometimes. I think there are people sometimes that don't have the mental power, and being in a lower phase kind of makes them feel inferior. I don't really think they are inferior, but I've had feelings like that sometimes.

Cathy: I've been in classes that were not phased, too. You do learn a lot, but still you feel held back because you have to go along with the class and lots of phase students are interested in just learning. I was in an unphased class and we just didn't move fast enough. You get bored so you just sit back and let things slide because you can easily keep up with them with no trouble at all, but it's still good to be in a class with different types of people.

Bev.: I'm inclined to agree with Cathy because I know this girl who, when she was in the sixth and seventh grades, wasn't in phasing. Although she was really young she was kind of slow. The teachers would give it to her and she's the kind of person that has to have care with it to show her that you want her to learn. And when she didn't, she just failed and failed. She was held back. So when they started the phasing, you know, most of the teachers in the lower phasing care about you a lot more, it seems like, and now she's almost an honor roll student. She's graduating this year and she's making almost straight A's. And I don't think she could have done it if she hadn't had phasing, because now everybody takes time with her and she feels like she can do it rather than they just give it to her. She's doing real well now.

Co.: So you think phasing helped her because she was performing at a low level, but the extra care motivated her to do better and she probably is achieving at her capacity now.

Bev.: Uh-huh.

Bill: When Cathy brought this up I was thinking of what I wanted to bring up in this group session and it was dealing with the teacher. Of course it didn't just affect me personally, it affected the whole class but it did affect me personally, too. She was the type that doesn't give anybody any attention. She goes up and stands in front of the classroom and talks to "it." You've got to have the teacher to encourage you, I think, no matter what phase you are or at what level of learning you are. You probably could do the work on your own but you've just got to feel like you have someone standing by you, willing to help you that you don't get lots of times in the school classroom. I feel like they are inefficient.

Co.: Do any of you have feelings similar to Bill?

Sue: I agree with him. In three of my classes—I have the same teacher for two of them—and in the one class my teacher will come in there and just give it to you, over and over and over. I'm not the kind of person that you have to say—well, I get along with my teachers, real good. But I don't like to be talked to like I'm just a machine sitting there—to feed me. One teacher did act like that, and I didn't do well at all. I didn't care if I had my homework done. It was a good thing I liked that subject or I wouldn't have done anything. I think I brought my book home twice. But in one class it was real hard for me and I knew this teacher cared about me, because she would stay after school to help me. I didn't do as well but I studied, where in my other class I didn't even try. I'd pay attention in class because you have to and that's how I got good grades in there, but in the other I didn't do as well but I tried a lot harder.

Co.: So whether your teacher cares or not is pretty important to you as to how you perform.

Cathy: That's my thing in school. If the teacher doesn't care about me, I just don't care about the subject.

Co.: Cathy, it sounds like you're saying the same thing as Sue. If the teachers care they turn you on, and if they don't, they turn you off.

Cathy: Yeah.

Bill: It sounds like we're saying that the teacher should be there all the time. But what I mean is that you should be able to feel like she is your friend, and you can go to her when you need her. You should be able to work individually, too, and not let your work depend on her cause it's not always going to be that way. I realize like when you get in college, everybody says, "Oh you've got to learn to do it on your own because you know it's really personal." But I do believe that a teacher should let you know that she cares about you as a person not just as a student.

Marsha: This may not be related but taking it out of the teacher-student context, you know you always perform better in just everyday life situations if someone cares.

Bill: I play some basketball and I think this is a very similar situation with the coach. You don't perform as well in the sport if you're not interested and the coach isn't interested in you and he doesn't care for you, encourage you to play and all. I think it affects your game.

Co.: So it is very much like the teacher situation.

Bill: Uh-huh.

Sue: I have two older brothers who had some trouble with high school teachers, but they got along fine in college. It seems funny, all of a sudden you have all of this self-realization, you know, and you're going out into the world. Is it the fear of college?

Bill: It might be the atmosphere in the classroom and all, 'cause I don't know, the teachers there just don't tolerate it.

Sue: Well they don't have the problem. They don't have the problem to tolerate. There's never a question.

Bill: I think you're privileged to be able to go to college. If you get thrown out of college, that's it.

(The group moves into a discussion of college requirements, academic, and interpersonal, and the first session ends on this note.)

GROUP COUNSELING FOR ADULTS[5]

The following protocol was taken from a group session with adults very early in the life of a group. The protocol illustrates the application of the core conditions of Carkhuff (1969ab) to a problem introduced by a group member in *interview group counseling*. Since there was no facilitative base built with the counselee, the group counselor and members were careful to begin with interchangeable responses, especially of empathy. The interaction covered only ten minutes of group time and yet led to a decision that the counselee felt was necessary and appropriate.

The counselee was in her mid-twenties. The group was composed of male and female members from their early twenties to their late fifties.

Protocol

Counselee: Every time the phone rings my heart jumps. I stay worried all the time.

Counselor: You're really pretty sure then that you're going to get some bad news every time the phone rings.

Counselee: Yes, it seems like that I just wait to hear some upsetting news from home.

---

5. From Gazda, G. M.: *Group Counseling: A Developmental Approach,* 1971. Courtesy of Allyn and Bacon, Inc., Boston, Massachusetts.

Group Member A (female): Something then is going on at home that makes you think that something bad is going to happen?

Counselee: Yes, my sister is ill and they're trying to find out what's wrong with her but they tell me that they don't know exactly what it is yet. I feel like maybe I should be there instead of eighty-four miles away, living my own life.

Counselor: You feel kind of guilty that in this time of crisis in your family that you're not there to help out.

Counselee: Yes, it seems like that every time they've needed me, that I was either away at school or not available. This really has me upset!

Group Member B (male): It is not the first time that they couldn't depend on you to be around? You've been away quite a bit sometimes.

Counselee: Yes. Maybe it wouldn't affect me so badly if this were the first crisis, but it seems like it's just been one a minute in the last five years, and I'm really feeling guilty. I'm married now, but I still feel like I have commitments to Mom and Dad.

Counselor: You feel that during these five years away from home you weren't doing enough to help your Mom and Dad. Now you are married and you're in less position to help them than you were before.

Counselee: Yes. This is it, and then this is the point that confuses me. They wanted me to go away to school and get an education and get a good job. But then being away from home and getting a good education caused me not to be there when they needed me. Now, I've got a good education and am working and I feel like I should be there with them.

Counselor: After they sacrificed for you, you stayed away and now you feel like you owe them something in return, but you haven't been able to pay them back in some way or other.

Counselee: I guess that's getting to the point. Just marrying and getting your own life, job, house—just how much can you participate in family situations when you are out of school, out of the house, without really feeling like you are giving them less than you really should?

Group Member C (male): You just wish you knew what was a fair return to them (interrupted here by counselee response).

Counselee: Yes.

Group Member C (male): . . . after you're married, and what married people owe their parents.

Counselee: Yes, especially after they've made sacrifices for me.

Counselor: I get the feeling that you feel that you do need to do more than you have done.

Counselee: Yes, but then on the other hand, I'm wondering if I really should.

Counselor: Sometimes you think you should, and other times you don't know what a fair return is.

Counselee: Yes, so if I could just work out this problem of not being so-so I wouldn't be so concerned with what's going on at home. If it just wouldn't occupy my mind so much. It really is upsetting me! It seems if I could adjust to the fact that Mom and Dad and my sister have a life, Jack (husband of counselee) and I have a life, and we can just do so much and then function normally.

Group Member D (female): Somehow if you can just get settled in your own mind that there has to be this separation and that you can feel comfortable about whether you've been fair to your parents.

Counselee: Do you think that it's normal to worry about a sister that is sick and ill, and is it normal to the point that you think about it 80 percent of the time and you really spend your time moping and wondering if something is deadly wrong with her? I just don't know what will become of me, nor would I know how to help Mom and Dad.

Group Member C (male): You really don't think it's normal to spend that much time worrying about her. You're also feeling quite a bit of guilt about her illness and the fact that you can't do more for her and your parents.

Counselee: That's why I'm coming and asking for help, because I don't know whether or not it's normal or not. I kind of feel it is normal, since I do have close ties, and I really do love them— love her and my family. But then I don't have guilt feelings about her illness, 'cause this is something that I did not have anything to do with. I do have a guilt feeling about whether or not I really did help them (parents) enough, or if I'm committing myself to home (when I say home, I mean to Mom and Dad and family) as much as I should. That is the essence of my problem. And then it seems like that because I do have these guilt feelings, and it stays on my mind . . . like I'm always wondering about if something is going to happen. If it is, I say, well I should be there. Then if I were there, I wonder how much I really could do.

Counselor: What could you do? You're kind of torn between the feeling that you need to be there on the one hand, and realistically if you were there, you couldn't do anything anyway to change your sister's health, but you might in some way be a comfort to your parents.

Counselee: Yes. Now what are your views on this?

Counselor: I guess all I can tell you, Marilyn, is what I hear you telling me—that you're pretty miserable right now the way things are, and it is not getting any better, and that you need to take some kind of action to feel better about this relationship between you and your parents, that you need to do something more than you have done. I don't know what's possible, but that is what I heard you telling me—that you feel like you owe more than you've been giving them back.

Counselee: I do feel that I have to do more. I guess now my next move must be to talk to my husband about my feelings and make plans to do something more for my parents but which will be acceptable to him.

SUMMARY

This chapter begins by defining group counseling through placing it in perspective with other group procedures. It is defined as lying on a continuum from prevention to remediation and including aspects of both plus growth-engendering dimensions.

The essence of this chapter is the explication of Developmental Group Counseling—an eclectic position that includes relationship and learning principles. This position rests on the hypothesis that group counseling must take into consideration the counselee's age and developmental levels—physical, psychological, social, vocational, cognitive, and moral—if it is to be relevant to varying age groups. The age groupings for which special forms of group counseling have been described are five to nine, nine to thirteen, thirteen to twenty, and adulthood. For each age grouping the preferred type of leadership, group size, setting and media, group composition, and length and duration of treatment are described. Protocols are used to illustrate group counseling with each age group.

The dynamics operative in counseling groups such as leadership, including essential conditions of a helping relationship, structuring, goal setting, norm setting and stages of group development are related to effective group functioning. Related topics include criteria for group selection and composition, ground rules for group operation, values and uniqueness of counseling groups, and limitations of counseling groups.

A list of carefully selected readings is given at the end of the chapter. These readings have been selected to provide specific references for each of the four age groupings dealt with in Developmental Group Counseling.

SUGGESTED READING

Amster, F.: Differential uses of play in treatment of young children. *American Journal of Orthopsychiatry, 13*:62, 1943.

Blocher, D. H.: *Developmental Counseling.* New York, Ronald, 1966.

Bandura, A.: Behavioral modification through modeling procedures. In Krasner, L., and Ullman, L. P. (Eds.): *Research in Behavior Modification.* New York, HR&W, 1965.

Berenson, B. G., and Mitchell, K. M.: *Confrontation for Better or for Worse!* Amherst, Massachusetts, Human Resources Development Press, 1974.

Blakeman, J. D., and Day, S. R.: Activity group counseling. In Gazda, G. M. (Ed.): *Theories and Methods of Group Counseling in the Schools.* Springfield, Thomas, 1969.

Boocock, S. S., and Schild, E. O. (Eds.): *Simulation Games in Learning.* Beverly Hills, Sage Publications, 1969.

Brammer, L. M.: Eclecticism revisited. *Personnel and Guidance Journal, 48*:192, 1969.

Carkhuff, R. R.: *Helping and Human Relations.* Vol. 1. *Selection and Training.* New York, HR&W, 1969(a).

Carkhuff, R. R.: *Helping and Human Relations.* Vol. 2. *Practice and Research.* New York, HR&W, 1969(b).

Carkhuff, R. R.: *The Development of Human Resources: Education, Psychology, and Social Action.* New York, HR&W, 1971.

Carkhuff, R. R., and Berenson, B. G.: *Beyond Counseling and Therapy.* New York, HR&W, 1967.

Corsini, R. J.: *Roleplaying in Psychotherapy.* Chicago, Aldine, 1966.

Crosby, M. (Ed.): *Reading Ladders for Human Relations,* 4th ed. Washington, D.C., American Council on Education, 1963.

Erikson, E. H.: *Childhood and Society,* 2nd ed. New York, Norton, 1963.

Flavell, J. H.: *The Developmental Psychology of Jean Piaget.* Princeton, D. Van Nostrand, 1963.

Gazda, G. M.: *Group Counseling: A Developmental Approach.* Boston, Allyn, 1971.

Ginott, H. G.: *Group Psychotherapy with Children.* New York, McGraw, 1961.

Glasser, W.: *Schools Without Failure*. New York, Har-Row, 1969.

Goldstein, A. P., Heller, K., and Sechrest, L. B.: *Psychotherapy and the Psychology of Behavior Change*. New York, Wiley, 1966.

Groups in guidance: special issue. *Personnel and Guidance Journal*, April, 1971.

Haas, R. B. (Ed.): *Psychodrama and Sociodrama in American Education*. New York, Beacon Hse, 1949.

Hansen, J. C., Niland, T. M., and Zani, L. P.: Model reinforcement in group counseling with elementary school children. *Personnel and Guidance Journal*, 47:741, 1969.

Harms, E.: Play diagnosis: preliminary considerations for a sound approach. *Nervous Child*, 7:233, 1948.

Havighurst, R. J.: *Developmental Tasks and Education*, 2nd ed. New York, Longmans, Green, 1952.

Havighurst, R. J.: *Human Development and Education*. New York, McKay, 1953.

Havighurst, R. J.: *Developmental Tasks and Education*, 3rd ed. New York, McKay, 1972.

Hinds, W. C., and Roehlke, H. J.: A learning theory approach to group counseling with elementary school children. *Journal of Counseling Psychology*, 17:49, 1970.

Kohlberg, L.: *Collected Papers on Moral Development and Moral Education*. Cambridge, Laboratory of Human Development, Harvard University, Spring, 1973.

Lilienthal, J. W., and Tryon, C.: Developmental tasks: II. Discussion of specific tasks and implications. In *Fostering Mental Health in Our Schools: 1950 Yearbook, ASCD*, Washington, D.C., Assn Supervision, 1950.

MacLennan, B. W., and Felsenfeld, N.: *Group Counseling and Psychotherapy with Adolescents*. New York, Columbia U Pr, 1968.

McGrath, E., and Altman, I.: *Small Group Research: A Synthesis and Critique of the Field*. New York, HR&W, 1966.

Middleman, R. R.: *The Non-verbal Method in Working with Groups*. New York, Assn Pr, 1968.

Moreno, J. L., and Kipper, D. A.: Group psychodrama and community-centered counseling. In Gazda, G. M. (Ed.): *Basic Approaches to Group Psychotherapy and Group Counseling*. Springfield, Thomas, 1968.

Murphy, G.: Play as a counselor's tool. *School Counselor*, 8:53, 1960.

Nesbitt, W. A.: *Simulation Games for the Social Studies Classroom*. Vol. 1, *New Dimensions*. New York, Foreign Policy Assoc., 1968.

Raser, J. R.: *Simulation and Society: An Exploration of Scientific Gaming*. Boston, Allyn, 1969.

Scheidlinger, S.: Three approaches with socially deprived latency age children. *International Journal of Group Psychotherapy, 15:*434, 1965.

Simulation Games. New York, Western Pub, School and Library Department (brochure n.d.).

Slavson, S. R.: Differential methods of group therapy in relation to age levels. *Nervous Child, 4:*196, 1945.

Sturm, I. E.: The behavioristic aspect of psychodrama. *Group Psychotherapy, 18:*50, 1965.

Super, D. E., Crites, J., Hummel, R., Moser, H., Overstreet, C. B., and Warnath, C.: *Vocational Development: A Framework for Research.* New York, Bureau of Publications, Teachers College, Columbia University, 1957. Monograph No. 1.

Super, D. E., Starishevesky, R., Matlin, N., and Jordaan, J. P.: *Career Development: Self-concept Theory.* New York, Coll Ent Exam, 1963. Research Monograph No. 4.

Truax, C. B., and Carkhuff, R. R.: *Toward Effective Counseling and Therapy.* Chicago, Aldine, 1967.

Tryon, C., and Lilienthal, L. W.: Developmental tasks. I. The concept and its importance. In *Fostering Mental Health in Our Schools: 1950 Yearbook, ASCD,* Washington, D.C., Assn Supervision, 1950.

Varenhorst, B. B.: Innovative tool for group counseling: the Life Career Game. *School Counselor, 15:*357, 1968.

Zaccaria, J. S.: Developmental tasks: implications for the goals of guidance. *Personnel and Guidance Journal, 24:*372, 1965.

Zaccaria, J. S.: Some aspects of developmental guidance within an existential context. *Personnel and Guidance Journal, 47:*440, 1969.

REFERENCES

Alper, T. G., and Kranzler, G. D.: A comparison of the effectiveness of behavioral and client-centered approaches for the behavior problems of elementary school children. *Elementary School Guidance and Counseling, 5:*35, 1970.

Anderson, A. R.: Group counseling. In Glass, G. V., and Thoresen, C. E. (Eds.): *Review of Educational Research: Guidance and Counseling, 39(2):*209, 1969.

Bach, G. R.: *Intensive Group Psychotherapy.* New York, Ronald, 1954.

Bass, B. M.: *Leadership, Psychology and Organizational Behavior.* New York, Har-Row, 1960.

Beck, D. F.: The dynamics of group psychotherapy as seen by a sociologist, part I: the basic process. *Sociometry, 21:*98, 1958.

Bell, G. B., and French, R. L.: Consistency of individual leadership position in small groups of varying membership. In Hare, A. P., Borgatta, E. F., and Bales, R. F. (Eds.): *Small Groups.* New York, Knopf, 1955.

Berenson, B. G., and Carkhuff, R. R. (Eds.): *Sources of Gain in Counseling and Psychotherapy: Readings and Commentary.* New York, HR&W, 1967.

Berenson, B. G., and Mitchell, K. M.: *Confrontation for Better or Worse!* Amherst, Human Resources Development Pr, 1974.

Berne, E.: *Principles of Group Treatment.* New York, Oxford U Pr, 1966.

Blake, R. R., Mouton, J. S., and Fruchter, B.: The consistency of interpersonal behavior judgments made on the basis of short-term interactions in three man groups. *Journal of Abnormal and Social Psychology,* 49:573, 1954.

Blake, R. R., and Brehm, J. W.: The use of tape recording to stimulate a group atmosphere. *Journal of Abnormal and Social Psychology,* 49:311 1954.

Blakeman, J. D.: *The Effects of Activity Group Counseling on the Self-evaluation and Classroom Behavior of Adolescent Behavior Problem Boys.* Unpublished doctoral dissertation, University of Georgia, 1967.

Blocher, D. H.: *Developmental Counseling.* New York, Ronald, 1966.

Bonney, W. C.: Group counseling and developmental processes. In Gazda, G. M. (Ed.): *Theories and Methods of Group Counseling in the Schools.* Springfield, Thomas, 1969.

Bonney, W. C., and Foley, W. J.: The transition stage in group counseling in terms of congruity theory. *Journal of Counseling Psychology, 10:*136, 1963.

Borgatta, E. F., and Bales, R. F.: Interaction of individuals in reconstituted groups. In Hare, A. P., Borgatta, E. F., and Bales, R. F. (Eds.): *Small Groups.* New York, Knopf, 1955.

Brammer, L. M., and Shostrom, E. L.: *Therapeutic Psychology.* Englewood Cliffs, P-H, 1960.

Carkhuff, R. R.: *Helping and Human Relations,* Vol. 1. *Selection and Training.* New York, HR&W, 1969(a).

Carkhuff, R. R.: *Helping and Human Relations.* Vol. 2. *Practice and Research.* New York, HR&W, 1969(b).

Carkhuff, R. R.: Systematic human relations training. In Gazda, G. M., and Porter, T. L. (Eds.): *Proceedings and a Symposium on Training Groups.* Athens, College of Education, University of Georgia, 1970.

Carkhuff, R. R.: *The Development of Human Resources: Education, Psychology, and Social Change.* New York, HR&W, 1971.

Carkhuff, R. R., and Berenson, B. G.: *Beyond Counseling and Therapy.* New York, HR&W, 1967.

Catterall, C. D., and Gazda, G. M.: *Strategies for Helping Students.* Springfield, Thomas (in press).

Cohen, A. R.: Communication discrepancy and attitude change: a dissonance theory approach. *Journal of Personality, 27:*386, 1959.

Day, S. R.: *The Effects of Activity Group Counseling on Selected Behavior Characteristics of Culturally Disadvantaged Negro Boys.* Unpublished doctoral dissertation, University of Georgia, 1967.

English, R. W., and Higgins, T. E.: Client-centered group counseling with pre-adolescents. *Journal of School Health,* p. 507, Nov., 1971.

Erikson, E. H.: *Childhood and Society.* New York, Norton, 1950.

Erikson, E. H.: Growth and crises of the healthy personality. *Psychological Issues, 1:*50, 1959.

Erikson, E. H.: *Childhood and Society,* 2nd ed. New York, Norton, 1963.

Festinger, L., Schachter, S., and Back, K.: *Social Pressures in Informal Groups.* New York, Harper, 1950.

Flavell, J. H.: *The Developmental Psychology of Jean Piaget.* Princeton, D. Van Nostrand, 1963.

Frank, J. D.: Group methods in psychotherapy. *Journal of Social Issues, 8:* 35, 1952.

Gazda, G. M.: A functional approach to group counseling. In Gazda, G. M. (Ed.): *Basic Approaches to Group Psychotherapy and Group Counseling.* Springfield, Thomas, 1968.

Gazda, G. M.: *Group Counseling: A Developmental Approach.* Boston, Allyn, 1971.

Gazda, G. M., Asbury, F. R., Balzer, F. J., Childers, W. C., Desselle, R. E., and Walters, R. P.: *Human Relations Development: A Manual for Educators.* Boston: Allyn, 1973.

Gazda, G. M., Duncan, J. A., and Meadows, M. E.: Group counseling and group procedures—report of a survey. *Counselor Education and Supervision, 9:*305, 1967.

Gazda, G. M., Duncan, J. A., and Sisson, P. J.: Professional issues in group work. *Personnel and Guidance Journal, 49(8):*637, 1971.

Gazda, G. M., Evans, L. P., and Kaltenbach, R. F.: *Instrumentation in Group Research.* Paper presented at Conference on Small Group Research, Indiana University: Bloomington, April, 1975.

Gazda, G. M., Walters, R. P., Childers, W. C.: *Human Relations Development: A Manual for Health Science.* Boston, Allyn, 1975.

Gendlin, E. T., and Beebe, J.: Experiential groups: instructions for groups. In Gazda, G. M. (Ed.): *Innovations to Group Psychotherapy.* Springfield, Thomas, 1968.

Gesell, A., Ilg, F. L., Ames, L. B., and Bullis, G. E.: *The Child from Five to Ten.* New York, Harper, 1946.

Gesell, A., Ilg, F. L., and Ames, L. B.: *Youth: The Years from Ten to Sixteen.* New York, Harper, 1956.

Ginott, H. G.: *Group Psychotherapy with Children: The Theory and Practice of Play Therapy.* New York, McGraw, 1961.

Goldstein, P., Heller, K., and Sechrest, L. B.: *Psychotherapy and the Psychology of Behavior Change.* New York, Wiley, 1966.

Havighurst, R. J.: *Developmental Tasks and Education.* Chicago, U of Chicago Pr, 1948.

Havighurst, R. J.: *Developmental Tasks and Education,* 2nd ed. New York, Longmans, Green, 1952.

Havighurst, R. J.: *Human Development and Education.* New York, McKay, 1953.

Hill, W. F.: *Hill Interaction Matrix Scoring Manual.* Pocatello, Idaho, Author, 1961.

Hill, W. F.: *Hill Interaction Matrix (HIM) Scoring Manual.* Salt Lake City, Dye, Smith, 1963.

Hill, W. F.: *Hill Interaction Matrix (HIM),* rev. ed. Los Angeles, University of Southern California Youth Studies Center, 1965.

Hill, W. F.: Group therapy for social impact: innovation in leadership training. *American Behavioral Scientist, 11(1):1,* 1967.

Hollander, E. P.: *Leaders, Groups and Influence.* New York, Oxford U Pr, 1964.

Hulse, W. C.: Dynamics and techniques of group psychotherapy in private practice. *International Journal of Group Psychotherapy, 4:65,* 1954.

Kohlberg, L.: *Collected Papers on Moral Development and Moral Education.* Cambridge: Laboratory of Human Development, Harvard University, Spring, 1973.

Kranzler, G. D.: Elementary school counseling: an evaluation. *Elementary School Guidance and Counseling, 2:286,* 1968.

Lieberman, M. A., Yalom, I. D., and Miles, M. B.: Encounter: the leader makes the difference. *Psychology Today, 6(10):69,* 1973.

Lowrey, L. G., and Slavson, S. R.: Group therapy special section meeting. *American Journal of Orthopsychiatry, 13:648,* 1943.

Mahler, C. A.: *Group Counseling in the Schools.* Boston, HM, 1969.

McGrath, J. E., and Altman, I.: *Small Group Research: A Synthesis and Critique of the Field.* New York, HR&W, 1966.

Muuss, R. E.: *Theories of Adolescence.* New York, Random, 1962.

Prados, M.: Some technical aspects of group psychotherapy. *International Journal of Group Psychotherapy, 3:131,* 1953.

Rogers, C. R., Gendlin, E. T., Kiesler, D. J., and Truax, C. B. (Eds.): *The Therapeutic Relationship and Its Impact: A Study of Psychotherapy with Schizophrenics.* Madison, U of Wis Pr, 1967.

Schachter, S., Ellertson, N., McBride, D., and Gregory, D.: An experimental study of cohesiveness and productivity. In Cartwright, D., and Zander, A. (Eds.): *Group Dynamics.* Evanston, Row, Peterson, 1960.

Schutz, W. C.: *FIRO: A Three-Dimensional Theory of Interpersonal Be-*

havior. New York, HR&W, 1960. Republished: *The Interpersonal Underworld.* Palo Alto, Sci & Behavior, 1966.

Slavson, S. R.: Differential methods of group therapy in relation to age levels. *Nervous Child,* 4:196, 1945.

Slavson, S. R.: Common sources of error and confusion in group psychotherapy. *International Journal of Group Psychotherapy,* 3:3, 1953.

Slavson, S. R.: *A Textbook in Analytic Group Psychotherapy.* New York, Intl Univs Pr, 1964.

Spotnitz, H.: *The Couch and the Circle.* New York, Knopf, 1961.

Stone, L. A., Coles, G. J., and Lindem, A. C.: *Multidimensional Evaluation Structure Analysis (MESA): A Complete Multidimensional Scaling System for a Multiplicity of Purposes.* Grand Forks, Judgmetrics, 1970.

Super, D. E., Crites, J., Hummel, R., Moser, H., Overstreet, C. B., and Warnath, C.: *Vocational Development: A Framework for Research.* New York, Bureau of Publications, Teachers College, Columbia University, 1957. Monograph No. 1.

Super, D. E., Starishevesky, R., Matlin, N., and Jordaan, J. P.: *Career Development: Self-concept Theory.* New York, Coll Ent Exam, 1963. Research Monograph No. 4.

Truax, C. B.: The process of group psychotherapy. *Psychological Monograph,* 75, 1961 (whole no. 511).

Truax, C. B.: *"A New Approach to Counselor Education."* Paper presented at the Canadian Guidance and Counseling Association Convention, Edmonton, Alberta, Canada, June, 1969.

Truax, C. B., and Carkhuff, R. R.: *Towards Effective Counseling and Psychotherapy: Training and Practice.* Chicago, Aldine, 1967.

Tryon, C., and Lilienthal, J. W.: Developmental tasks: I. The concept and its importance. In *Fostering Mental Health in Our Schools. 1950 Yearbook of ASCD.* Washington, D.C., Assn Supervision, 1950.

Varenhorst, B. B.: Innovative tool for group counseling: the Life Career Game. *School Counselor,* 15:357, 1968.

Yalom, I. D.: *The Theory and Practice of Group Psychotherapy.* New York, Basic, 1970.

Yaryan, R., and Festinger, L.: Preparatory action and belief in the probable occurrence of future events. *Journal of Abnormal and Social Psychology,* 63:603, 1961.

Zaccaria, J. S.: Developmental tasks: implications for the goals of guidance. *Personnel and Guidance Journal,* 24:372, 1965.

Zimbardo, P. G.: Involvement and communication discrepancy as determinants of opinion change. *Journal of Abnormal and Social Psychology,* 60:86, 1960.

IV

CHILD DRAMA FOR GROUP GUIDANCE AND COUNSELING

Prentiss M. Hosford and Elizabeth Acheson

COUNSELORS CAN USE DRAMA as an ego-building, role-playing activity, especially with children and youth whose potential to play out situations has not been inhibited or crippled. Moreno (1949) introduced psychodrama and sociodrama as forms of therapy, but he recommended that they be incorporated in education as spontaneity training. The importance of play for children in the attainment of an integrated personality has been stressed by Axline (1969), Ekstein (1966), Erikson (1963), Ginott (1961), Piers (1969), Smilansky (1968), and Winnicott (1971). School counselors are not typically trained in play therapy or psychodrama, but they have been influenced by the work and writings of these therapists and can see the relationship between those processes and improvisational drama.

Dorothy Heathcote of the Institute of Education, University of Newcastle-upon-Tyne, England, introduced to American educators a model of child drama which can serve as a process for group guidance and as a group counseling technique. The procedure allows children, guided by a skilled leader, to improvise and develop their own dramas about any issue or topic that can capture their attention and imagination or that may be of concern to them. Any theme they might choose could be classified as belonging in one of three sources of conflict situations: the human being against the environment, person against person, and the individual against his or herself.

This form of drama has a natural entry into the elementary curriculum through both the cognitive and affective areas. It can motivate and extend learning, modify behavior, and enhance the self-concept of children. As a group guidance procedure with a creative leader, it can introduce opportunities for reflective and creative thinking. Through role taking around universal themes, children are in an ideal position to learn to understand and value themselves and ways of relating to others in a healthy manner. Leaving such learning to chance, or as a concomitant outcome of the curriculum, is taking a risk. Since the pressure for cognitive learning has dominated education in recent years, and little attention has been given to meeting children's affective needs, numerous efforts have been made to include units of mental health as an integral and separate part of the curriculum. Drama as a guidance and counseling tool or technique is not presented here as a substitute for the activities which are presently being used with success by counselors with materials such as Developing Understanding Self and Others (DUSO) kits, puppets, films, pictures, toys, stories, and the like, but it is introduced as an additional option. It builds primarily not on materials to be purchased but on the resources of the counselor and counselees alike and stretches the mind, sharpens the senses, and deepens feelings.

Heathcote uses drama successfully with delinquent youth, emotionally disturbed and mentally retarded children and adults, in classrooms with normal children, and in special classes of talented youth. The outcomes of the spontaneous improvisations have revealed the modification of perceptions and behavior and have increased responsibility for one's behavior (Heathcote, 1971). The structural model of this form of drama consists of a concept or generality, which is narrowed into segments of meaning by the leader and children. One segment is then selected and developed through questioning to focus on the children's particular interest, concern, or need, and the drama begins.

Through the drama the leader directs the children to face problems by confrontation, and the full range of interaction processes comes into play. Through both subtle and overt behavior, the leader withholds expertise or gives information, strengthens the group, raises status of individuals, manages the leadership, exposes thoughts and feelings, slows or accelerates the action, gives individual scope, probes, presses and creates tension, manipulates the environment, extends vocabulary, and facilitates responsible behavior. Children can be helped to see them-

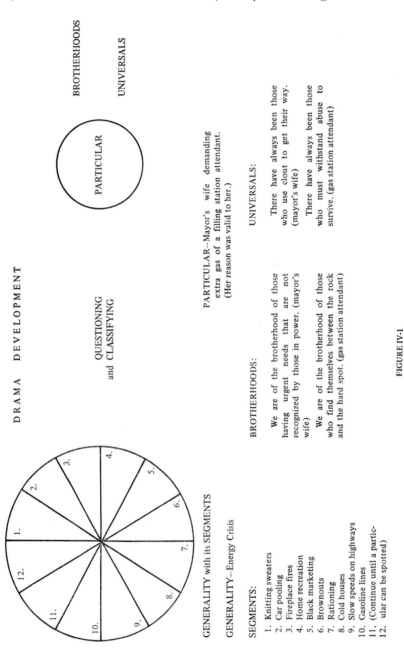

DRAMA DEVELOPMENT

QUESTIONING
and CLASSIFYING

BROTHERHOODS

PARTICULAR

UNIVERSALS

GENERALITY with its SEGMENTS

GENERALITY—Energy Crisis

SEGMENTS:

1. Knitting sweaters
2. Car pooling
3. Fireplace fires
4. Home recreation
5. Black marketing
6. Brownouts
7. Rationing
8. Cold houses
9. Slow speeds on highways
10. Gasoline lines
11. (Continue until a partic-
12. ular can be spotted)

PARTICULAR—Mayor's wife demanding
extra gas of a filling station attendant.
(Her reason was valid to her.)

BROTHERHOODS:

We are of the brotherhood of those
having urgent needs that are not
recognized by those in power. (mayor's
wife)

We are of the brotherhood of those
who find themselves between the rock
and the hard spot. (gas station attendant)

UNIVERSALS:

There have always been those
who use clout to get their way.
(mayor's wife)

There have always been those
who must withstand abuse to
survive. (gas station attendant)

FIGURE IV-1

selves as decision makers and responsible persons, and through their play they arrive at universals and feel a part of various brotherhoods. The drama makes explicit what was implicit in their needs and in their role taking and acting out. Since drama can be used in almost any situation and with most pupils, it can become one of the counselor's most useful and effective tools.

DEFINITION OF GROUP GUIDANCE AND GROUP COUNSELING

Group guidance and group counseling are growth-enhancing activities. When practiced with children in the schools, they provide a framework in which concern for pupils' affective and cognitive development is primary. A definition of developmental guidance incorporates assisting children to accomplish the tasks which are appropriate and necessary at certain stages of development in a given culture (Havighurst, 1972). A definition of group counseling builds on an eclectic point of view and allows for both individual children and the entire group to develop through interaction and reflective thinking. It allows children opportunities to try on roles as it builds on their natural ability to play out experiences.

Child drama is improvisation based on the participants' concerns, led by a leader usually in role, for the purpose of exploring ideas and situations. It is a group guidance and group counseling technique for meeting the objectives for personal development or helping to bring about the fullest possible realization of human potential. The participants become more aware of their own strengths and abilities and of the qualities other people possess. Drama can generate a desire to communicate with others in a shared experience. It encourages the recollection of experiences which can lead to new discoveries when the leader directs the group to seek information and helps to relate it to what they already know.

Children can act out fantasies together in child drama, as a form of therapeutic intervention, and identify with figures that meet their needs. They have an opportunity to learn to delay gratification. They can learn that one may win one time and lose another; they can see that it is not always the powerful one who has his/her way; and they learn that working together can accomplish more than separate efforts by single individuals. They learn tolerance. If they see other children accepting an "outcast" or "isolate," they can try out their own feelings without drawing attention to themselves, or they can suspend judgment while observing group reactions.

Opportunity is given within a play situation for making choices or taking decisions and, equally important, the accepting of the consequences of decisions. Children can gain insight into other people's experiences and develop sympathetic understanding, and they may test the possibilities of their responses to other people. Thus social development, a function of group guidance and counseling, is facilitated.

When children have had experience in drama through developmental guidance or group counseling, they have in many instances rehearsed life episodes and even crises. Only chance would allow for acting out what would later be a real life situation, but the transfer or application may come through with insight and clarity. If a child has raised his/her level of language to converse with the king of the land, he/she may be more at ease when he/she is addressing the mayor of the city on a class field trip. If children have discovered they have power without being aggressive, they have learned one of the principles of nonviolence.

RESEARCH RELATED TO THE PROCESS

Research related to the particular form of drama which the authors recommend has not been reported in this country, and the use of child drama as a guidance activity or a counseling technique is in an embryonic stage. Research on related forms of drama and group work supports further exploration and use of this process, and evidences of the value of dramatic play, improvisation, and role playing in education and mental health appear in the literature.

Sacks (1973) stated that psychodrama is an underused resource in group counseling. He identified parallels between the therapeutic and the educational function. Corresponding to analytic psychotherapy, psychodrama attempts to release repressed ideas or affects, and like educational methods, it attempts to expand the behavioral repertoire by teaching. Sacks warned against the abuse of the procedure in the educational setting, since psychodrama should never be used to probe, thus creating an antitherapeutic atmosphere.

Play, or useful adaptive behavior that maximizes the capacity for variability and builds on the child's reaction to experience (Sutton-Smith, 1974), can mediate novelty and lead to creativity. Sutton-Smith stated that play can prepare children for demands which will be made on them later. Play in a universal sense embraces exploration, self-testing, and imitation. Saltz and Johnson (1973) studied the effects of fantasy play intervention on socially and economically disadvantaged preschoolers. They found children who engaged in role enactment of imaginary stories to be significantly higher than a control group on a number of measures of social and cognitive development and to show higher incidence of spontaneous sociodramatic play. They also made higher scores on Borke's Revised Interpersonal Perception Test and performed better than controls on tasks designed to measure story sequence memory and story verbalization skills. They did not improve significantly on several subtest measures of intelligence or in ability to recall pictures as opposed to objects; but the investigation concluded that fantasy play is a promising and practical intervention method. Moulin (1970) reported significant gains in nonlanguage responses on an intelligence test and on six of nine subtests of psycholinguistic ability for underachieving primary children after they experienced twelve one-hour weekly therapy sessions of client-centered group counseling using play therapy media.

Second and third-grade children, who were identified as having average ability but were underachieving because of identifiable emotional factors such as passivity, fear of authority, or poor self-image, participated in group counseling sessions twice a week for twenty sessions (Reisman and Beyer, 1973). Various media such as role playing, games, and toys were used to help the children express their feelings. They played out roles of parents at report card time and were encouraged to test behavior and to interact with the sex group that had inhibited them. The goals of helping underachievers utilize their potential, encouraging appropriate expression of feelings and behavior, and providing psychological insights to teachers appeared to be attainable, and both parents and teachers recommended the continuation of the practice.

Selman (1973) described five stages of role taking development based on Piaget's stages of cognitive development and Kohlberg's levels of moral development. During Stage 0, ages four to six, children can separate themselves from others but still expect the perspective of others to be the same as theirs. Upon reaching Stage 1, approximately ages six to eight, children learn that besides being separate from themselves, others see things from their point of view and they realize that they see things from the point of view of others. At about ages eight to ten the children come into Stage 2 when they recognize that they are viewed by others as subjects having their own thoughts, feelings, and motives, just as they can view others as subjects. Between the ages of ten and twelve, children enter Stage 3 and are able to step outside themselves to see themselves as others do, while simultaneously maintaining their own perspective. Children then recognize that others can do the same. Finally the adult stage, Stage 4, is reached between ages twelve and fifteen. During this final development the adult accepts that even though one recognizes the perspective of others, this does not guarantee his or her understanding of others; therefore social conventions are necessary to keep communications open.

Hoffman's study (1973) of empathy, role taking, guilt, and the development of altruistic motives was based on Flavell's belief that egocentrism in the young child begins to diminish by seven or eight years of age. Flavell considered perceptual role taking as a means of providing one an estimate of how another person perceives a situation rather than one's own thoughts or feelings about it. Hoffman observed the awareness of perspective differences in children younger than six years.

Literature related to dramatics and the moral development of latency-age children was reviewed by Morse and Simmons

(1973). They were primarily interested in the nature and development of play and the contribution play and drama can make to children's emotional and moral development. Piaget's model, which includes accommodation or registering of information from reality and assimilation or the integration of new material, forms a basis for investigating whether children experience anxiety because of their fantasies and whether these fantasies are then suppressed. Children have two kinds of fantasies—one kind is free from conflict and the other causes anxiety. Symbolic play and fantasy in latency-age children show less distortion of reality to the ego in the sense that imitation becomes reflective. One of Erikson's developmental tasks characteristic of this phase is the acquiring of a sense of industry while fending off a sense of inferiority. Participation in dramatics makes a positive contribution to emotional and moral development and can help children overcome feelings of inferiority. In the process they can better understand the behavior of others; thus the interplay of action and reaction can provide insights into social relationships.

The effect of dramatic play in social studies teaching was investivated by Hartshorn and Brantley (1973) to determine if second and third-grade pupils' understanding of cause-and-effect relationships and everyday social situations, their sense of responsibility, and their ability to generate alternative solutions could be improved. A post-test-only control group design was used, and the treatment was assessed by a series of comprehension-type questions, half of which were taken from standardized tests and the remainder devised to relate to content explored through the dramatic play. Experimental pupils were those pupils who had shown limited social and verbal skills on the Verbal Performance Test and sociometric measures. The treatment involved dramatizing the content of the social studies program which centered around community workers. Experimental pupils participated once or twice weekly, choosing their own roles and acting and speaking spontaneously, with discussion afterward. On other days research activities were coordinated with the children's play, and other school subjects were integrated and interrelated. Questions on the posttest were analyzed to measure correct response, incorrect response, and assumption of responsibility for solving the problem. There was a significant treatment effect, but no significant grade or interaction effects. The study supported earlier work that postulated role playing and dramatic play as an effective way to teach social studies, not only from the standpoint of knowledge acquisition but also as a means of helping children develop problem-solving skills.

Dyer and Vriend (1973) used the term role work instead of role play in group counseling to differentiate between the art form and the therapeutic act. VanScoy (1972) used videotape to enable four latency-age boys in a residential school for emotionally disturbed children to experience the responsibility for operating complex equipment and the subsequent viewing of themselves in activity group therapy. The group was formed to help the members see the transition from play-oriented childhood to the work-oriented world of adults, and to allow the children to see that work can be as satisfying as play. Operation of the equipment required attention to precise tasks and gave the children a chance to see the consequences of irresponsibility. Since their objective included script writing and all of the tasks that accompany theater production, the filmed twelve-minute videotape represented more than six of the ten sessions the group met. The leader concluded that the experience contributed to a lessening of "silly behavior." The boys were able to function as a group, and three of the four were discharged shortly afterward. Knudson (1971) found that when low-achieving rural students engaged in specialized language activities and role playing, which they videotaped, they experienced a significant increase in IQ, reading, writing, and oral language. The experimental children handled all production tasks, with jobs rotated so that all were involved in research, reading, writing, and interviewing.

Levin (1972) found drama to be beneficial in a college classroom in allowing students to pursue their own emotions through identification. Students were able to see commonalities and universals in life as they enacted classic works. Levin also recommended role playing and psychodrama to develop bases for personal understanding and insight, and in helping students appraise reciprocal actions between themselves and others. She used role playing to promote discovery, and she guided and terminated it when the audience (class) seemed ready for a discussion.

The effect of group processes in improvised drama when groups were determined by two procedures was investigated by Gilmore (1973). Seven-year-olds in a mixed primary class were given a sociometric test and grouped in a ratio of two girls to three boys into three groups: the most cohesive, the least cohesive, and a random group. Groups in isolation participated in a common problem-solving improvisation with the same leader, and pupils were observed by a single investigator who recorded verbal communication on a modification of the Bales model which showed socio-emotional positive reactions, tasks or attempted answers, tasks or attempted questions, and socio-emotional negative reactions. Results indicated that the random grouping of pupils for drama activity does not reduce or increase harmony within the group, but that the activity is enhanced when pupils are grouped as cohesively as possible, as through sociometry. The usefulness of a cross-grade group which can be easily accommodated in child drama is supported in a study by Kern and Kirby (1971) of the utilization of fifth- and sixth-grade children as peer helpers in group counseling.

Research results with group counseling that lend credibility to the use of child drama include a study by Gibbons and Lee (1972) who worked with ten boys referred because of teacher-observed problems. The goal was to help the problem children become more aware of their behavior and its consequences; and the group chose to discuss mutual concerns, share ideas and suggestions for solving problems, make individual and group decisions, and determine their course of action. The primary recurring theme was powerlessness. The children were able to feel less powerless when they made suggestions, and especially when later they presented them to their teacher, who accepted them. The counselor perceived greater feelings of mutual respect between counselor and teacher, and the boys' behavior changed in that they could use their collective strength appropriately and found out that the democratic process could work, but that certain rules were nonnegotiable.

Studies of counselor function (MacDougall and Brown, 1973; Miller, Gum, and Bender, 1972) show that guidance and counseling tasks could incorporate drama as a means of helping children meet developmental needs related to self-concept enhancement, self-understanding, social skills, value clarification, and career development. Among the duties reported by Miller et al. (1972), in which child drama would be an effective medium, is assisting children to (1) derive positive personal meaning from learning, (2) become more aware of their being and develop a positive attitude toward themselves and toward life, (3) develop the competence to cope with frustration and conflict in their personal life, (4) experience satisfaction from relations with adults and other children, and (5) become aware of the place of values in life and to develop a system of their own but one which is consistent with a pluralistic society.

Problems generated by the lack of trained personnel have led to innovative uses of staff. Ivey and Alschuler (1973) recommended that counselors share with teachers some of the techniques used in group guidance and counseling. Kranz (1972) reported that inadequate numbers of persons who could give psychological guidance to primary school children precipitated the utilization of teachers as play therapists. The program was based on Axline's premises that play is a natural medium for self-expression and that children need the opportunity to "play out" their feelings and problems, that play therapy may be directive or nondirective, and that the therapist may allow the child to assume some responsibility and direction. Teachers had a ten-week training course in play therapy, followed by a ten-week practicum during which each teacher could work with one child for two one-hour sessions each week and then present the case to the psychologist. Rooms were equipped and set aside as playrooms in two schools. Evaluations by teachers who observed the children were highly favorable. Foley (1970) studied parents' perceptions of the behavior of their emotionally disturbed sons who had undergone an experimental treatment which consisted of nondirective play therapy led by undergraduate education majors trained in eight one-and-one-half-hour sessions. These boys produced more positive changes than those treated by experienced therapists, a placebo treatment group with education majors trained "to be friendly," or a no-treatment group. Student-therapists gained in positive attitudes towards children, as measured by the Minnesota Teacher Attitude Inventory.

THEORETICAL FOUNDATIONS OF THE PROCESS

Adults learn new roles by vicarious role playing at a pre-conscious level. Little children participate in dramatic play to explore their future conditions. Professions have recognized the use of role taking to teach their members how to function professionally. While learning the counseling role, students try on the roles of counselor and counselee before actually working with persons who would be dependent on their skill. Child drama is a way of role taking. It does not teach roles laid down in a curriculum or suggested in a guidance package; it deals with those that currently meet the participants' needs and interests, thus incorporating the unique excitement of the children. Emotional investment keeps the learners involved in overcoming the barriers confronted in the drama and ensures that learning ensues.

Child drama is focused on the school-age child from kindergarten to secondary school. It can also be adapted and applied for use with preschool children and for older adolescents. The framework in which child drama is placed as a group procedure is described by Gazda (1971) (see also Chapter III in this text). It can be a means of evaluating a child's developmental progress and/or providing a means of helping a child learn and practice developmental tasks and coping behaviors in the areas of affective, physical, social, intellectual, moral, and vocational development.

The elementary school curriculum in its broad connotation is a panorama against which skilled and perceptive counselors and teachers can, using history, literature, and the social sciences, meet children's needs for "psychological education" (Alschuler and Ivey, 1973). Education in human behavior, whether it is recognized as affective education, mental health education, or by some other name, is usually not formally recognized and included as a separate subject with regularly scheduled teaching times. Consequently, it is frequently neglected. The special programs which have been developed involving toys, puppets, games, role playing, and the like (Bessell and Palomares, 1967; Dinkmeyer, 1971; Ojemann, 1959; Peters, Shelly, and McCormick, 1966; Shaftel and Shaftel, 1967) are used by teachers who are in schools where such training is valued, and by others who can inject them into their programs. Producers of textbooks have "humanized" their offerings (Follett, 1970; Harcourt Brace Jovanovich, 1970).

The developmental tasks children need to accomplish during late childhood place demands on cognitive processes. The development and refinement of thinking skills require that teachers and counselors who work with children be highly skilled in ways of provoking thought and questioning, to model critical and reflective thinking, and be able to place children in situations where they must use the skills which are considered to be desirable and, in fact, necessary for survival. Thinking, defined by Raths, Jonas, Rothstein, and Wassermann (1967), includes observing, comparing, classifying, looking for assumptions, hypothesizing, collecting and organizing data, summarizing, criticizing, interpreting, imagining, applying facts and principles in new situations, coding, designing projects or investigations, and decision making. These thinking operations may be practiced through drama in a context which has been generated by the children's own needs. The bringing together of many of these operations in child drama is indeed a feat that requires a skilled leader, and teachers and counselors who work in drama develop their own thinking at the same time that they assist children in improving in these skills.

Eight behavioral syndromes (Raths et al., 1967) may be associated with faulty thinking: impulsiveness, overdependence upon the teacher, inability to concentrate, rigidity and inflexibility, dogmatic, assertive behavior, extreme lack of confidence, missing the meaning, and resistance to thinking. Children who exhibit behavior characterized as one of these types are frequently referred to the counselor, who can classify their dominant manner of coping and form groups in which they may be helped to overcome these problems or faulty thinking operations. Such problems which may not have crystallized may be attacked through group guidance within the classroom. One way which either teacher or counselor may use is the class meeting (Glasser, 1969). Another is role playing. Drama involving the entire class offers a challenging way to help children see the consequences of faulty thinking and consider alternatives which might work. The dramatic experience can take place in situations which allow them to explore the human condition outside the domestic parameters of their own lives. They can use the insights gained from their experience with universal conditions, examined in the classic setting, to apply to their personal situation. Corsini (1966) defined the educational connotation of role playing, "whereby people act out imaginary situations for purposes directed to self-understanding, improvement of skills, analyses of behavior, or to demonstrate to others how one should act" (p. xi).

Gray and Mager (1973) have taught teachers and counselors to use improvisational drama in dealing with interpersonal relationships, racial conflicts, prejudices, and other problems of youth. They stated, "Because of the way some schools are organized, counselors frequently have more flexibility in their schedules than do teachers, and are in a better position to try new things. Public school counselors who have combined improvisational drama with other group dynamics techniques report new counseling effectiveness" (pp. 188-189). In contrast to child drama, the framework of improvisational drama that Gray and Mager recommend consists of physical freeing, concentration, believability, and relationships. They emphasize that the teacher "does not teach psychological values, and he or she does not analyze students' experiences and tell them what they should learn about themselves from the experiences" (p. 7), but their work has shown that drama "has enormous potential for freeing people to develop capacities they might not have known they had" (p. 2). Gray and Mager would essentially follow this format: warm-ups of short improvisations or simple exercises, richer or longer improvisations, and closing.

Introducing the concept of psychological education as a means of alleviating psychosocial problems among children and young people, Ivey and Alschuler (1973) urged the teaching of healthy coping skills through increasing pupils' intentionality, or ability to anticipate experiences, make choices, and attain their goals. Thus children would be able to act on more than one perspective and use a variety of problem-solving strategies. They recommended the introduction of psychological techniques into academic subject areas so that psychological and academic goals enhance or complement each other.

> By introducing here-and-now use of imagination, touching students' feelings, and translating ideas into action, traditional subject matter areas become more personally relevant. For example, the Pilgrims' leaving England because of intolerance is usually presented and discussed as a fact. Students fail to see the relevance of this experience for their own lives. However, students wake up and become involved when they are asked value-clarifying questions such as "Did you ever experience a similar intolerance in your own life?" or "If you are persecuted or teased by someone, what do you do?" When an approach such as this is used, the academic context provides a stimulus for reflective thinking (p. 595).

Drama in education is both an ego-enhancing technique and a learning experience. As a means of building self-concept, it meets some of the goals of group play therapy as practiced by Ginott (Hosford, 1973). Ginott (1961, 1968) based his work on the experiences of Slavson who viewed the function of the group as encompassing three areas: play and activity, association with same-age children, and the role of the worker. Group as opposed to individual play therapy provides an opportunity for the child to relate to others and test him or herself against them, to move into the human environment or from egocentricity to object relationships, and to identify with others in ways that lead to comfort and security.

The uses of child drama are compatible with the six uses specified by Amster (1943) and abstracted by Gazda (1971): for diagnostic understanding; to establish a working relationship as a basis for self-expression; to break through a child's way of playing and defenses against anxiety; to help a child verbalize certain conscious material and associated feelings; to act out unconscious material and relieve tension (catharsis); and to develop play interests which can extend into the child's daily life. At first glance this compatibility may not be apparent, but as the procedure is described and illustrated, similarities will be noted and insights gained as to benefits inherent in drama in education.

Child drama helps children develop empathy with others. Smilansky (1968) found that underprivileged children did not participate in playing roles common to the mainstream of society. She felt that a prerequisite for functioning effectively in society is lacking in these children's experiences, and recommended direct instruction by a therapist in role to teach them how to role play. Counselors are expected to take children where they are in terms of their ability to role play and expand their skills, and counselors who work with young culturally different children may expect to first teach children "how." To learn new roles or to modify old behaviors requires opportunities to try them out in supportive surroundings, such as that afforded in child drama.

Gazda (1971) compared sociodrama, psychodrama, and behavioral therapies. All three forms have been used with positive results (Barclay, 1961; Gittleman, 1965), and these action techniques, on the basis of research, seem promising.

The developmental approach recommended by Gazda (1971) shows how modeling by the leader can encourage children's relationships, development, and problem resolution. The leader would move from less threatening situations to the relevant procedures as children showed indications of growth.

Procedures that involve action, as opposed to interview-type counseling, can be analyzed to show that the principles of learning are an underlying factor, and as the technique is learned and practiced by counselors, trained teachers, and therapists, it can be subject to research.

Research, observation, and practice of child drama support the theories of Mead (1936), Dewey (1943), and Goffman (1959) that claimed that the human's innate capacity to learn lies in the ability to take on or try out roles. The more complex the society, the more roles each person must learn. Goffman saw all interpersonal exchanges as productions in which actors carry out roles. Success in these roles depends partly on the opportunity one has had for rehearsals. Role taking, as it occurs in child drama, presents open-ended situations for which participants try out optional solutions, and their own decisions are used. The leader helps the children follow their decisions to experience the consequences of having lived by them. Confrontations are presented when strictures of the role are not respected. When children seem thwarted in proceeding with roles because conditions are foreign or too demanding, the leader challenges with questions, usually framed as nonquestions, and encouragement. The participants' situations are always reversible because they are dealing with a form of play. No decision can cause real damage; other solutions can be tried by replaying the situations. At times during the drama and at its close, reflective thinking on the part of children is encouraged and elicited. At this point the learning through identification is reinforced.

The learning of new roles or modification of behaviors requires opportunities to try out roles in supportive surroundings. Child drama is an ideal medium for doing this. Child drama has a theoretical framework which leads to the belief that the technique can be extremely useful in developing mature behavior and modifying that which is immature. Practitioners who have lively imaginations and intellectual curiosity and who have supportive, open personalities can be easily trained to use child drama. So little work has been done using this process as a counseling technique that any counselor or guidance-oriented teacher who works with it in group guidance and counseling, or as psychological education, will, for a while, be on the frontier of what appears to be a highly promising practice.

STRUCTURING CHILD DRAMA

Counselors who want to use child drama and who have participated in a workshop or related experience which provided a basic understanding of the process are almost ready to start. Final preparations for working in child drama include: (1) taking stock of his or her own strengths and needs; (2) looking at what the group brings to the drama; and (3) preparation for working with drama.

Taking Stock of Strengths and Needs

An experienced counselor is aware of his or her own style of working with groups, and his or her own strengths and limitations.

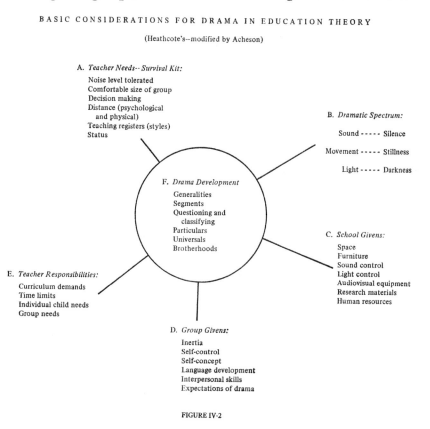

BASIC CONSIDERATIONS FOR DRAMA IN EDUCATION THEORY

(Heathcote's—modified by Acheson)

A. *Teacher Needs-- Survival Kit:*
Noise level tolerated
Comfortable size of group
Decision making
Distance (psychological and physical)
Teaching registers (styles)
Status

B. *Dramatic Spectrum:*
Sound - - - - - Silence
Movement - - - - - Stillness
Light - - - - - Darkness

F. *Drama Development*
Generalities
Segments
Questioning and classifying
Particulars
Universals
Brotherhoods

C. *School Givens:*
Space
Furniture
Sound control
Light control
Audiovisual equipment
Research materials
Human resources

E. *Teacher Responsibilities:*
Curriculum demands
Time limits
Individual child needs
Group needs

D. *Group Givens:*
Inertia
Self-control
Self-concept
Language development
Interpersonal skills
Expectations of drama

FIGURE IV-2

He/she will not use a technique if he/she sees that it requires skills or emotional components which are not in his or her repertoire. Once the counselor has assessed him or herself, he/she can plan dramas that can be led successfully.

Heathcote (1972) refers to a portion of her theoretical "wheel" as a leader's "survival kit." A modification of it will be useful for the counselor to consider.

The counselor should use his or her answers to the following questions to establish the parameters for drama in his or her guidance and counseling sessions.

Leader Needs

NOISE. How much noise can I tolerate? What kinds of noise can I abide? What kinds of noise bother me?

SIZE OF GROUP. How many children will I feel comfortable working with? the smallest number? the largest number?

DECISION MAKING. What kinds of decisions can I allow children to make? Which decisions must I make myself? Which decisions must be made beforehand so plans can be made? Which ones can be left for spontaneous development?

LEADER REGISTERS. How many registers or styles of leadership can I use effectively? In which registers do I feel most comfortable?

STATUS. What are my status needs? Must I be the one who always knows?—the one who is in control? Or can I be content being the one who has created a good time while exploring some interesting, productive situations? (See Figure IV-2, A.)

Once the counselor knows the limits of operation, he or she can imagine the kinds of dramatic situations in which he or she would feel comfortable. The dramatic spectrums of sound/silence, movement/stillness, and light/darkness (see Figure IV-2, B.) will give him or her ideas about how action can be effective and plots modified through dramatic moments. If the activities need to be quiet, perhaps the exciting contrasts can come from shifts on the movement/stillness or light/darkness continuums.

There may be little space in which to move around (see Figure IV-2, C.); but perhaps occasional shouts or cheers, in contrast to stark silence, or lighting effects can provide the dramatic excitement. If lighting must remain constant—if the room has a glass wall without draperies—and noise and movement are disturbing to the teachers in adjoining rooms, verbal dramas are still possible; e.g., courtroom scenes, board meetings, class meetings, labor/management disputes. The counselor, as leader, can still exert stirring presses on the participants by working from a low power but highly verbal role in the drama. The children can unravel these problems from their seats, speaking one at a time, in "broad daylight." Initial emotional involvement comes more easily, however, when appropriate noise and movement can be allowed. Ways to provide the children more freedom and responsibility will be seen as the counselor gains confidence in working with drama. The participants gain competence in their developmental tasks by taking responsibility in drama as they work through universal problems.

Group members exercise responsibility as they take part in making decisions about their drama. The first session should be kept short—just long enough to learn the drama's setting, the attitudes inherent in its roles, its problems, and perhaps to initiate some action. The intervening time between sessions is used to plan possible plot development and to accomplish the various group and individual goals. Decisions that are necessary to achieve the goals will be made by the counselor. Diverse means for accomplishing various ends are obvious after continued work in drama. Work done with Action Mazes (Gazda, 1971) will help the counselor see how behaviors at one point in a problem influence the behaviors that follow. This also shows how the counselor's skill can turn decisions which seem to be heading the action towards disastrous results into productive learning situations.

Looking at the Group

After the counselor has assessed his/her own style of working he/she should analyze the makeup of the group. Sometimes counselors can select the composition of the group; at other times someone else determines it. Either way, he/she will need to know his/her group. (See Figure IV-2, D.)

*   *   *

Two thirds of the children enrolled in a school were children from upper middle income/high education local families, and one third of the children lived in other parts of the city. Some of these bused-in children came from very poor families. Thus two quite different socioeconomic levels were represented. To compose a drama group four teachers had selected a few children from their classrooms; some of these children were leaders and some had overt problems but might benefit from working with other children and an outside resource person. There were fourteen fourth and fifth graders—nine boys and five girls, of whom five boys and two girls were black. In intelligence they ranged from very superior to dull normal, and in background from the son of a psychiatrist to a child whose family was receiving public assistance. Five of the children had emotional problems or observable maladjustment.

The children who were brought from their neighborhoods by bus to this school to achieve racial balance were slowly adjusting to their new classes. They were experiencing the effect of a decision made concerning them by people who did not know them. The school board had moved them around to meet the demands of the federal government. The children knew they had been removed from their familiar school, one in their neighborhood, to an unfamiliar school. They may not have known why this had happened, but they and their parents had been powerless to prevent it. The children from the school's neighborhood felt inundated with outsiders. They, too, had been powerless to prevent this invasion. All the children needed an experience in which they, as individuals, could feel they would be listened to (see Figure IV-2, E.).

The drama leader read them *The King's Fountain*,[1] the story of a poor man who tried to get influential men in the

---

1. Alexander, L.: *The King's Fountain*. New York, Dutton, 1971.

city to protest the building of a fountain by their king. The water required for the fountain would take away the water supply of the city. Eventually it was clear that if this man wanted this injustice protested, he would have to go to the king himself. The poor man's sincerity and humility persuaded the king of his folly, thus saving the citizens' water supply.

The fourth- and fifth-grade children saw this as a story of bravery and tyranny. They decided to make a play about these traits and set it in Rome at about 100 AD.

The leader's notes on the children after their first session reported:

Angela: a bright, beautiful, well-adjusted child.

Barbara: quiet and self-sufficient; the only one who brought her paper about herself that was assigned.

Carol: independent and bright; can be antagonistic and still seems to vie for attention and seek negative reinforcement.

Debbie: quiet but seems to have depth of perception and feeling.

Ellie: quiet and serious, imaginative.

Frank: has had many experiences, such as travel in Europe; speaks of Rome, Paris, London; seems bright and outgoing.

George: tall, handsome, bright; many good ideas.

Hal: did not come until 12:50 because he was with the EMR teacher; less attentive at first; probably not really retarded except in achievement; was a bit ill at ease at first.

David: a change from last year; laughs more; other children seem fond of him and look to him; he is paying more attention to what they say about themselves and identifying or reacting to information; example of humility in choice of roles is great.

Jim: very secure and has a great deal of leadership potential; independent in thinking and cooperative when his idea is not accepted; has broad knowledge as David has.

Kenny: bright and handsome; seems to want to cooperate and will be able to assume some leadership in time.

Larry: gets attention by bothering other children or involving himself in random behavior; holds back right now as if afraid his ideas will not be accepted; not sure of his ability level yet.

Mike: large boy, less attractive than David and Jim; bids for attention; seems bright but unmotivated towards leadership; seems to want to cooperate but unable to discipline himself.

Norman: missed school today; attendance has been erratic; school phobia? brother just enrolled in private school.

❋   ❋   ❋

The drama is to facilitate children in their development. During the elementary school years children are establishing their identities and developing a sense of responsibility as well as skills in problem solving.

Establishing Identity

The developmental tasks of childhood (Havighurst, 1972) require children to develop independence and individuality during their elementary school years. Children need to break the excessively strong bonds they have had with their parents and develop ties with their communities—with peers and adults—as well as maintain their family ties. Their values are established during these years. Ginott (1972) stated, "Ethical concepts such as responsibility, respect, loyalty, honesty, charity, mercy cannot be taught directly. They can only be learned in concrete life situations from people one respects" (p. 152). Child drama involves children in roles of responsible adults in situations that demand mature behavior. Children, animals, or incompetents that may become necessary to the drama can be imagined or played by a guest resource person, since children could learn little about desirable identities while in these roles.

One of the greatest contributions as a counselor in child drama is the modeling of respect for the individual. This takes place when he or she is in role and is weaving the children's contributions into the drama, and when he/she turns a child's out-of-role behavior into a positive contribution, thereby showing the child positive regard.

❋   ❋   ❋

Joe, an active seven-year-old who had difficulty getting into role, started climbing the bookcases near his peers who were struggling to establish believability in their ancient village.

"Look, Joseph is climbing the lookout tower! Do you see any sign of danger, Joseph?" shouts the leader.

"A band of robbers is coming this way!" reports back the instantaneous lookout. And Joe was involved in the drama for a time. His contribution was an important one, for believability then came easily to a threatened village. Joe's comment had developed a focus for the group.

✿   ✿   ✿

Group experiences such as this in which the counselor's imagination transforms negative or passive behavior to positive action promote self-concept enhancement and peer acceptance. Children are influenced by the way their power figures regard them, and they learn respect for themselves as they experience it from others.

Establishing a Sense of Responsibility

Children learn to take responsibility for their actions when they must experience the consequences. The leader, in role, might question obviously unwise decisions of the participants, but if time permits, opportunities are provided for learning by playing through poor choices and their repercussions. Leaders may have difficulty allowing the participants to make apparently immature decisions. No *deus ex machina* can rescue the dramatists; once decisions are made, realistic results must follow. So, if a family with a low income purchases a color television on "time," they may be in for trouble. When there is no money to pay the monthly installment, the television will be returned to the store. No rich uncle or fairy godmother will appear with the money. The participants must live through the loss of their television; otherwise, understanding of the developmental task of learning responsibility will not be aided.

Drama is a way to test decisions and explore their consequences. The counselor's eye and ear are constantly testing the authenticity of each behavior in the drama and the responses to it, and he or she will find that some responses will need exploring.

Developing integrity in expressing displeasure to the appropriate person, for example, is an important achievement. Through drama children can try out mature ways of behaving.

Similarities between the real problems faced by the counselees and those they experience in drama roles should neither be pointed out to them nor to the group. The plot provides protection that prevents unintentional psychological damage to a participant. Through reflective thinking children will be helped to view the situation from the perspective of various roles at the same time that they can see the composite result.

Problem Solving

One of the developmental tasks of latency is the gradual achieving of independence from adult control. Problems arising from this transition may be of a cognitive, moral, or affective nature. By removing the children's problems to another time and/or place, the counselor can deal with them with impunity and provide children with a stimulus for identification and reflective thinking. He or she can also train classroom teachers to use this technique, since child drama avoids the dangers for a nonprofessional worker that are present in psychodrama or sociodrama where an individual's or a group's problems may be explicitly explored. In child drama the group's focus is on the plot of the drama—the attitudes of the "responsible adults" in the play, and it is the behavior of the responsible adults who live at another time in another place that is modified. Each child learns as much from this experience about him or herself and his or her relations with others as he/she can afford to.

Preparation for Working with Drama

Even the most experienced drama leader prepares for each session carefully, focusing on both long and short-term goals.

Short-term Planning

Short-term goals require specific preparations for each group meeting. They include collecting information and perhaps an object or two, writing a chart or letter that reviews for participants what happened during the previous drama, planning specific goals for individuals and for the group, and speculating on potential dramatic development of generalities, particulars, brotherhoods, universals, questioning techniques, and presses and probes. Speculations may not always be accurate, but working through potential developments is a good warmup.

Long-term Preparations for the Leader

Long-range preparations are more demanding but can be more satisfying as the counselor sees his or her own growth. These preparations are developing a lively, flexible mind and a wide range of reading. They began long before he/she thought of child drama and will continue for a lifetime.

Keeping the Mind Flexible

A drama leader's mind is busy. He or she must classify, generalize, cite specifics, spot universals and symbols, or concrete examples of these, switch negative situations into positive framework, and test dialogue, probes, and presses. Often his or her mind does two or three of these operations simultaneously. Limbering up exercises pay off in livening up thinking habits and in providing some forethought about situations that may eventually be useful in a drama. The counselor may explore situations suitable for drama as his or her mind idles and his/her body goes through routines—showering, doing dishes, driving, raking leaves, or waiting for a bus.

Generalities

As an exercise to avoid surprise suggestions from the group, the counselor could list all the generalities he or she thinks the counselees might find interesting (see Figures IV-1 and IV-2, F). An example might be travel, for various reasons—to freedom, for riches, for adventure—and by various means—anything from walking to a rocket ship. Children are interested in circuses, monsters, rockets, current event topics (energy crisis), and themes from books, such as bravery, loneliness, honesty.

There are a number of ways to start children on a drama. All dramas have *generalities*—themes or topics of the play. A generality may come from the children directly, or from them through the counselor, as when he or she recognizes a concern of theirs which he/she feels they would benefit from exploring. To learn directly from them what generality they would be interested in working with, he/she might start by asking them, "To make a play, you need to have a problem. What problem would you like to explore?"

"Plays, as stories, are based on three themes," the counselor might say, "the human being against the environment, person against person, and the individual against himself or herself. In which situation would you like to work?"

The leader could ask the children if they would like to make a play about a "pudding of feelings." To do this the children list feelings in each of three categories: feelings that made them feel good (happiness, love, joy), feelings that they do not enjoy (hate, greed, anger), and feelings that cause people to take action (anxiety, frustration, concern). The group selects one feeling from each of these sets (ingredients of the "pudding") to explore, and the feelings are sequenced in their play (Heathcote, 1972). The setting of the drama determines the kinds of people they will be and their relationship to one another. The generality evolves from the selected, sequenced feelings and will be established by further exploration of the participants' interests.

If a generality is to come indirectly from the group, the leader needs to be cognizant of the lives of the group members outside of school as well as in. A generality can be introduced with a news clipping or by reading a story which shares a theme with the group's concern. The plot of the story would not be used, but the theme would.

❖   ❖   ❖

In the case of the cross-grade group of children who listened to *The King's Fountain* and looked at the pictures that illustrated it, the discussion of what they perceived the story to be about transcended the plot which was related to a city's water supply. The theme, the group decided, was "someone in power wants to do something that would be hard on a large number of common people"; or "bravery and tyranny" as one child abstracted. On this generality they built their Roman drama. This activity seemingly helped to overcome their frustration with their own uncontrollable life situation.

* * *

Problems and deficits the leader recognizes in the group may as yet be unrecognized by its members. It is not necessary to bring pupils' needs to their attention when using one or more of them to form a generality. The drama itself should ring true to the children, helping to divert the development of tendencies that might crystallize into problems. If working through the drama in developmental guidance sessions is not therapeutic enough, the problem may be dealt with directly later in a counseling situation.

The leader must remember that child drama is based on the assumption that the learner is the originator of the focus of the play. How it is introduced is unimportant. The group also helps determine in what manner the generality will be explored.

Segments and Particulars

Any generality can be examined from a variety of points of view. When working with a group, the leader should ask the members to *segment* that generality, to tell him or her what comes to mind when they think about that topic or theme (see Figures IV-1 and IV-2, F). Their responses show their points of view. The leader can add to their responses what he or she knows about these children and about their interests. By knowing their expectations about the topic and their sources of excitement, he/she can arrive at the *particular*, or point of entry to the drama. Three exercises can prepare the leader for doing this.

1. List all the segments or aspects of a generality.

* * *

When we asked our fourth and fifth graders what they thought *The King's Fountain* was about, they said they per-

ceived the theme to be "bravery and tyranny." They had seg-
mented the generality (book) for the leader. Once the leader
learned when and where the children wanted to be, the particular could be determined and the drama could start.

❖   ❖   ❖

2. The second exercise would be classifying the segments of a
generality in ways to establish diverse points of view.

❖   ❖   ❖

No classification by the leader of segments for *The King's
Fountain* was necessary. A child with a unique abstracting
ability immediately suggested "bravery and tyranny," and the
others agreed. Usually the leader must listen for segments that
go together and be able to label the category to determine the
group's point of view.

❖   ❖   ❖

3. Finally, try creating particulars for each point of view.

❖   ❖   ❖

The particular for the drama in ancient Rome surfaced as
the leader, in role as a slave, approached a group asking if
they had heard the news. Caesar was raising the taxes. The
leader then asked who they were, and they identified themselves—one was a tailor, another owned a clothing shop; two
were palace guards; three were Caesar's own children. The
leader made closer inquiries of them. Did they know why the
taxes were being raised? A scholar and a slave merchant and
slaves were in the group. They immediately suggested that the
tax increase was necessary so more slaves could be bought for
the palace. The discussion shifted to what this would do to the
common people. They said they had a hard enough time keeping food in the mouths of their families and roofs over their
heads without paying higher taxes. The drama began. The
participants had accepted the problem of how to prevent taxes
from being raised by their ruler.

❖   ❖   ❖

The first two processes, deciding on a generality and generat-
ing segments, are routine, but practice will make them easier for

the leader when working with a group. The final process demands imagination and daring, for a particular is the situation into which the leader, in role, plunges the group to orient it to the problem. The role must be highly vocal to make the leadership heard; however, it must be limited in power. All may be lost if the group associates the power of the leader's role in life with the power of the leader's role in the drama. The leader may be a secretary, noncommissioned officer, servant, messenger—any person who must appeal to a higher authority for orders. The "higher authority" may be present in the person of a child, or if the participants do not feel the need for its embodiment, it can be referred to rather than seen. By taking low-powered roles the leader reduces the chance of the children expending their energies fighting his or her power in real life under the protection of the drama. Instead, their attention can be focused on exploring the humanity of others.

Another limbering-up exercise would be to look in each particular for the brotherhoods and universals suggested. What brotherhoods does it hold?

* * *

A brotherhood implicit in *The King's Fountain* particular might be, "We are of the brotherhood of those who must take destiny into our own hands for our own salvation and that of others."

* * *

What universals are implicit?

* * *

A universal implicit in *The King's Fountain* might be: "Throughout time there have always been the powerful who would profit from those under their jurisdiction."

* * *

Reading Widely

Counselors who read widely in history, the social sciences, and folklore have an advantage when working in drama. Today's problems have their counterparts in most periods of history all over the earth. In child drama, the leader or the group projects the group's concern, or perhaps one that he/she sees brewing under the surface, into another, or a classic setting, to handle it as the group will. For example, he or she may be aware that interracial marriage is a community concern. The children want a drama to take place long ago in the northwestern part of the United States, so this particular might come to mind if the leader had been reading about American Indians:

❊ ❊ ❊

A handsome strange man has just ridden into the village. He doesn't have our people's sloping forehead, and the symbols on his jacket are not ours. His retinue is large and well out-fitted, and he claims much wealth in his home village. He wants to marry my sister. My mother thinks it a good match, but my father will not permit it. "It is better to marry poor and know the ways of your man than to marry rich into the unknown," is his point of view.

❊ ❊ ❊

This could be an opening situation based on a theme the leader selected in a setting chosen by the group. Before the next session he/she and the children would read to learn about marriage customs of this tribe and other information that would lend veracity to their drama. Next, they would explore the group's solutions to the problem. Participants would not be second-guessing what Chinooks would have done; they would be working through how they think *they* would have acted had *they* lived during those times and under those circumstances. No mention needs to be made of the current issue, interracial marriage. If any participant notes a similarity, he/she does so for him or herself. The leader, through his or her sensitivity to community concerns, has recognized an issue and has offered the children an opportunity to explore it to whatever depth their maturity will take them. Reflective thinking is important here. If questions are raised and children wish to make comparisons between the community's concern and their drama, the counselor will guide their speculations and help them clarify their values. Knowledge of Chinook lore will help focus on the universal implicit in the classic situation.

These preparations will give the leader confidence in his/her first attempts at child drama and support his or her continuing efforts.

GOALS FOR THE TREATMENT

The goals for which child drama can be used in guidance and counseling are varied. They range from pure enjoyment of children working together, combining their knowledge and creativity, to serious counseling that can be carried out in a small group. Drama can lead to self-concept enhancement, language development, cognitive learning, and social development. Short-term and long-term objectives can be divided into increments which can be incorporated into the counselor's planning of each session.

Almost any of the short-term goals can be set for either a large or small group developmental guidance experience or a group counseling drama. A short-term goal can often be achieved during a single drama session or improvised play. This does not imply that changes in behavior can necessarily be accomplished so easily, but gains in perception and learning can be initiated to be further reinforced. Expectations for a short-term experience might include such objectives as (1) teaching specific vocabulary and meanings in context, (2) developing the meaning of certain concepts, (3) becoming familiar with and develop respect for a given level of language or a regional or cultural dialect, (4) clarifying or applying cultural or moral values, (5) realizing another point of view, (6) releasing tension, (7) establishing cohesion within a group, and (8) motivating activities required or desired by one or several group members such as reading a book, keeping a diary, painting or some other art activity, writing a letter or story or poem, and carrying out research.

The counselor can use drama effectively in establishing interest in a curriculum topic which a class will be moving into with their teacher. Interesting the classroom teacher in drama and assisting him or her in developing skill to further extend the class experience is one of the greatest services the counselor can render to the teacher. This will in turn help in meeting the developmental needs of children and interrelating curriculum areas. The importance of this was appropriately stated by the Government of Northern Ireland Ministry of Education (1956):

> Dramatic activities transcend the traditional but largely artificial boundaries of school subjects, fusing them into a unified and significant whole. The broader sympathy and the wider knowledge of one's fellows which dramatic activity inculcates enrich understanding (p. 34).

Goals may differ for the individual members of the counseling group. For one child the goal may be to elicit verbal expression. His or her need may stem from a hesitancy to express him or herself or from a difficulty that will be diminished by safer opportunities to use and explore his or her own language. Another child may need to learn cooperation and to practice getting along with other children; for him/her an objective would be to grow more tolerant and accepting of others. Learning to live with the memory of a traumatic experience by reliving it as a bystander or in a nonthreatening role can be also achieved by drama.

One of the conditions that reinforces the feeling of alienation that some children feel when they are bused to a school outside their neighborhood is the lack of time to actually play with the children from the school's neighborhood—to get to know their new classmates out of school. In a southern city, steps have been taken to try to reduce this social distance. The long-range goal set up for working with a group of these children in drama was to develop a cohesive group, representing the various backgrounds in the school, who would serve as models to their classmates in interpersonal relations. As a short-term goal the leader wanted the children to confront issues wherein they would all be assertive and realize that any one of them could have some effect on what happens around them.

Drama in the context of group counseling might be considered psychodrama, but it would not follow the original Moreno model (Sacks, 1973). However, the classic model has been adapted for a number of purposes: diagnosis—to analyze a group and individuals in a given situation, therapy—to facilitate the correction of problems which would be expected to respond to catharsis through drama, and education—to direct or guide normal behavior toward desired goals. In group counseling, child drama is a useful way for participants to act out past and present problems, either symbolically or in a realistic situation, with spontaneity and freedom. This is a form of reality-testing. If an idea does not work in a dramatic activity, one would have to consider that it might not work in actuality and that alternatives should be planned. Or if a child is able to anticipate later reaction to a behavior or an idea by experiencing the effect it has in the drama, he/she will be able to modify it to incorporate or consolidate what he/she has learned.

Drama extended over a period of time (e.g., the Skylab experience of nine-year-olds which lasted seven weeks) can accomplish long-term objectives, with short-term goals interwoven. Long-term objectives for the participants can be grouped as (1) the development of self-concept, (2) the development of language, (3) the appreciation of culture and humanity, and (4) the development of social dynamics and skills. In meeting these objectives the leader would be alert to the modification of behavior related to evidences of decision making and concept formation, increased skill in rhetoric, a higher degree of attentiveness to what occurs or is said, group recognition of universals, increased interest and appreciation of conditions, themes, or persons, and evidences of common bonds between individuals in the group.

Outcomes for children who experience drama in group guidance and counseling might embrace sharpened cognitive powers and greater sensitivity to persons and situations, more skill at anticipating reactions, and an enlarged repertoire of responses. Through the reversibility of roles, they will have experienced being the antithesis, perhaps, of the role they customarily assume. Chronic fears in some children may be alleviated when in the safety of their peer group they encounter a problem and are helped to combat it. When the counselor organizes a group where a problem such as this is apparent (e.g., separation anxiety, fear of a tonsillectomy, fear of flying), and yet the severity of the neurotic fear is not so pronounced as to require psychiatric treatment, careful planning by the leader can make the ideas initiated by the children work to a point that what was implicit in their fears has been made explicit, and therefore something that can be confronted and handled.

SELECTION AND GROUP COMPOSITION

Guidance groups in a school setting will usually consist of heterogeneously assigned members. One would expect a fairly even ratio of boys and girls and a range of ability with an approximately normal mean. If the school follows a neighborhood assignment pattern, there could be a clustering around one socio-economic level, race, and possibly religion; but if the school is involved in widespread busing, there may be heterogeneity in all factors. Counseling groups would be selected by the counselor with particular attention to each child, all of whom would not necessarily be expected to have problems.

In child drama there has been no research on selection. Demonstrations in the United States by Heathcote and groups shown on films have involved a variety of combinations. The authors' work has included cross-grade groups, child-chosen groups, children selected by teachers, entire classrooms, Sunday school classes, two classes combined, and classes for the gifted.

Ginott (1961, 1968) stated the specific characteristics of children who would be included in group play therapy and those who would be excluded. Gazda (1971) recommended guidelines for selecting children for play group counseling, with particular attention to the applicability of Ginott's requisites, but with a more liberal view in terms of less separation by sexes. Ginott's and Heathcote's practices were compared by Hosford (1973); the differences are prescribed by the definition of the group process—therapy or drama—but the possible outcomes of these processes are congruent or similar.

A wide variety of drama group combinations is available, ranging from combined classrooms of assorted students to a small group chosen by the counselor. The following suggestions may be useful.

1. The counselor should observe the students in their classrooms

in order to have some first hand information about their maturity, problems, coping behavior, strengths, and interests. Also, prior to the firm commitment to include a child in the group, he/she should verify his/her feelings with the child's teacher. He or she may play a hunch; nonetheless, if he/she finds that a child has difficulty adapting to the activity, let the child be responsible for continuing. However, a mischosen participant should not be allowed to ruin the experience for the other members.

2. If the group is organized to be purposefully therapeutic for three to six children, the counselor may select the same number of healthy children to balance those and to serve as models and facilitators. If the counselor is to be in role with the group rather than out of role, this balancing is not as important. Another alternative for completing a group is to let the children choose who will work with them. With rare exceptions, this will be an interesting and workable arrangement.

3. If a drama begins and moves for a session or two, but the need for an additional child is noted; if, for example, the counselor senses the need for a stable, self-directed youngster, another can be brought into the activity. In child drama, roles can easily be added without radical modifications.

❋   ❋   ❋

NASA has sent two more scientists to join the Skylab I project. The leader said, "We welcome you. Introduce yourselves to us and tell us your research interests."

"I am Astronaut Fernando, and I want to investigate the plant life I think is in space, and study the effect of space atmosphere on these plants I brought from Earth."

"I am Astronaut Kimberley, and I'm a zoologist. I don't know what to expect yet, but I'll be working with Astronaut MaKay."

Thus two members are added to the nine-member group who had begun a drama about Skylab I.

❋   ❋   ❋

If children are absent from the group, the action can continue. They have simply occupied themselves elsewhere, and it is even possible for ideas attributed to them to be presented by others. They can return another day without loss of continuity since each session is written in narrative form, to be read and affirmed or amended at the start of the next session.

4. It is the leader's responsibility to keep the group from containing an imbalance of children who present a particular problem, such as hyperactivity, or who are too reticent to move into the action in a satisfying or contributing manner. The leader, in role, may engage those children in productive activities that modify the problem behavior.

*　*　*

A flood is rising on the river, and a mobile radio reporter (leader) alerts two passive housewives that their children had been seen playing too close to the river bank. Later, through the TV newscast (leader), men and women are summoned to a hotel which has been converted into a temporary shelter to help evacuees from a town which has been inundated by flood waters. The "housewives" then set about handing out dry clothing and cooking for the flood victims.

*　*　*

Thus the leader enticed reticent participants to become involved.

5. There may be times when a child must be excluded from a group after repeated trials have not worked out.

*　*　*

Matt's aggression was controlled while he was a palace guard. He held a spear and steadfastly refused to allow entry—although at times he needed an in-role confrontation to remind him of his responsibility and duty to Caesar. In a later drama that developed when the group learned that *Jonathan Livingston Seagull*[2] was banned in China, the children were engaged in living and working in the Peoples Republic of

2. Bach, R. *Jonathan Livingston Seagull.* New York, Avon, 1973.

China. Matt's behavior finally caused the group to ask that he be removed.

Children similar to Matt who really need the experiences drama can provide may be poor risks because of severe lack of interpersonal skills. From time to time Matt was included in the drama group, and the prognosis is promising since he is receiving individual therapy and his interest in drama activity is high.

6. No problem has been encountered in the mixing of sexes in child drama groups either in the authors' practice or in their observation of Heathcote. If action takes place on the high seas in the seventeenth century, girls can be sailors. If boys are all one has to work with, girls (women) can be alluded to and considered to be in the drama.

* * *

Heathcote asked a young boy what his wife thought—what she would do if she knew that he was planning to shoot the President. The boy answered that he wouldn't tell her, but if she knew she wouldn't tell anyone.

* * *

The authors agree with Gazda (1971) and Heathcote (1972) that separation by sex of school-age children is generally unnecessary. Gazda, however, warned of the interference in a mixed sex group by the more rapidly maturing girls during latency. He does not recommend mixing the sexes for group counseling with latency-age children. The problem, however, would be less likely in drama than in other forms of group counseling, since the girls' aggressiveness could be channeled in a nonthreatening way, and also the status of the boys could be raised to a desired level by the leader in role.

7. The youngest children in a cross-grade group should possess qualities that will allow them to move with the older ones, such as social maturity, facility with language, or creative ideas. Yet they should not be so aggressive as to discourage other members who may be lacking in one factor or another.

The cross-grade heterogeneous group can be a simulation of a society and thus offer a realistic problem-solving situation.

8. Differences in race and religion have created no problems in child drama groups with which the authors are familiar. Conversely, they lend credibility to action and dialogue based on what children actually bring to a situation. Moments may arise to challenge the leader's ingenuity.

❀ ❀ ❀

Pre-latency-age children of mixed age, sex, race, and religion were involved in a play about Roman life and the buying and selling of slaves. Some opted for roles of buyers. Others were slaves, and the leader took the role of a slave merchant. At the first session of this two-day drama no black child was a buyer, but several were among the slaves. Each "slave" stated his or her country of origin, from options given by the leader who, in role, described every slave. These descriptions gave the slave's background, talents, and skills, whether he or she was from Britain, Africa, Mesopotamia, or Syria. For example, the Britons were described as good farmers, and a slave from Africa was an artisan with the unique ability to smelt iron and highly skilled in the making of articles from copper and jewelry from semiprecious stones; while another was a talented musician with a rare instrument made of the finest tropical woods. The following day some of the roles were reversed, and a white child chose to be a slave from Africa and two of the black children decided they were slave buyers (Heathcote, 1972).

❀ ❀ ❀

9. Ginott (1961) specified that children with certain problems would not be eligible for group play therapy. Such children are not likely to be in a typical school. Heathcote has worked in special schools and institutions with delinquent children, groups of unwed pregnant girls, and mentally retarded children and adults. Even with trainable mentally retarded children she has used the fundamentals of drama when teachers who were studying with her worked one-to-one with a group

of youngsters whose average mental age was about three and one-half years.

Opportunities are unlimited for using drama with all ages and types of children. Research in group selection would be timely and helpful at the present time.

GROUP SETTING

Child drama can be done wherever counseling usually takes place; a classroom or office can easily accommodate it. Even less likely places such as a supply closet, porch, or parking lot can sometimes be used. If furniture appears to be in the way, it becomes incorporated into the drama as hills, trees, or houses; or else the drama can lean heavily on contrasts in lighting and sound/silence elements of the spectrum to make up for the lack of movement (see Figure IV-2, C).

Ideal conditions for working in drama would include a carpeted room to make sitting on the floor comfortable and to reduce the noise level. About 900 square feet of open space with a storage area and two or three alcoves off to the side for individual or small group action is a comfortable size. Soundproof walls and ceilings would be appropriate. Movable, sturdy work tables and stack chairs are useful to have when writing or research is to be done. No stage is needed or desired. Cabinets or shelves hold supplies, books, and equipment. Window hangings that can block out daylight make darkness possible, and a dimmer switch on the room lights helps create various moods for drama. Chalkboards are useful for plotting, mapping, listing, and diagramming. Bulletin boards display solutions to drama-based problems, maps, diagrams, lists, poems, paintings, or any other work of the children. The best settings cannot salvage superficial drama; and good drama can be done in the most unlikely settings.

GROUP SIZE

The size of the group may vary when child drama occurs in a classroom. To develop a concept from the curriculum, the whole class participates. Even with the emphasis on content, guidance benefits are likely to occur for some pupils. In the counselor's office drama may be restricted due to lack of space; but the counselor can use some other part of the school as the locale for group counseling.

Group Size for Drama as a Guidance Technique

The leader's personal preference for group size limits the number of participants. Some counselors and guidance-oriented teachers enjoy the dynamics of a large group. Others want the security of small numbers. The theme to be explored, the interest of the children, and their maturity also influence the group size. If only part of a class is to be involved in a drama, the group's composition would be determined by the number of pupils who show the need to explore an issue or to participate in a small group. Many class problems can be lived out in a drama fantasy by placing a conflict in the classic mode. From a time and place other than their own, the universality of the problem becomes explicit, and the problem and its solution may be clarified for some children.

Sometimes the group size is influenced by the physical space available or the number of pupils already grouped for certain types of instruction. The authors find it unsatisfactory to engage part of a class in drama while the remaining pupils are assigned seatwork. Those doing seatwork want to watch the action and unwittingly become an "audience" which detracts from the effectiveness of child drama for the participants. Because the seatwork pupils watch the drama instead of doing their work, they fail to finish their assignments, a failure which hurts their self-concept. Either the drama, or those children not participating in it should be removed from the room.

Group Size for Drama as a Counseling Technique

When using drama as a medium for group counseling, fewer pupils would be involved, from two to twelve. The size of the group depends on the nature of the children's needs, the makeup of the group in terms of intragroup compatibility, and the characteristics of the pupils, such as hyperactivity or docility. If the counselor feels that he or she wants to work with five children whose problems can be dealt with in a drama, two or three well-adjusted children would be invited to join the group. They would serve as models, as responders to ideas, as buffers, or as initiators, when it is clear that no harm will occur from this arrangement. This is not a new notion. Axline (1969) allowed children in play therapy to select friends to join the play. Children teaching other children, not a new concept in education, is being encouraged.

In child drama the leader exercises control either in or out of role. In-role participation allows the leader to be closely involved with the counselees. The leader can note their specific reactions in situations set up by a preconceived crisis in the drama, or to problems relevant to the children's own lives.

The group is small enough in group counseling drama for the counselor to be aware of significant inter- and intrapersonal dynamics of the counselees.

FREQUENCY, LENGTH, AND DURATION OF DRAMA GROUPS

The frequency, length, and duration of group sessions depend on a variety of variables: the needs of group members, the needs of the drama, and the school's schedule. Some needs of group members would be determined by their cognitive and language ability, self-concepts, interpersonal skills, and attention span. The drama may sometimes be stopped temporarily for children to locate information or carry out ancillary activities; or the occurrence of the "right moment" for reflective thinking might necessitate a break. The school schedule does not always permit flexible planning; yet drama can be productive even when restricted to an hour-a-week schedule.

Guidance Groups

In a group guidance program, child drama would be used whenever it appears to be an appropriate medium. A group of nine- and ten-year-olds may spend one session each week, with activity time in between, for three or four weeks on the problem of "action that can be taken by people who are oppressed."

Someone's interest in achieving excellence, or in assuring freedom of self-expression without public sanction, may cause a group to take four to six weekly sessions to consider why a nation might want to inhibit certain forms of creativity. Some daily sessions may be planned if a counselor or teacher feels that a group of primary children need play activities that will develop their language and loosen up their oral modality for self-expression. These might be short sessions of twenty to thirty minutes duration during which children will speak and interact with each other and the leader in a nonthreatening situation that would seem unlike school.

When drama is part of the developmental group guidance program, it can be carried out from kindergarten, as a very play-oriented activity, through the secondary school, where it evolves into a form more closely related to sociodrama. As children grow older they will consider the activity as moving from play to improvisation. Their needs will change and their attitude toward the activity will become more sophisticated and peer and contemporary problem oriented. Drama in group guidance would be an ongoing activity, with its use, frequency, and duration determined by the children's interest and enjoyment and the leader's evaluation of its effectiveness to cause change in counselees. More positive self-concepts, greater tolerance of ambiguity, willingness to share attention and activities, and willingness and ability to assume leadership and show initiative would be behaviors the counselor would assess.

Counseling Groups

Counseling-oriented dramas might be shorter in duration, and the themes explored more relevant to the needs of the particular counselees at that specific time than the themes from literature and contemporary events might seem. Depending on the severity of the child's problem, individual or "part of group" sessions may be needed in order to ascertain what application of the child's learning and coping behavior is taking place, and to allow him or her follow-up activities which contribute to catharsis, such as writing about what happened, drawing or painting a picture, reenactment with a puppet, and the like. A plot is kept between the counselee and his or her problem. Ideally the counselor's schedule will be flexible enough to accommodate an increased number of sessions if they seem necessary, especially to fit around scheduled absences from school such as Christmas or spring holidays and vacations. When children are referred by the counselor for psychotherapy outside of school, their continued participation in child drama should be determined by the counselor and therapist jointly. There are likely to be periods in therapy when participation in another treatment would be specifically suspended or recommended.

MEDIA

No media are specifically necessary to work in child drama. Drama used in group counseling can make good use of recording equipment though, and books and selected objects can be helpful. Therefore, media that can facilitate child drama in guidance and counseling situations can be grouped under two headings—counselor aids and media to enhance the dramatic experience (see Figure IV-2, C).

Counselor Aids

A tape recorder is almost a necessity. Audiotapes of a session are reviewed by the counselor after each session to (1) recall the sequence of the drama for charts with which to introduce the next session, thus freeing the counselor's mind from having to retain content, (2) acquaint the counselor with pupil comments that might have been missed during the press of the drama, and (3) recall details of specific counselor-counselee or counselee-peer interactions to determine the more productive forms of exchanges and note which participants should be given greater support during the next session.

A videotape recorder (VTR) costs more than an audio recorder and requires a person to operate it. The initial expenditure to buy a VTR can be justified because it can do all an audio recorder can and also provide a visual record for later study of nonverbal cues. Having a second person to redirect the sound pickup, as well as to focus the camera on the appropriate activity can be an advantage of VTR over the audio recorder. Anyone can easily learn to operate the camera. Counselors beginning to use drama need a camera operator who is sensitive to the counseling process and who is supportive of the participants. For example, a teacher or aide working with the counselor, or an older and mature student can be of immense assistance. The camera's focus will be on the productively involved children and occasionally the counselor's most effective work. During initial attempts, counselors need to see what is going right with their work. Once they feel comfortable with drama, the camera can be helpful in the counseling task. No person can see and hear all that goes on while running a group. Well-made tapes provide the counselor with multiple diagnostic opportunities. Furthermore, there may be occasions when the replay of a session for the participants may assist in meeting the counseling goals.

Shelf paper or experience chart paper and felt-tipped pens are used by the counselor to record what happens in each session. This record helps the participants recall what happened during the preceding episode, and may be useful in a number of ways: as language experience, reading material for young children or underachievers, to facilitate group cohesiveness, to give status to children by color-coding their names or quoting pertinent dialogue, to transcribe on book-sized paper to be illustrated and bound by the children, or to duplicate for each child to have a copy.

Media to Facilitate or Enhance the Dramatic Experience

Books, writing supplies, artifacts, and technical devices can be used to enhance the dramatic experience for the children. Books provide themes for dramas and information for the children to refer to when curiosity aroused by the drama compels them to learn more of the historic or geographic situations in their play. Stories are never reenacted; rather, themes are reset in situations and times determined by the participants.

Tablet paper, shelf paper, pencils, felt-tipped pens, and crayons are useful in connection with the drama. Felt-tipped pens or crayons used on shelf paper are sometimes more freeing than a ballpoint and lined paper. Leaders and participants write records or plans quickly on shelf paper. Documents to be read in large groups are more legible on this big paper, which can be rolled up for easy storage. Some children may still prefer the familiar tablet and ballpoint or soft lead pencil. Chalk and chalkboard are helpful for the participants to plot and map out their operations as the drama progresses. Lists of supplies to take on an expedition, a map of the village, or a diagram of the monster they fear or want to create—all need this easily amended technique.

Artifacts may be brought in by the counselor or discovered on site: anything from bits of trash which distract a child to jewelry someone is wearing or a piece of pottery or carving brought from home. Each piece is symbolic of a lifestyle. These create speculation.

❖   ❖   ❖

Bits of trash—threads, dust, and tiny scraps of paper—that were distracting some young participants were called for by a leader as part of the ritual of cleansing the house for the Seder (Heathcote, 1974).

A participant's bracelet became evidence of contact with an Indian tribe's disabled chief.

Sculpture and pottery aroused curiosity about the level of the culture in which the group found itself.

A collection of cloths and clothing sometimes remind a child who and where he or she is and may interest him or her in those whose clothing is different.

❖   ❖   ❖

Props that distract rather than draw the participants' attention to their work are put aside.

There is little necessity for hardware in child drama, but if it is available, it can be used effectively. A tape recorder can serve as a radio or as a spying device; a light dimmer helps develop moods. Levels or risers (platforms) can elevate participants and help them to gain the feeling of importance before their believability and the reactions of other participants can convince them of their own power. Media can help, but none is necessary.

The typical toys of the play therapist are absent. Instead, access to materials for use mainly between drama sessions should be on hand since plays lead to inventing, composing, constructing, painting, and other activities that challenge children's creativity and facilitate desirable sublimation.

LEADER QUALIFICATIONS

A child drama leader needs to be flexible, accepting, secure, supportive, hardworking, and persistent. The leader should be a certified teacher, counselor, school psychologist, or school social worker who would be ethically self-limiting. Child drama leaders who wish to use the technique in developmental guidance and counseling must know the characteristics and needs of the age pupils they are dealing with and avoid making assumptions which could decrease the effectiveness of the process. People should not attempt child drama unless they are able to take what children bring to a situation and build on it. Child drama is used for the child. The leader must be trained to recognize vulnerability to hurt in the child. This insight should be a safeguard and should help the leader move the drama in such a way as to circumvent a potentially harmful situation. The leader must be alert to the implied direction for further work with the child or indications that the child should be referred for therapy.

Reading about this mode of child drama is unlikely to make a counselor or teacher an effective child drama leader. An intensive workshop followed by abundant practice, or a course with practicum arrangements is necessary. An internship, personal study, and exposure to films and tapes which are available in some universities and school systems in the United States will all contribute to a leader's knowledge about using the technique. Training in the value of any of the expressive arts in child development and therapy can also be very helpful and add to the leader's expertise. These experiences are more useful than training in theatre. Courses in creative dramatics and role playing can provide helpful supplemental training, but they will not show a teacher or counselor how to carry out this form of child drama.

A leader should be well read in the social sciences, history, and folklore, in order to be able to place the drama in a universal perspective. A broad background is necessary to move problems from the domestic to the classic and help children sense the oneness of man and the commonality of experience. The leader's personality and experiences play a large role in working with children in this medium. Heathcote (1972) listed eighteen attributes needed by persons who work with children in child drama:

1. ability to draw upon one's own life,
2. ability to relate the particular to the general,
3. ability to be natural in the present moment,
4. ability to identify at different levels,
5. ability to use logic,
6. a sense of time/timelessness,
7. a sense of theatre,
8. an understanding of conflict in action,
9. an understanding of symbolism and brotherhoods,
10. a fine control of language,
11. a fine control of physical relationships,
12. a fine control of intake,
13. ability to believe,
14. ability to see all the attitudes which are explosive,
15. a strong sense of body image,
16. ability to nurture ideas, i.e., develop a seed,
17. ability to see the directional potential of a seed in relation to a group,
18. ability to receive and upgrade ideas by putting them into action.

The child drama leaders who can accomplish the most with children are open, intuitive persons who will be able to mentally classify the information which is being produced by the group. This helps in planning how to move the action, sensing the particular needs of individual children and the group so that appropriate experiences can be arranged, and helping the children think critically and with reflection.

ETHICAL CONSIDERATIONS

In the practice of child drama as a guidance and counseling technique it is not anticipated that problems would be encountered with reference to ethical considerations. Child drama will be most often used as a developmental guidance experience, and as such would be a part of the regular school curriculum. When drama is used in counseling and play groups or activity therapy groups, children who are under the care of a psychiatrist should participate only when the professional who is working with them is fully aware of and in agreement with their participation. As a rule, such a child would be excluded until the therapy is discontinued or the therapist desires to see what the patient can do with the group of children.

In using drama in group guidance and group counseling, the leader is expected to be self-limiting with regard to ethics. No problems would be expected within the realm of developmental guidance, but situations might arise in the counseling group or the play therapy activity which would require extreme caution.

Care should be taken to ensure the psychological safety of all participants. Children's right to privacy should not be invaded or their problems of a personal nature exposed in a manner that could bring harm. Parental permission should be obtained when group counseling or play or activity therapy would involve exceptional children if such a policy exists in the school. The counselor should always be aware of the progress and condition of children involved and allow time for the independent resolution of any problems which may be apparent in the drama or revealed by any other means to the counselor. The leader in role should be sensitive to possible problem areas and arrange for them to be handled in ways which would make children feel competent and secure in trying to cope, or to help them see, directly or through inference, a belonging to a brotherhood of those who have in common a given anxiety or concern. The leader's role is to help bring out what is implicit in the playing out of the group so that benefits for all children are available. Since the course of action is directed toward universals and participants are helped to view the human condition as common to all people across all time, domestic situations can be placed in a less threatening perspective. While children will be able to identify with external problems that are related to situations in their own lives, they can act them out in a reversible situation and try out solutions without the fear of disaster. Both in role and out of role, then, the counselor will respect and protect the counselee, and the counselor and any other leader will be governed by ethical professional standards (APA, 1968; APGA, 1974).

LIMITATIONS OF THE TREATMENT

Almost any child who is attending a regular school would be a candidate for drama as a guidance or counseling activity. Some few children who lack the self-discipline to participate in a large group may, nevertheless, be brought into a smaller group where more structure is imposed and where the content will be shaped to meet their particular needs. Severely disturbed children would not be expected to participate with pupils from a normal classroom except when two or three are included as a therapeutic measure for those few. Then the behavior of the normals would serve as a model.

Child drama is a promising form of educational therapy when practiced by a qualified teacher of exceptional children or a counselor. Retarded children who are handicapped to a degree that they require a self-contained classroom will respond well to drama that involves only their classmates. Sometimes a few retarded children can be integrated successfully into a regular class activity, especially if the class has been prepared and realizes that they will be in a position to help their peers. Insights to be gained at the maturity level of the largest number of participants in a group are usually the desired outcomes; therefore care should be taken to ensure that any handicapped children included would have the benefit of interpretative behavior and language that they can fully understand.

Children who need psychotherapy should not be arbitrarily involved in drama as a counseling measure. They should be referred to a mental health facility or professional for therapy. However, if they have impulse control and the desire to participate in drama, they can be expected to gain from it if recommended by mental health professionals.

Since cross-grade groups can be set up, there are greater opportunities for the use of drama by counselors to work with the assortment of children who may be referred to them by teachers. Benefits to the children will be commensurate with their abilities to perceive and think. As they are given practice in thinking (Raths et al., 1967), limitations will be lessened and greater gains can be expected.

SUMMARY

Research has not yet been reported in this country on the use of child drama as a guidance and counseling technique. However, counselors have been successful using dramatic techniques with developmental guidance and counseling groups. Dramatic play is recognized as a productive activity for young children, and social psychologists stress the importance of language in the development of personality and self-concept. Meaning can only be established as a consequence of communication, and in child drama the overt spontaneity of the individual confronts the community sanctions and strictures presented by the leader in role, providing greater commitment for the learner than individual vicarious role playing might. This is why a school counselor or a classroom teacher with whom children feel comfortable can be more effective as a leader than a visiting drama specialist.

Developmental guidance and counseling, as referred to in this chapter, can be carried out with all the children in a class to help assure the accomplishment of developmental tasks. As an intervention, it helps children to withstand problems caused by slow or inadequate achievement of developmental tasks. Guidance activities are those dealing with problems that concern the whole class; counseling is carried out with individuals or small groups, focusing on personal problems relevant to the individual participants. Child drama is spontaneous improvisation developed from the interests of the participants, led in such a way as to confront problems as universal concerns. The skilled leader, who is usually in role, provides a therapeutic climate. Participation in this problem-solving situation can develop positive self-concepts and language and interpersonal skills.

Drama can help the counselor achieve long-term and short-term goals with children. Some long-term goals that drama has the potential for accomplishing are the development of language ability and social skills and a sense of responsibility, as well as the enhancement of self-concept. Short-term goals, such as vocabulary and concept development and the modification of minor personality traits and ineffective behavior, may be achieved in one or two sessions.

As a developmental guidance experience, entire or combined classes can participate in child drama. The technique can also be used effectively with small groups of children (two or three) with like personal problems matched with healthy models to form groups of four to six. No special setting or materials are required. A tape recorder is useful to have, and a carpeted, soundproof area that can be darkened is helpful, but not essential, for working in drama. Neither a stage nor the traditional play therapy playroom equipment would be useful. The equipment from an activity therapy room, however, would be useful for ancillary projects springing from the drama.

Counselors probably need a workshop and practicum or a laboratory course in child drama to be able to use it effectively. The growing body of articles, books, and films on the subject here in the United States provides supplementary learning aids. Observations or demonstrations are helpful but cannot replace actual experimentation with the technique when a supportive supervisor is available to assist.

Any qualified counselor or teacher who is flexible, accepting, secure, supportive, hard working, and persistent, with a good imagination, sense of humor, and a universal outlook on life, can develop the skills to work effectively as a child drama leader. This professional person needs to be familiar with child development and sensitive to the needs of the individuals in the group, so that referrals of seriously maladjusted children can be made. The ethical guidelines of the leader's profession must be followed. Children who lack impulse control and the need for approval will benefit little from drama. They will need more intense therapy. Retarded children benefit from drama when it is carried out at a level meaningful to them. Groups mixed in mental abilities, religions, races, national origins, sexes, economic backgrounds, and chronological ages work together effectively. All are a part of the cultural tapestry of this country, and child drama is preparation for life in its diverse society.

SUGGESTED READINGS

Axline, V. M.: *Dibs: In Search of Self*. Boston, HM, 1964.

Birdwhistell, R. L.: *Kinesics and Context*. Philadelphia, U of Pa Pr, 1970.

Britton, J.: *Language and Learning*. Coral Gables, U of Miami Pr, 1970.

Courtney, R.: *Play, Drama & Thought*. London, Cassell, 1968.

Duke, C. R.: *Creative Dramatics and English Teaching*. Urbana, National Council of Teachers of English, 1974.

Fines, J., and Verrier, R.: *The Drama of History: An Experiment in Cooperative Teaching*. London: Clive Bingley, 1974.

Ginott, H. G.: *Between Parent and Child*. New York, Macmillan, 1965.

Ginott, H. G.: *Between Parent and Teen-ager*. New York, Macmillan, 1969.

Films

British Broadcasting Company: *Improvised Drama: Part I*. New York, Time-Life, 1965.

British Broadcasting Company: *Three Looms Waiting*. New York, Time-Life, 1971.

Northwestern University: *Dorothy Heathcote Talks to Teachers: Parts I and II*. Evanston, Viewfinders, 1973.

Northwestern University: *Building Belief: Parts I and II*. Evanston, Northwestern Film Library, 1974.

Videotapes

National College of Education: *Teaching through Drama: Parts I and II*. Evanston, National College of Education, 1972.

University of Georgia: *Dorothy Heathcote Demonstration (Middle School) and Followup: Parts I and II*. Athens, U of Georgia, 1974.

University of Georgia: *Dorothy Heathcote Lecture and Demonstration (Elementary School): Parts I, II, and III*. Athens, U of Georgia, 1974.

REFERENCES

Alschuler, A. S., and Ivey, A. E.: Getting into psychological education. *Personnel and Guidance Journal, 51*:682-691, 1973.

American Psychological Association: *Ethical Standards of Psychologists.* Washington, D. C., American Psychological Association, 1968.

American Personnel and Guidance Association: Ethical standards. *Guidepost, 17(extra)*:4-5, 1974.

Amster, F.: Differential uses of play in treatment of young children. *American Journal of Orthopsychiatry, 13*:62-68, 1943.

Axline, V. M.: *Play Therapy.* New York, Ballantine, 1969.

Barclay, J. R.: Effecting behavior change in the elementary classroom: an exploratory study. *Journal of Counseling Psychology, 14*:240-247, 1967.

Bessell, H., and Palomares, U. H.: *Methods in Human Development.* San Diego, Human Development Training Institute, 1967.

Corsini, R. J.: *Roleplaying in Psychotherapy.* Chicago, Aldine, 1966.

Dewey, J.: *The School and Society,* rev. ed. Chicago, U of Chicago Pr, 1943.

Dinkmeyer, D.: Top priority: understanding self and others. *The Elementary School Journal, 72*:62-71, 1971.

Dyer, W. W., and Vriend, J.: Role working in group counseling. In Vriend, J., and Dyer, W. W. (Eds.): *Counseling Effectively in Groups.* Englewood Cliffs, Ed Technology, Pub 1973.

Ekstein, R.: *Children of Time and Space, of Action and Impulse.* New York, Appleton, 1966.

Erikson, E. H.: *Childhood and Society,* 2nd ed. New York, Norton, 1963.

Foley, J. M.: *Training Future Teachers as Play Therapists: An Investigation of Therapeutic Outcome and Orientation Toward Pupils.* Chicago, Loyola University, 1970. (ED 067 794)

Follett Educational Corporation: *The World of Language.* Chicago, Author, 1970.

Gazda, G. M.: *Group Counseling: A Developmental Approach.* Boston, Allyn, 1971.

Gibbons, T. J., and Lee, M. K.: Group counseling: impetus of learning. *Elementary School Guidance and Counseling, 7*:32-36, 1972.

Gilmore, S.: Group processes in educational drama: report of a pilot study. *Educational Review, 25*:106-111, 1973.

Ginott, H. G.: *Group Psychotherapy with Children.* New York, McGraw, 1961.

Ginott, H. G.: Group therapy with children. In Gazda, G. M. (Ed.): *Basic Approaches to Group Psychotherapy and Group Counseling.* Springfield, Thomas, 1968.

Ginott, H. G.: *Teacher & Child*. New York, Macmillan, 1971.

Gittleman, M.: Behavior rehearsal as a technique in child treatment. *Journal of Child Psychology and Psychiatry, 6*:251-255, 1965.

Goffman, E.: *Presentation of Self in Everyday Life*. Garden City, Doubleday, 1959.

Glasser, W.: *Schools Without Failure*. New York, Har-Row, 1969.

Gould, R.: *Child Studies Through Fantasy*. New York, Quadrangle, 1972.

Government of Northern Ireland Ministry of Education: *Provision for Primary Schools*. Belfast, Her Majesty's Stationer's Office, 1956. Cited by Duke, C. R.: *Creative Dramatics and English Teaching*. Urbana, National Council of Teachers of English, 1974, p. 77.

Gray, F., and Mager, G. C.: *Liberating Education*. Berkeley, McCutchan, 1973.

Harcourt Brace Jovanovich, Inc.: *The Social Sciences: Concepts and Values*. New York, HarBrace J, 1970.

Hardy, M. P., Sr.: Drama in the classroom. *Elementary English, 51*:94-102, 1974.

Hartshorn, E., and Brantley, J. C.: Effects of dramatic play on classroom problem-solving ability. *Journal of Educational Research, 66*:243-246, 1973.

Havighurst, R. J.: *Developmental Tasks and Education*, 3rd ed. New York, McKay, 1972.

Heathcote, D.: *Drama in the Education of Teachers*. Newcastle, University Printing Services, Ltd., 1971.

Heathcote, D.: Lectures and demonstrations at Northwestern University, Evanston, Ill., 1972.

Heathcote, D.: Lectures and demonstrations at the University of Georgia, Athens, Georgia, 1974.

Herron, R. E., and Sutton-Smith, B.: *Child's Play*. New York, Wiley, 1971.

Hoffman, M. L.: *Empathy, Role-taking, Guilt, and Development of Altruistic Motives*. Bethesda, National Institute of Child Health and Human Development, 1973. (ED 085 109)

Hosford, P. M.: *Two Views of the Heathcote Mode of Child Drama: As Exemplary Teaching and in Contrast to Traditional Group Play Therapy*. Paper presented at the American Personnel and Guidance Association Convention, Atlanta, May 1973.

Hosford, P. M.: Magic of drama. In Berger, A., and Smith, B. H. (Eds.): *Language Activities*. Urbana, National Council of Teachers of English, 1973.

Hosford, P. M., and Acheson, E.: Child drama . . . and Jonathan Livingston Seagull. *The English Record, 25*(3):70-73, 1974.

Ivey, A. E., and Alschuler, A. S.: An introduction to the field. *Personnel and Guidance Journal, 51*:591-597, 1973.

Jennings, S.: *Remedial Drama.* New York: Theatre Arts, 1974.

Jones, R. M.: *Feeling and Fantasy in Education.* New York, NYU Pr, 1971.

Kelley, E. Y.: *The Magic IF.* Baltimore, Natl Ed Pr, 1973.

Kern, R., and Kirby, J. H.: Utilizing peer helper influence in group counseling. *Elementary School Guidance and Counseling,* 6:70-75, 1971.

Kessler, J.: *Psychopathology of Childhood.* Englewood Cliffs, P-H, 1966.

Knudson, R. L.: The effect of pupil-prepared videotaped dramas upon the language development of selected rural children. *Research in the Teaching of English,* 5:60-68, 1971.

Kranz, P. L.: Teachers as play therapists: an experiment in learning. *Childhood Education,* 49:73-74, 1972.

Kramer, E.: *Art as Therapy with Children.* New York, Schocken, 1971.

Lederman, J.: *Anger and the Rocking Chair.* New York, McGraw, 1969.

Levin, B. S.: Drama for the disadvantaged. *Improving College and University Teaching,* 20(3):164-166, 1972.

Lowndes, B.: *Movement and Creative Drama for Children.* Boston, Plays, 1971.

MacDougall, M. A., and Brown, J. A.: *The Impact of Social Skill Training on the Affective Perceptions of Elementary School Children.* Paper presented at the American Educational Research Association Annual Meeting, New Orleans, Feb., 1973. (ED 074 166)

Massialas, B. G., and Zevin, J.: *Creative Encounters in the Classroom.* New York, Wiley, 1967.

Mead, G. H.: *Mind, Self & Society from the Standpoint of a Social Behaviorist.* Chicago, U of Chicago Pr, 1934.

Millar, S.: *The Psychology of Play.* New York, Aronson, 1973.

Miller, G. D., Gum, M. F., and Bender, D.: *Elementary School Guidance: Demonstration and Evaluation.* St. Paul, Pupil Personnel Services Section, Minnesota State Department of Education, 1972. (ED 072 371)

Moreno, J. L.: The spontaneity theory of learning. In Haas, R. B. (Ed.): *Psychodrama and Sociodrama in American Education.* New York, Beacon Hse, 1949.

Morse, R., and Simmons, H. C.: Dramatic and moral development in latency-age children: a bibliographical summary. *Religious Education,* 68:69-83, 1973.

Moulin, E. K.: Effects of client-centered group counseling using play media on the intelligence, achievement, and psycholinguistic abilities of underachieving primary school children. *Elementary School Guidance and Counseling,* 5:85-98, 1970.

Ojemann, R. H.: *Developing a Program for Education in Human Behavior.* Iowa City, State U of Iowa, 1959.

Peters, H. J., Shelly, M., and McCormick, R.: *Random House Program for Elementary Guidance.* New York, Random, 1966.

Piers, M. W.: Play and mastery. In Ekstein, R., and Motto, R. L. (Eds.): *From Learning for Love to Love of Learning.* New York, Brunner-Mazel, 1969.

Raths, L.: *Meeting the Needs of Children.* Columbus, Merrill, 1972.

Raths, L. E., Jones, A., Rothstein, A., and Wassermann, S.: *Teaching for Thinking.* Columbus, Merrill, 1967.

Reisman, E. F., and Beyer, L. M.: Group counseling in an elementary school setting. *Child Welfare, 52*:192-195, 1973.

Sacks, J. M.: Psychodrama: an underdeveloped group resource. *Educational Technology, 13(2)*:37-39, 1973.

Saltz, E., and Johnson, J.: Training for thematic-fantasy play in culturally disadvantaged children: preliminary results. *Studies in Intellectual Development.* Detroit, Wayne State University, Michigan Center for the Study of Cognitive Processes, 1973. (ED 081 486)

Selman, R. L.: *A Structural Analysis of the Ability to Take Another's Social Perspective: Stages in the Development of Role-taking Ability.* Paper presented at the biennial meeting of the Society for Research in Child Development, Philadelphia, March, 1973. (ED 081 486)

Shaftel, F. R., and Shaftel, G.: *Words and Action.* New York, HR&W, 1967.

Smilansky, S.: *The Effects of Sociodramatic Play on Disadvantaged Preschool Children.* New York, Wiley, 1968.

Sutton-Smith, B.: *The Folkgames of Children.* Austin, U of Tex Pr, 1972.

Sutton-Smith, B.: *Play as Variability Training and as the Useless Made Useful,* 1974. (ED 084 008)

University of Newcastle-upon-Tyne: *Drama in Education,* Newcastle, University Printing Services, Ltd., 1971.

VanScoy, H.: Activity group therapy: a bridge between play and work. *Child Welfare, 51*:528-534, 1972.

Vinton, I.: *The Folkways Omnibus of Children's Games.* Harrisburg, Stackpole, 1970.

Wagner, B. J.: Evoking gut-level drama. *Learning, 2(7)*:16-20, 1974.

Ward, W.: *Playmaking with Children.* New York, Appleton, 1957.

Way, B.: *Development Through Drama.* London, Longman, 1967.

Winnicott, D. W.: *Playing and Reality.* New York, Basic, 1971.

V

COUNSELING ADOLESCENTS IN GROUPS[1]

MERLE M. OHLSEN

E VERYONE CAN PROFIT from counseling when confronted by problems that he or she feels cannot be solved alone or with the assistance of relatives, friends, and coworkers. Being hurt by a loved one or feeling guilty about hurting someone, questioning the love of a loved one, grieving for someone, being conscious of a problem without the courage, self-confidence, or skills to attack it or being confronted with a problem whose solution will disappoint an esteemed person, not being able to meet up to others' expectations, failing to achieve desired goals —obviously these are problems for adults as well as adolescents.

Inasmuch as adolescents are engrossed with their search for identity, McCandless (1970) believes that rapid social changes and relaxation of moral values have complicated their lives even more than adults' lives. He believes that many of adolescents' problems involve frustration in achieving their major goals— status, sociality, adequate sexual adjustments, and self and society-fulfilling values and morals.

> Status may be more highly valued for boys, sociality for girls. Both are probably more important in the long run than sex, although the importance of sexuality is likely to be underplayed within the core, middle-class culture. While often neglected by scholars, an individual's moral values development is likely to be more important than anything else in determining the quality of his life. These four major goals are achieved in all life settings, whether family, school, community groups, or job.
>
> The point that needs greatest emphasis in a psychology of adolescence is that a drive-change theory predicts that the period is one in which great personal change can occur. Such change can be malign

---

1. This is a revision of Chapter 10 in Merle M. Ohlsen's *Group Counseling*, New York, Holt, Rinehart and Winston, 1970, and will appear as Chapter 8 in the forthcoming revision.

or benign, and it is society's responsibility to maximize the latter while minimizing the former (p. 36).

ADOLESCENTS' NEEDS

Adolescents are trying to determine who they are, what they would like to do, and what they can do. They are also trying to develop the will and self-confidence to do these things. Adolescents are trying to learn how to recognize their problems early and solve them rather than to ignore them until they erupt into crises. Although they are struggling for independence from significant others such as parents and teachers, there are times when they prefer to lean on them. At the same time they are changing their reference group from family to peers. Because of rapidly changing times, and the adolescents' consuming demands for independence, peers encourage adolescents to question many of their parents' values.

Unlike Hall (1904), who described adolescence as a period of storm and stress, Hurloch (1967) cited the findings of Gesell, Ilg, and Ames (1956) to support the notion that the period could better be described as a period of heightened emotionality. Ausubel (1954) characterizes adolescence as a period of testing the adequacy of the personality structure laid down during childhood. Ackerman (1955) believes adolescents tend to be extraordinarily sensitive to others' judgment of their worth. Being caught between the twin horns of conformity and defiance explains their trigger-edge irritability. Nowhere is their rawness and their need to prove themselves more vivid than in their relationships between the sexes. Each sex is acutely aware of the other, is highly sensitive to the other, and lacks the confidence of the more experienced, mature adult. Adolescents tend to get excited or threatened more easily than mature adults. When, therefore, their significant others vacillate from treating them as children to treating them as adults, and when the significant others try to get them to fulfill their needs, adolescents often lack the self-confidence and interpersonal skills to react maturely. On the other hand, Ausubel found that although personality defects appear to be more glaring during this period, they tend to be only transitory disturbances. Even when the personality defects are more basic, he concludes that the appearance of the most serious personality disorders occur after rather than during adolescence. Except for those who experienced markedly deviant sexual development, Hurloch concludes that most learn to cope with the problems with which they are confronted as adolescents. Adolescents often give their parents and teachers "a hard time," thus causing these adults to wonder whether they will ever "find themselves." Kirkpatrick (1952) agrees that most do, and without any permanent scars.

Garrison's (1965) review of the research on adolescents suggests that much of adolescent anger results from frustration of some goal-seeking activity. They feel that they are pressured to work for the goals others have for them, that they are not allowed to make their own important decisions, and that they are expected to work for goals which are not appropriate for them. On these occasions they often feel that their significant others bully them. Lacking the verbal and social skills to cope with these confrontations, they tend to strike back as a restrained and tormented animal would.

By contrast, adolescents want to be participating members of society (Ayer and Corman, 1952). Their interest in national and world affairs has long been fostered by high school and college teachers, and it has been greatly increased by television. Adolescents are more concerned about social problems than most adults realize. They appreciate support and encouragement from significant adults when they try to solve social problems (and under these circumstances they will listen to adults' suggestions), and they thrive on genuine opportunities to solve social problems and on recognition for *real accomplishments*. However, when adults ignore obvious social problems, adolescents tend to become disappointed, disillusioned, and even cynical with adults' complacency (Neidt and Fritz, 1950). Some feel that they must protest with demonstrations, strikes, and even riots to get adults' attention and to bring about desired changes. Others give up and withdraw by separating themselves from these adults, by quitting school, by staying in school but withdrawing from the learning process, or by turning to drugs.

Adolescent needs which provide general goals for group counseling may be summarized as follows:

1. Search for identity,
2. Essential information about their interests, abilities, and aptitudes,
3. Essential information-seeking skills to identify opportunities and to evaluate them in terms of their own interests, abilities, and aptitudes,
4. The interpersonal skills and self-confidence required to recognize and deal with their conflicts,
5. The interpersonal skills and self-confidence to recognize when decisions are required, how to make them, and how to implement them,
6. Sensitivity to others' needs and improved skills to help others satisfy their needs,
7. The communication skills to convey their real feelings directly to relevant persons, and with considerations for their feelings,
8. Independence to examine what they believe, to make their own decisions, to take reasonable risks, to make their own mistakes, and to learn from their mistakes,
9. The interpersonal skills to deal with authority figures in a mature manner—e.g., employers, police, government officials, as well as parents and teachers,
10. The opportunity for meaningful participation in developing and maintaining limits on their own behavior,
11. Improved understandings and skills for coping with their physical and emotional changes associated with maturation, and
12. Improved skills in learning to live adult roles.

As much as adolescents want their independence from parents, there are times when they feel very dependent upon them. They are ambivalent about their financial dependence; they resent it, and at the same time they are reluctant to relinquish it. When they want to lean on adults they must know they can count on them. For example, they are willing to pretend to act out of deference to their parents in order to cope with peer pressure to do something which they do not want to do anyway. They feel more secure when they realize that their parents have the ego strength to enforce limits when they are not able to do so.

Some adolescents feel that no one has ever tried to teach them to behave independently. Others feel that they are forced to rebel to escape from their parents' control. Though at some times most adolescents rebel to avoid conformity, the rebellious tend to conform more than the conformists. The difference is that they are controlled by peers rather than by their family's values and traditions. Sometimes the rebellious are used by unprincipled demagogues who may be approximately their own age, but more likely are adults who pretend to understand them in order to use them.

When rebellion serves no purpose except to fight conformity or to revolt against the establishment and its traditions, it is a neurotic reaction to authority. Healthy rebellion arises out of love for something—a recognition that something must be changed and a commitment to change that which is wrong. Healthy rebels have goals. Furthermore, they want to participate in the planning and the implementing of change, and most are willing to accept adults' assistance.

Unfortunately, many adults seem to assume that adolescents must rebel to earn their independence, and hence parents must learn to tolerate it. When parents and teachers learn to empathize with adolescents, to listen to them when they want to talk openly, to respect adolescents' ideas, and to enlist their assistance in solving problems and in defining meaningful limits and enforcing them (and changing limits as the adolescents are able to function more responsibly), many of the heartaches and conflicts with which adolescents are confronted in growing up can be resolved without rebellion. Adolescents can accept from strong, understanding adults the assistance which they require to meet their increasing responsibilities. They are searching for meaning in their daily lives in their communities as well as in their schools and homes. They cherish meaningful group experiences with peers in student government, personal growth groups, and in counseling groups. Competent counselors, whom the adolescents perceive as unequivocally trustworthy confidants, are required to provide them counseling and to provide parent education for their parents.

THEORETICAL FOUNDATIONS

The treatment model described in this chapter is developed upon the notion that it meets adolescents' needs and uses the change agents within the group. For his purposes here the writer labels these as therapeutic forces. To the extent to which a leader trusts members and shares leadership responsibilities with clients determines the extent to which he or she teaches them to recognize and help manage these forces in counseling groups. The forces are described briefly here.

Attractiveness

"The more attractive the group is to its members, the greater is the influence that the group can exert on its members" (Cartwright, 1951, p. 388). Cartwright and Zander (1968) also concluded from a review of the research that group attractiveness is determined by whether its goals are perceived as important, its members' needs are met, these members are valued and accepted, the membership includes prestigious members, the membership is relatively homogeneous, and whether its membership is small enough to communicate and relate effectively. Later sections in this chapter on selection and size illustrate how the model takes cognizance of these data in order to increase group attractiveness.

Belonging

As the feeling of belonging increases within a counseling group, clients experience growing commitment to change, to participate more meaningfully, to listen to others, and to respond more honestly to each other. Observing peer clients struggling with similar problems contributes to a feeling of belonging (Beck, 1958; Powdermaker and Frank, 1953) and increases identification with other clients and commitment to therapeutic norms (Kelman, 1963). Hobb's (1962) observations concerning the importance of intimacy in individual therapy is even more important for adolescents in group counseling. Unlike most other groups, Dreikurs (1957) observed that talking openly in a counseling group does not lower one's status. Instead clients are valued for looking at themselves as they really are. They sense genuine human fellowship with others who are able to give of themselves without ulterior motives. Membership in such a group in which adolescents experience intimacy desensitizes them to the fear of intimacy, teaches them relationship skills, and encourages them to establish mature relationships with significant others including peers outside of their counseling group.

Acceptance

Genuine acceptance by peer clients enhances clients' self-esteem; and increases their confidence that they can be helped (especially when clients realize they have been selected for a model with much care). Though acceptance by peer clients is not as predictable nor as unconditional as it is from the counselor, it is even more powerful when it is experienced because it is not paid for and it comes from other lay persons like themselves (Kelman, 1963). When adolescents are accepted in such a group and realize the degree to which others try to understand them, believe in them, and *can help them,* they discover that others can be tolerant of solutions which are most appropriate for them—that they *can develop mature relationships* with peers as well as with most adult relatives and friends.

Security

Beck (1958) presented a number of reasons why clients feel safe within their treatment group (and her reasons apply especially to adolescents in group counseling): (1) Trust is learned more readily in a group; (2) untrained peers provide an uncensored, more realistic response to trust; and (3) they learn readily to listen to each other. Very soon all discover that others have problems that are as bad or worse than their own, and that others also expect to be helped. Moreover, within this counseling model, clients are helped from the beginning to accept responsibility *for getting themselves ready for counseling,* for convincing themselves as well as their counselor in the intake interview that they are committed to discuss their problems openly and to change their behavior, and for accepting responsibility for learning to trust their peer clients and their counselors. They also realize what will be done within their group to maintain confidence. With the definition of specific behavioral goals, *they recognize that group counseling is designed to help them learn new behavior* rather than to change their personality (and consequently their search for identity will not be disrupted; Holmes, 1964).

When clients feel secure within their counseling group, they can discuss their problems openly, share ideas on tentative solutions, solicit feedback, accept feedback from others, and express their own genuine feelings toward each other. The safer clients feel in a group, the easier it is for them to learn from their members. When they do not feel safe they tend either to become inactive (present, but nonpatient members) or to drop out of the group (Sethna and Harrington, 1971). Furthermore, the nonparticipation not only deprives them of assistance, but it poses a threat to other members. Although secure clients realize that at times they must deal with painful material, they are not threatened by participation; they are willing to tolerate the pain in order to reap the benefits which accrue from improved adjustment.

Expectations

Clients profit most from group counseling when they realize what will be expected from them and what they can expect from others prior to deciding whether to participate in group counseling (this also is essential to ensure truth in packaging of services). In order to achieve this goal counselors must be able to define meaningfully the helping process for their prospective clients. A counselor must realize under what conditions he or she functions best and what decisions he/she feels comfortable permitting clients to make; he/she must encourage prospective clients to ask any questions that they may have, and encourage them to accept responsibility for clarifying expectations and for getting themselves ready for counseling. When prospective clients realize what is expected of them in order to increase their chances for success in their group, they perform better as clients and as helpers, accepting more responsibility for creating and maintaining a therapeutic climate, and for implementing their desired new behaviors. Thus, they discover early that not only must they decide whether to participate but they must convince themselves as well as their counselor that they want to join a counseling group and learn specific new behaviors; they become convinced of what they must do to achieve their goals.

Commitment

Those who profit most from group counseling accept their need for assistance and are committed to discuss their problems openly from the beginning, to define and implement desired new behaviors and help peer clients do the same. They discover early that the counseling group is a safe place to talk openly about their problems and to practice new behaviors. Even when it is painful, they are determined to follow through in meeting the terms of their agreement with their counselor and peer clients to establish a good working climate and to implement their goals. These clients are determined to achieve their own goals and to help their peer clients achieve theirs.

Responsibility

With increased acceptance of responsibility for developing and maintaining therapeutic group norms, for their own growth, and for encouraging peer clients' growth, clients' chances for growth will be enhanced. Most group members of even task-oriented groups thrive on meaningful participation and on being given real responsibility for their behavior. Such experiences discourage reactive behaviors, but for adolescent clients this is more crucial. When adolescents are offered a chance for help, allowed to decide whether to participate, and are called upon to demonstrate their own readiness for group counseling, they recognize that they are being given real responsibility and they like it. Moreover, those who most readily accept responsibility for helping others as well as themselves tend to profit most from the therapeutic experience (Lindt, 1958). Clients' participation in developing and revising group norms also is one of the most effective elements in producing cohesiveness (Bach, 1954).

Open Communication

Effective group members communicate openly. Thelen and Stock (1955) reported that one effective group had hammered out agreements on questions such as these: What can we expect from each other? How freely may we express our feelings? Who will settle disputes and how? How wide a range of behavior can we tolerate? Though most adolescent clients recognize that they must accept some responsibility for developing their own trust, they must perceive the counselor as unequivocally trustworthy. They also appreciate an opportunity to report their preferences on who will be included in their group. Usually they demand a very clear understanding of confidentiality. When the counselor explains why it is important for them to come to counseling prepared to talk openly, how to accept this responsibility, and what they will be permitted to decide, open communication in counseling in enhanced. Counselors also enhance communication by encouraging clients to ask them questions and answer questions in a nondefensive manner. Dreikurs (1957) concluded that talking openly enhanced a client's status. Weigel, Dinges, Dyer, and Straumfjord (1972) found a positive relationship between mutual liking on the part of peer clients and the extent of self-disclosure. Their clients also tended to rate self-disclosing peers as healthier.

Congruence

Effective communication is essential for successful group counseling, and congruence within each individual is essential for good communication. Unfortunately, sometimes everyone requires external feedback to detect lack of congruence. Individuals are congruent when there is accurate matching of those feelings of which they are aware and those which they are experiencing. If, therefore, the message senders are to send a clear message, they must experience congruence while communicating their message (otherwise they will send a garbled one), and if receivers are to receive a clear message, they must be congruent while they are receiving (or they will garble even a clear message). When, for example, individuals are angry at someone but for some reason cannot own their anger, they deny the anger, fail to deal with the conflict involved, and usually communicate poorly. From his research and clinical experience Rogers (1961) generalizes as follows:

> Assuming (a) a minimal willingness on the part of the two people to be in contact; (b) an ability and minimal willingness on the part of each to receive communication from the other; and (c) assuming the contact to be continued over a period of time; the following relationship is hypothesized to hold true.
>
> The greater the congruence of experience, awareness and communication on the part of one individual, the more the ensuing relationship will involve: a tendency toward reciprocal communication with a quality of increasing congruence; a tendency toward more mutually accurate understanding of the communications; improved psychological adjustment and functioning in both parties; and mutual satisfaction in the relationship.
>
> Conversely the greater the communicated incongruence of experience and awareness, the more the ensuing relationship will involve: further communication of the same quality; disintegration of accurate understanding, less adequate psychological adjustment and functioning in both parties; and mutual dissatisfaction in the relationship (pp. 344-345).

Sometimes, early in the life of a counseling group, counselors may have to teach their clients to recognize incongruence and to use considerate feedback to cope directly with it. Usually clients recognize incongruences but often they require assistance in learning how to handle them. Bach and Deutsch's (1971) pairing technique also can be used to teach clients to deal with lack of congruence as well as to help them achieve genuine intimacy.

Tension

Clients must experience some tension and dissatisfaction with their present state to be motivated to change their behavior. On the other hand, excessive tension can debilitate clients to such an extent that they cannot use their own resources for achieving desired changes.

When clients come into counseling committed to discuss their problems they must not be allowed to merely cathart, thus experiencing relief and losing motivation for behavior change. Instead they should be helped to implement new behaviors as they discuss their problems—gradually experiencing relief from catharting while experiencing pleasure from implementing their desired new behaviors.

CLIENTS' GOALS

For those who use this model, goal setting is initiated when counselors describe the treatment process for prospective clients. Besides describing the process and prospective clients' responsibilities as clients and helpers, counselors draw upon their past experiences with similar clients to review the types of problems former adolescent clients discussed (and use appropriate language to relate them to adolescents' needs). They do this to illustrate how they discussed their problems, and to point out precisely how they developed and implemented their behavioral goals. Thus, counselors not only help clients decide whether to participate but also encourage them to prepare for discussion of their worries and upsets and to think about their own behavioral goals even before they have had their intake interviews. Such a presentation also helps prospective clients begin to accept responsibility for their own growth.

In the opening statement of an intake interview, a counselor reviewed what was covered in a classroom presentation for eleventh graders and structured for the intake interview as follows:

*   *   *

Perhaps you will recall that when I visited your class I described what goes on in a counseling group, gave you a number of examples of what persons your age talk about in counseling groups, reviewed how they were helped, and answered your questions. I also indicated that I schedule these interviews to give you a chance to practice talking about what worries and upsets you, *to help you decide precisely how you would like to change your behavior* (counseling goals), and to help you decide precisely how you will be able to recognize when you have achieved your goals for counseling (criteria for evaluating your own growth). With such clear understandings you will be able to determine *for yourself* whether you want to participate and, if you do, whether group counseling is helping you, and precisely *how* it is helping you. Although I try very hard to help everyone who requests counseling, I accept for group counseling only those *who can convince themselves* and me that they are ready for counseling—that they are committed to discuss what really worries and upsets them, to learn desired new behaviors, and to expect and to help peer clients to implement desired new behaviors. You see, I want to do everything I can to increase the chances of my clients getting *real help*. The better I know you, the better I can help you define clear goals *for yourself*, the better I will be able to place you with others with whom you can expect to be helped (Here I often comment on who needs to be placed with whom and for what purpose—both as models and as appropriate persons with whom to practice desired new behaviors.) Tell me about you, what worries you, and what new behaviors you want to learn. I will listen very carefully, guess how you feel, and help you talk openly about what worries you.[2]

❖   ❖   ❖

Such interviews take considerable time (30 to 60 minutes), but they are worth it. Those who are selected begin counseling with behavioral goals that they understand and accept. The counselor *helps them* discuss where they hurt; he or she helps them decide precisely how *they want to change their behavior;* he/she helps

2. For those who have difficulty opening up discussion of the problems which worry and upset them, the writer usually responds in either of these two ways: (1) "Perhaps it would help if you could tell me what you wish you could share with me and what is keeping you from doing it"; or (2) "Close your eyes, think about your earliest memories that you can visualize vividly (preferably before age ten), and tell me about them."

them identify whose assistance and reinforcement would enhance their chances for achieving *their goals;* and he/she helps them celebrate *their success.* Consequently, they are motivated to achieve their own goals and to accept considerable responsibility for therapeutic group norms and for their own personal growth.

For those who are not ready for group counseling, the counselor helps them explore whether group counseling may be a good future source of assistance, and if so, what they can do to get themselves ready for it. If it is not recommended, the counselor should explain what are the other sources of help for them. Thus, the counselor exhibits genuine caring for those who decide either that they do not want or that they are not ready for group counseling.

SELECTION AND GROUP COMPOSITION

In terms of what is known about adolescents' needs the method described above for selecting clients makes sense (1) by respecting their right to decide for themselves whether they accept assistance, (2) by making them responsible for developing their own readiness for treatment, for defining their treatment goals, for making the commitment to learn new behaviors, for helping others learn new behaviors, and for establishing therapeutic norms, and (3) by helping them develop criteria to appraise their own growth. This selection method also minimizes the threat of external evaluation introduced by diagnostic testing (Ackerman, 1955) and takes cognizance of Johnson's (1963) point that it is easier to help those who are experiencing pain and who seek treatment on their own than it is to help those who have been coerced into treatment by relatives and friends. Beck (1958), Ewing and Gilbert (1967), Johnson (1963), and Rickard (1965) concluded that volunteers are the best bets for successful treatment. Lieberman, Yalom, and Miles' (1973) clients who profited most from treatment were open and trusting and gave others frank but considerate feedback. They requested frank feedback for themselves and at the same time they recognized the curvilinear nature of openness—with whom and under what conditions it is appropriate to be open. They also were willing to take risks in dealing with their problems and in implementing desired new behaviors outside of their counseling group. Stranahan, Schwartzman, and Atkin (1957) deduced that those who profit most from group treatment must have some capacity for insight, a degree of flexibility, a desire for growth, and some wholesome experiences early in life with an authority figure who possessed some measure of steadiness, helpfulness, direction and maturity. Allport (1960) decided that ability to become ego involved is an essential characteristic of any good group member. Such a member is able to invest in helping others and reap satisfaction from seeing others solve their problems. Moreover, Ryan (1958) discovered that ability to become meaningfully involved in a treatment group seems to be related to a member's ability to empathize with others, to form relationships with others, to delay gratification of one's own needs, and to derive satisfaction from gratifying others' needs. On the other hand, Sethna and Harrington (1971) reported those who failed to disclose and to become *meaningfully involved early* either tended to lapse from treatment or to become nonpatient members. Spielberger, Weitz, and Denny (1962) decided that those who profited most from group counseling possessed personality characteristics which enabled them to participate fully (and possessed the commitment to attend sessions regularly). Lindt (1958) found that those who were helped were able to make an emotional investment in helping at least one other client. Finally, the author has found that those who are able to define precise, behavioral goals are most apt to be helped (and those who cannot or will not do so are more apt to become resisting clients). Bach (1954) also questioned including in group treatment the decidedly resisting types of clients: the culturally deviant, the chronic monopolist, and the impulsive individual.

Perhaps even reluctant clients can be helped when they are included with others who are strong enough to prevent them from curbing or destroying the therapeutic climate for growth of others as well as themselves. These others may encourage them to change, and be willing to accept them and learn from them, too. Furthermore, many who at first appear to be "poor bets" (and have not volunteered themselves for group counseling) can become good treatment risks when the method is described for them and their questions about it are answered. If they are allowed *to decide for themselves* to participate, they accept responsibility for convincing themselves and their counselor that they are committed to discuss their problems openly, to learn new behaviors, and to encourage peer clients to do the same. In other words, they truly accept and help establish therapeutic norms for their group.

For those who use this method, the primary source of selection data are prospective clients. In addition to using the data described above, counselors encourage clients to explore the following questions: "With whom do I need to learn to cope with and with reference to what? From whom do I believe I could learn best how to cope with these problems or concerns? With whom would I like to be in a group? With whom would I not feel comfortable, or at least, I feel would interfere with my open discussion of my worries and concerns?" Clients selected from organized groups such as school or youth organizations can answer these questions. Obviously, a counselor also must honestly ask himself/herself with reference to each prospective client, "Is this someone I can help within this group in this setting and with these prospective clients?" Though the elaborate type of diagnostic testing endorsed by Bach (1954) is rarely required by those who counsel reasonably healthy adolescents, there are occasions when a counselor may wish to solicit additional information. For example, a school counselor may occasionally wish to supplement the intake interview with usual school sources (and only with prospective client's permission): the cumulative folder, case conference (Ohlsen, 1974), and interviews with teachers and parents. From such interviews a counselor can learn what primary roles a prospective client plays with peers, siblings, and adult authority figures. These significant others also may know problems with which a prospective client requires assistance and from whom the client is best able to accept assistance.

Once counselors have their data they try to put together the best possible combination of clients who are ready for counseling. Usually they ask who needs what from whom? From whom can each learn best (and who are required as models for whom)? Where several counselors regularly accept responsibility for encouraging each other's growth, they should meet as a group and staff the cases of each prospective client, cooperatively helping each other select the best combination of clients for each group.

Most counselors who counsel adolescents in groups tend to assign both males and females to the same group, but otherwise work for considerable homogeneity. Adolescents tend to be very sensitive to evaluation by peers of the opposite sex and have a very strong need to prove themselves (Ackerman, 1955). Because they want to learn to relate to the opposite sex, they are interested in participating in mixed-sex counseling groups. They also learn quickly to discuss frankly their socio-sexual development problems and to practice skills required in role-played scenes, and with less need to test limits with obscene language than in groups composed of either boys or girls.

Most counselors work with clients of about the same age, but the crucial factor is social maturity rather than chronological age. Even counselors who work with adults seem to feel that a wide age range may impede discussion and reduce the chances of clients experiencing affiliative feelings.

For similar reasons some authorities caution counselors to make groups reasonably homogeneous with reference to intelligence. To the extent that individual verbal ability hampers communication with peer clients, it negates the ability to profit from group counseling. When most clients have greater verbal facility than a given member, they tend to talk over his or her head. When, on the other hand, some clients talk down to the rest of the group, they often reject, and in turn are rejected by their peer clients. For some bright adolescents, especially those who want to be leaders, it may be desirable to learn to communicate with a wide range of persons.

Discovering other clients within their group who have similar problems helps clients of all ages feel that they belong and that they are understood. Even though they may soon discover that each one's problems have very different underlying causes, adolescents experience genuine affiliation feelings when a peer client assigns the same name to his/her problem. Seeing others discuss similar problems openly and watching them learn new ways to behave motivates still other group members to discuss their problems too. Some counselors enhance this feeling by reviewing common problems with which previous clients have learned to cope. Some also have prospective clients complete a problem check list to identify clients with similar concerns.

Useful as it is to include those with similar problems in the same group, homogeneity with reference to personality dynamics and/or type of client is not recommended. It tends to encourage group resistance. For example, to counteract this problem, gifted underachievers tend to be counseled most effectively with peers whom they admire, e.g. who are searching for ways to improve their academic performance, and who also may be highly motivated to adjust to their situation rather than to rebel against it. Bach (1954) also argued for some heterogeneity on the grounds that it provides clients with the opportunity to learn to relate to and to aid persons different from themselves.

GROUP SETTING

Effective counselors recognize and use the therapeutic forces within a counseling group and know how to train clients to recognize and use them. They also recognize the antitherapeutic forces and are able to help clients recognize them and learn to cope with them.

Effective group counseling can be provided with minimal space and equipment. There must be adequate space for a circle of eight or nine chairs in a room in which clients can speak freely without being overheard. An attractive, spacious, well-equipped room conveys institutional support for the service (and a successful practice for the private practitioner). Furthermore, a carpeted floor encourages members to move back their chairs and sit on the floor when they feel that it is appropriate. A spacious room is appreciated by those who use considerable role playing, informal exercises, dance, and music as part of the treatment process (Ohlsen, 1973). Additional space is also appreciated by those who encourage exercises such as trust walks. Regular audio recordings are essential in order to enable clients to review what happened in any given session, to critique a proposal and/or role-played action, and to help individuals, including the counselor, appraise their impact on the others. Video recordings are highly valued for these purposes; often they are essential in order to help members recognize their incongruence and to confront them with their own behavior and unverbalized needs. Increasingly counselors are beginning to recognize the value in soliciting feedback from their clients—even young children—and especially when it can be provided in conjunction with video recordings: "(1) Watch for specific instances in which you were helped and/or hurt; (2) For each indicate whether you were helped or hurt; (3) Watch for what was done that especially helped or hurt you; and (4) How did you feel when it was happening?"

GROUP SIZE

Loeser (1957) reported that as groups increase in size, transference reactions become weaker and weaker until members experience no meaningful relationships with each other. He concluded that a group of four to eight is ideal for group counseling and group therapy, and that such a size is a natural group, being the largest that can function without a leader and some strong rules. Larger groups break up into subgroups without strong leadership. With increased size the members tend to experience their only meaningful relationship with the leader, speaker, or performer. As a group's size increases from eight to thirty, Loeser noted that members tend to function like a class with increasing dependence on the leader. This situation gives the central figure power. The degree to which the counselor can establish meaningful relationships with members determines the extent of his or her ability to arouse emotion for a cause or to quiet unrest.

Psathas' (1960) review of the literature also suggests that with increased group size, members experience less direct involvement and participation. Instead of interacting with each other they tend as the group gets larger to direct their communications to the highest-ranking initiator, who in turn responds to them as a group rather than to them as individuals. Most communications in large groups flow through a selected or appointed leader.

In order for a counseling group to function effectively, members must be able to capture the floor to speak, to feel safe to discuss their feelings openly, to interact meaningfully with other individuals, and to solicit and accept feedback. When making a decision on group size, a counselor must consider each client's maturity, attention span, and ability to invest in others. All clients must feel that adequate time has been allowed for them, that they will not have to wait too long to get the floor, and that the group is small enough for them to know other members and for them to be known. Those who counsel children in groups tend to work with smaller groups for shorter periods and meet them more frequently than those who counsel adults. Usually adolescents are counseled in groups of six to eight.

FREQUENCY, LENGTH, AND DURATION OF GROUP SESSIONS

Many studies have demonstrated that high school and college clients can be helped in eight to ten weekly sessions of approximately ninety minutes. Nevertheless, many counselors still prefer two sessions per week for adolescents. Both counselors and psychotherapists are coming to accept the notion that clients who are ready for counseling can be helped in six months or less. There is broad support for short-term treatment today (Adler, 1972; Ansbacher, 1972; Barten, 1971; Buda, 1972; Carney, 1971; Godbole and Falk, 1972; Mann, 1973; Rhodes, 1973; Schafer, 1973; Sifneos, 1972; Stewart, 1972; Thomas, 1973; Torre, 1972; Wolberg, 1965). In general, the length of therapy does not influence results (Carney, 1971).

> With the development of health insurance programs to finance a limited number of psychotherapeutic sessions, interest is being focused on short-term treatment methods. This economic stimulus merely highlights a growing conviction among many psychotherapists that there are disadvantages in long-term approaches in many cases. Indeed short-term therapy may be the treatment of choice for many (Wolberg, 1965, p. 4).

BEGINNING A GROUP

One of the best ways to introduce group counseling is to describe it for prospective clients at some regular meeting. For high school and college students this can be done in relevant classes such as high school social studies classes and in college beginning psychology classes. When counselors make such presentations they can increase the attractiveness of a counseling group by (1) using examples of problems discussed by other similar adolescents to convey that persons like themselves do seek help, (2) arranging for successful clients to produce a videotape in which they role play a beginning session to illustrate how a group functions and then answer prospective clients' questions concerning expectations and how they were helped, (3) including in their presentation a description of problems of prestige figures such as student leaders and athletes (but being careful not to break confidence), and (4) telling how they try to help prospective clients get ready for group counseling, and explaining how they try to select the best possible combination of clients to maximize clients' chances for obtaining help. After they have made their presentation, counselors answer the questions of prospective clients. Adolescents' questions tend to deal with expectations, selection of members, and keeping of confidences. They ask: How does one get into counseling groups? Why do adolescents join groups? What can members expect from each other and from their counselor? Where will the group meet? For how long and how often will it meet? Who will know who the participants are? How does group counseling differ from various types of group guidance, sensitivity groups, and encounter groups? Finally, the counselor distributes slips of paper to everyone. All report the following information: (1) Whether they want to be included in a counseling group: (a) yes, definitely, (b) no, not interested, and (c) maybe, still uncertain; (2) what would be the best meeting times for them; (3) whom would they like to have included in their group; (4) with whom would they prefer not to be in a group; and (5) where could they be most easily reached at the beginning of the school day?

Those who write "yes" are contacted first and scheduled for

intake interviews. In the meantime some who wrote "maybe" will seek out the counselor to indicate that they are definitely interested, and consequently they are scheduled for intake interviews. Others will report either that they are no longer interested or not interested for the present. Some also are referred by parents, teachers, and friends. As indicated earlier, special precautions are taken with the referred to convey precisely what is expected and how they could possibly be helped; then they are helped to decide *for themselves* whether to continue the intake interview and try to convince themselves and the counselor that they are ready for group counseling and committed to make the group function well, to define functional goals, and to define criteria which they can use to appraise their own growth.

After the intake interviews are completed the counselor reviews each client's case (preferably with a colleague) and selects the best possible combination of clients for each group. Occasionally, counselors conclude that they must reinterview some clients to clarify expectations, to help them develop more precise behavioral goals, or to help them practice verbalizing those problems for which the clients' behavior suggests that they may have difficulty sharing. Each client is then contacted and told when and where the group will meet.

At the beginning of the first session, the counselor asks all members to introduce themselves, describing briefly what worries and upsets them, and telling precisely how they would like to change their behavior. Usually those who otherwise would speak last are prepared in the intake interview to speak first. They also are encouraged to discuss first those problems with which they anticipate they will have greatest difficulty. For this courageous behavior they are reinforced by peer clients and by the counselor. As a consequence they feel better about themselves, feel that the worst is over, discover that they can face those problems which worry them most, and sense peer clients' increased acceptance of them. They realize that such openness and commitment enables others to be courageous too.

After all have shared their major concerns and described major new behaviors they want to learn, clients are encouraged to discuss what they can expect from each other (including some precise agreements on confidentiality). Whenever the counselor notes early instances in which a client functions especially well as a client or helper, he or she notes the specific productive behaviors and reinforces these behaviors. Some counselors also make video recordings of these first few sessions and play back those parts of the sessions in which clients exhibited especially good client and helper behaviors in order to teach these roles early, and thereby decrease the normal time it takes for clients to discover good models and to copy their behaviors. When, for example, in the first session with a group of delinquents Jean detected in Darlene's behavior a highly therapeutic feeling and reflected it well, the counselor said, "Jean, you seemed to pick up from the way Darlene was sitting, squirming, and looking around that she was really hurting, you guessed accurately how she felt, and you had the courage to say it. You made it safe for Darlene to cry and to talk openly about what worries and upsets her. That's great. Darlene used your help, talked openly, and decided on a couple of things on which she can begin working today. Jean, I also sensed that Darlene's struggle with her problems uncovered something in you." Thus, the counselor reinforced Jean's good helping behavior and also helped her face what was troubling her. Had the guess been wrong that Jean had something related to Darlene's problems to discuss, Jean could have said so. Already she realized that the counselor's reflections were educated guesses and that he/she would not be troubled to discover either that he/she was wrong or that she was not ready to own and to discuss that problem at this time.

Perhaps some counselors will have difficulty accepting the idea that clients can begin immediately discussing the topics that genuinely worry and upset them. The considerate and meaningful discussions which result from effective presentations and intake interviews really do get clients ready for the group counseling behavior change process. Furthermore, leaping into what really worries them enables clients to face problems which they previously had not been able to face and resolve. They are genuinely reinforced by peer clients and their counselor. Feeling that they have faced the big test and passed it, the clients are assured they will profit from this help.

RESEARCH RESULTS

Although it is difficult to appraise outcomes of counseling and psychotherapy, nevertheless, professionals have no other choice. All counselors and psychotherapists must try to determine how efficacious their treatment methods are. Furthermore, it is not sufficient to ask, "Is group counseling effective?" Instead, counselors must ask, "For whom was a particular treatment effective? Who profited most from it? Who was hurt by it? How were those who were helped different from those who were hurt? To what extent were results influenced by selections of clients, the combination of clients, or special professional skills and/or deficiencies of the counselor? To what extent did the clients understand what was expected from them and what they could expect from others when they decided to join a counseling group? Did they define precise, meaningful goals and criteria that they could use to assess their own growth? To what extent were the clients committed to discuss their problems openly, to change their behavior, and to help peer clients change? Did clients expect to be helped? To what extent did the treatment provided help clients with their goals? To what degree was the counselor able to develop a therapeutic relationship with each client, to help each relate therapeutically to peer clients, and to help each accept responsibility for developing and maintaining a therapeutic climate with the group? Were adequate criteria developed to appraise clients' growth in terms of their own goals? Were adequate appraisal techniques used to evaluate clients' growth in terms of criteria relevant for them? Were the data collected under scientific conditions and analyzed by use of defensible statistical procedures?"

Bergin and Garfield (1971) also endorse strongly the notion that efforts to appraise outcomes of counseling and psychotherapy must focus upon precise behavioral changes. They contend that vague, global measures of change are obsolete for assessing outcomes of counseling. They recommend two promising techniques: experimental analogue and elaborate, objective case studies. They also call for systematic follow-up of research subjects in order to determine the extent to which their gains are maintained and are influenced by intervening experiences.

Few researchers have considered adequately the questions listed above in attempting to appraise the worth of group counseling. On the other hand, they have done about as well as researchers in all applied psychology. Moreover, Meltzoff and Kornreich (1970) concluded that there has been a marked improvement in the outcome studies during the past decade.

> From every point of view (design, sampling, criteria, nature of controls, data analysis), the quality of research has improved along with the quantity. . . . Among the adequate studies, 84 percent showed positive effects of psychotherapy that were statistically significant. Similarly 75 percent of the questionable studies reported significant benefits . . . (p. 174).
>
> . . . Far more often than not, psychotherapy in a wide variety of types and with a broad range of disorders has been demonstrated under controlled conditions to be accompanied by positive changes in adjustment that significantly exceed those that can be accounted for by the passage of time alone . . . (p. 175).
>
> . . . There is little existing evidence of any systematic differences in efficacy between group and individual therapy. Studies that purport to show advantage of combination of the two methods are not conclusive either in design or analysis, to permit such conclusion (p. 183).

Recently considerable research has been reported which supports group counseling for adolescents (Ohlsen, 1970; Ohlsen, 1974). The better the clients accept their need for counseling, participate in defining meaningful behavior goals, and take on the responsibility for their own growth and for developing a therapeutic climate, the more they are apt to be helped.

Precise measures also are required to detect changes related to behavioral goals. Furthermore, evidence was cited earlier to support the methods presented in this chapter for initiating, selecting clients, and beginning group counseling.

Poorest results have been obtained by school counselors working with underachievers and disruptive adolescents (De Esch,

1974; Mitchell and Piatkowska, 1974). These clients are usually coerced into participation and frequently do not perceive themselves to be the problem. They view teachers and counselors as trying to perpetuate values which do not make sense to them. Some, especially the underachievers, question whether they can do better in school (or whether it is worth trying at all).

Three studies have been designed to appraise this particular model of group counseling. All obtained significant results with adolescents (Bartell, 1972; Bush, 1971; De Esch, 1974). Though Bush found that efforts to ensure some participation time for everyone in every counseling session did not affect results, he did conclude that the intake interview probably contributed to his positive findings. Bartell's subjects made significant growth, but he did not demonstrate that the intake interview accounted for his significant gains. De Esch demonstrated for his research subjects that they were referred to the discipline office less frequently, exhibited improvement on the two scales used in the Tennessee Self-Concept Scale, improved their scores on the Idiosyncratic Goal Rating Form, and improved their grades, but did not demonstrate improved behavior on a teacher's rating sheet. Few will be surprised by the last point. Even when clients improve their behavior it takes considerable time for teachers to change their perceptions of underachieving and disruptive students. Broedel, Ohlsen, Proff, and Southard (1960) urged strongly that counselors set aside time during treatment to help clients convey to significant others how they are changing and to enlist the assistance of significant others in reinforcing desired new behaviors.

De Esch observed that those studies which obtained significant results had three things in common: (1) The researcher presented clients with a clearly defined treatment model; (2) clients were given the opportunity to decide whether to participate; and (3) the treatment model concentrated on helping clients achieve specific goals.

COUNSELOR QUALIFICATIONS[3]

Like all others who educate persons for the helping professions, those who prepare professionals for group counseling face

---

3. This brief presentation reviews the highlights of another paper by the writer (Ohlsen, 1975).

certain common problems: (1) defining the treatment process, (2) determining precisely what facilitative skills the helper must possess in order to provide the specified treatment, (3) deciding how to organize the essential knowledge and skills into instructional components, (4) selecting good prospects for the professional education, (5) appraising trainees' progress at carefully determined check points, (6) encouraging their continuing personal and professional development in practice, and (7) enlisting their assistance in periodic evaluation of their preparation. Important as it is to recruit promising students, good recruitment must be supported by a staff who can teach, encourage trainees' personal and professional development, care deeply about trainees as persons and still practice selective admission-retention policies, excite their intellectual curiosity, and do the necessary research required to improve their professional services.

The task of those who prepare leaders for groups is complicated by the variety of effective groups which to the naive appear to be similar but require different professional skills. This is further complicated by some leaders who resist their professional organization's efforts to define their treatment, to screen candidates for preparation, to screen applicants for license, and to implement ethical standards.

For each group treatment which leaders use, they must realize who is most likely to profit from the technique (and to be hurt by it) with whom and under what circumstances; they must select only those clients who they believe can be helped by them; and they must have confidence in the technique and recognize its limitations. In order to help prospective clients decide whether to participate (and to ensure truth in packaging of the service), a leader must be able to describe the treatment process, what will be expected from clients, and its potential benefits for them.

Originally the program described below as a minimal program for those who do group counseling was planned for experienced counselors who had completed a master's degree in an approved graduate program, including at least three semester hours of counseling practicum. Though successful completion of a practicum in individual counseling with endorsement by the practicum supervisor is still a requirement, increasing numbers of inexperienced counselors are now being admitted to the program, usually as a part of some post-masters' degree level program. Most complete the four components included in the ten-week summer workshop during the regular academic year. For these students the group counseling course is a prerequisite for the group practicum.

❊   ❊   ❊

The two-week *group dynamics laboratory* was provided at the beginning of the workshop to increase trainees' sensitivity to others' needs, to increase their knowledge of group dynamics and to practice their interpersonal skills. The group of twelve was divided into subgroups for skill-building activities and for helping trainees explore the relevance of this knowledge for their personal as well as their professional lives.

A therapeutic experience as clients in group counseling was provided for trainees for the entire ten-week period. In the intake interview with the counselor whom the client chose, all assessed their commitment to discuss openly those problems which worried them most, defined specific behavioral goals for themselves, defined criteria to appraise their own growth, clarified expectations, and examined their commitment to change their behavior and help peer clients change theirs. From the beginning clients learned to help others, to celebrate successes, to seek reinforcement for desired new behaviors, and to reinforce peer clients' desired new behaviors. In general, most trainees seemed to achieve their personal goals. They also reported that these group counseling experiences as clients improved their helping skills.

The group counseling course included considerable reading in professional journals and in supplementary texts in addition to the text. Although the class discussion tended to focus upon clarifying and implementing ideas in group counseling, considerable time also was devoted to group dynamics, various leadership styles, and appraisal of outcomes of group counseling. Case materials and class demonstrations were used frequently by the instructor.

For the practicum all trainees, with the assistance of their supervisor, defined specific behavioral goals for the improvement of their group counseling skills and criteria which they used to appraise their professional development. All prepared and critiqued their description of group counseling for prospective clients, conducted their own intake interviews, and selected the best combination of clients for each group with the assistance of their supervisor and play-back partner (a peer trainee). Each served as leader of one counseling group[4] for the entire workshop period. Besides individual supervision of sixty to ninety minutes by their staff supervisor and by their peer supervisor twice a week, each was supervised once a week by one of the other two staff supervisors. Each also participated in group supervision twice a week with his or her subgroup of seven. Though audio recordings were usually used for supervision each was expected to submit periodically a video recording of a counseling session.

* * *

Two staff members were allocated half-time for the first summer session for group dynamics laboratory. Another two and one half full-time equivalents were allocated for the entire ten weeks for the group counseling course, the practicum, and the counseling groups.

Counselor educators in quality programs are increasingly expected to screen prospective professionals and endorse for license and employment only the competent. Although most counselor educators probably would prefer to use all their energy to furthering their trainees' personal and professional development, they recognize that someone must accept the responsibility for endorsement. Even where the formal licensing process includes a performance test (e.g. demonstrating counseling skills) which is judged by a competent committee of practitioners, the practicum and internship supervisors' detailed descriptions of trainees' behaviors can be useful supplementary data, especially

---

4. Since the first workshop conducted at Indiana State University, everyone has been required to counsel two groups.

in those programs for which every practicum and internship experience is evaluated by an evaluation team of at least three supervisors.

ETHICAL CONSIDERATIONS[5]

The use of group procedures by various persons in widely different settings has increased rapidly during the last decade. Unfortunately, this has enabled some poorly qualified and irresponsible persons to pose as professionals and to lead groups. Even some of the qualified leaders have been criticized for confronting members, for thoughtlessly uncovering hurtful material, for tearing away members' defenses, and for pressuring members to abandon their moral code and act upon their impulses. Leaders of groups also have been criticized for their failure to screen participants, to help prospective participants define personal goals, to help them generalize from what they learned in groups and to apply it in daily living (rather than to return repeatedly to treatment groups for peak experiences), and to appraise their results with systematic research.

Recently, however, a number of professional organizations have developed guidelines for professional preparation, for operating of groups, and for appraising ethical behavior in order to protect the public and their own profession's welfare. These organizations are the American Group Psychotherapy Association, American Personnel and Guidance Association, International Association of Applied Psychologists, Inc., National Training Laboratories, and University and College Counseling Center Directors.

In the opinion of this writer, each of these professional groups must decide the following:

1. For which of the leaders of groups does its professional organization have something to offer?
2. For which can each assume primary responsibility for accrediting training programs, for licensing leaders, and for disciplining unethical behavior?

---

5. Inasmuch as the author agrees in general with Gazda's presentation in Chapter Two, this section will be brief.

3. How may the association involve its members in defining the group procedures for which it accepts responsibility (and where appropriate, shares responsibility with some other professional group or groups)? How does each treatment differ from other acceptable treatment methods? What precisely are the implications of these differences for preparing those who will lead the groups?

4. What competencies must one possess to lead each type of group for which the professional organization accepts responsibility? How may the organization assess a leader's competencies prior to endorsing him or her and supervising his or her behavior to ensure quality service for his or her clients?

5. What are the basic components for a professional education program? How may these be organized into a meaningful program? What provision should be made for permitting licensed personnel to learn the essential skills from supervision on the job and stand examination by a committee of qualified practitioners? How may institutions' programs be best accredited and/or appraised periodically?

6. What can it do to encourage practitioners to appraise the outcomes of their services and to grow on the job?

7. What must it do to encourage ethical behavior of its members and to discipline those who behave unethically?

8. What legislation must it introduce to ensure that only qualified persons are licensed or certified?

LIMITATIONS OF THE TREATMENT

So far this treatment model has been used primarily with reasonably healthy clients who vary in age from first graders to senior citizens. For children who lack the verbal skills to convey what they are feeling, counselors have used play techniques and role playing. They also have tried to teach those clients who seemed to want to express themselves verbally the words they require to do so. Furthermore, when children are taught desired words with consideration rather than with pressure to verbalize, the experience tends to encourage vocabulary development, to encourage those who have a learning disability in this area to correct it. Ohlsen (1973) reported that even those writers who endorsed the use of nonverbal techniques agreed that most children can discuss their problems.

The method also has been used successfully with couples in marriage counseling and in a more limited way with delinquents, behavior-problem students, and hospitalized veterans.

For the various settings in which the method has been used and for the various types of clients, perhaps the single most important factor has been counselors' competencies, their acceptance of their competencies, and their willingness to use them confidently in helping their clients. Other important components which seem to have influenced results have been clients' readiness for counseling (including their acceptance of their need to learn new behaviors), their commitment to talk openly and change their behavior, their ability to define precise behavioral goals, and their being placed with others who accept them, need them, and are strong enough to encourage them to implement desired new behaviors.

SUMMARY

Adolescents can be counseled successfully in groups. In group counseling they are given the opportunity to define their own desired new behaviors, to assume responsibility for implementing their own desired new behaviors, and to experience genuine participation. They thrive on the support and encouragement from their counselor and peer clients and from recognition of their own real accomplishments. The counselor enhances these therapeutic conditions by communicating to prospective clients what they can expect before they decide whether to join a group, by selecting clients carefully, by teaching them to function as helpers as well as clients, and by helping them learn to accept responsibility for their own growth.

SELECTED READINGS

Gazda, G. M.: *Group Counseling: A Developmental Approach.* Boston, Allyn, 1971.

Mahler, C. A.: *Group Counseling in the Schools.* Boston, HM, 1969.

Ohlsen, M. M.: *Group Counseling.* New York, HR&W, 1970.

REFERENCES

Ackerman, N. W.: Group psychotherapy with a mixed group of adolescents. *International Journal of Group Psychotherapy, 5*:249-260, 1955.

Adler, K.: Techniques that shorten psychotherapy illustrated with five cases. *Journal of Individual Psychology, 28*:155-168, 1972.

Allport, G. W.: *Personality and Social Encounter.* Boston, Beacon Pr, 1960.

Ansbacher, H.: Adlerian psychology: the tradition of brief psychotherapy. *Journal of Individual Psychology, 28*:137-151, 1972.

Ausubel, D. P.: *Theory and Problems of Adolescent Development.* New York, Grune, 1954.

Ayer, F. L., and Corman, B. R.: Laboratory practices develop citizenship concepts of high school students. *Social Education, 16*:215-216, 1952.

Bach, G. R.: *Intensive Group Psychotherapy.* New York, Ronald, 1954.

Bach, G. R., and Deutsch, R. M.: *Pairing: How to Achieve Genuine Intimacy.* New York, Avon, 1970.

Bartell, W. R.: *The Effect of the Intake Interview on Client Perceived Outcome of Group Counseling.* Doctoral dissertation, Indiana State University, 1972.

Barten, H. H.: *Brief Therapies.* New York, Behavioral Pub, 1971.

Beck, D. F.: The dynamics of group psychotherapy as seen by a sociologist. *Sociometry, 21*:98-128, 180-197, 1958.

Bergin, A. E., and Garfield, S. J.: *Handbook of Psychotherapy and Behavior Change.* New York, Wiley, 1971.

Broedel, J., Ohlsen, M., Proff, F., and Southard, C.: The effects of group counseling on gifted underachieving adolescents. *Journal of Counseling Psychology, 7*:163-170, 1960.

Buda, B.: Utilization of resistance and paradox communication in short-term psychotherapy. *Psychotherapy and Psychosomatics, 20*:210-211, 1972.

Bush, J.: *The Effects of Fixed and Random Actor Interaction on Individual Goal Attainment in Group Counseling.* Doctoral dissertation, Indiana State University, 1971.

Carney, F. J.: Evaluation of psychotherapy in a maximum security prison. *Seminars in Psychiatry, 3*:363-375, 1971.

Cartwright, D.: Achieving change in people: some applications of group dynamics theory. *Human Relations, 4*:381-392, 1951.

Cartwright, D., and Zander, A.: *Group Dynamics: Theory and Research.* New York, Har-Row, 1968.

De Esch, J. B.: *The Use of the Ohlsen Model of Group Counseling with Secondary School Students Identified as Being Disruptive to the Educational Process.* Doctoral dissertation, Indiana State University, 1974.

Dreikurs, R.: Group psychotherapy from the point of view of Adlerian psychology. *International Journal of Group Psychotherapy, 7*:363-375, 1957.

Ewing, T. N., and Gilbert, W. M.: Controlled study of the effects of counseling on scholastic achievements of students of superior ability. *Journal of Counseling Psychology, 14*:235-239, 1967.

Garrison, K. C.: *Psychology of Adolescents*. Englewood Cliffs, P-H, 1965.

Gesell, A., Ilg, F. L., and Ames, L. B.: *Youth: The Years from Ten to Sixteen*. New York, Har-Row, 1956.

Godbole, A., and Flak, M.: Confrontation—problem solving therapy in the treatment of confusional and delirious states. *Gerontologist, 12*:151-154, 1972.

Hall, G. S.: *Adolescence*. New York, Appleton, 1904.

Hobbs, N.: Sources of gain in psychotherapy. *American Psychologist, 17*: 471-747, 1962.

Holmes, D. J.: *The Adolescent in Psychotherapy*. Boston, Little, 1964.

Hurloch, E. B.: *Adolescent Development*. New York, McGraw, 1967.

Johnson, J. A.: *Group Therapy: A Practical Approach*. New York, McGraw, 1963.

Kelman, H. C.: The role of the group in the induction of therapeutic change. *International Journal of Group Psychotherapy, 13*:399-432, 1963.

Kirkpatrick, M. C.: The mental hygiene of adolescents in the Anglo-American culture. *Mental Hygiene, 36*:394-403, 1952.

Lieberman, M. A., Yalom, I. D., and Miles, M. B.: *Encounter Groups: First Facts*. New York, Basic, 1973.

Lindt, H.: The nature of therapeutic interaction of patients in groups. *International Journal of Group Psychotherapy, 8*:55-69, 1958.

Loeser, L. H.: Some aspects of group dynamics. *International Journal of Group Psychotherapy, 7*:5-19, 1957.

Mann, J.: *Time-Limited Psychotherapy*. Cambridge, Harvard U Pr, 1973.

Mitchell, K. R., and Piatkowska, O. E.: Effects of group treatment for college underachievers and bright failing students. *Journal of Counseling Psychology, 21*:494-501, 1974.

McCandless, B. R.: *Adolescents: Behavior and Development*. Hillsdale, Dryden, 1970.

Meltzoff, J., and Kornreich, M.: *Research in Psychotherapy*. New York, Atherton, 1970.

Neidt, C. O., and Fritz, M. F.: Relation of cynicism to certain student characteristics. *Educational and Psychological Measurement, 10*:712-718, 1950.

Ohlsen, M. M.: *Group Counseling*. New York, HR&W, 1970.

Ohlsen, M. M.: Preparation of leaders for group counseling. *Counselor Education and Supervision*, 1975 (in press).

Ohlsen, M. M. (Ed.): *Counseling Children in Groups: A Forum.* New York, HR&W, 1973.

Ohlsen, M. M.: *Guidance Services in the Modern School.* New York, HarBrace J, 1974.

Powdermaker, F. B., and Frank, J. D.: *Group Psychotherapy.* Cambridge, Harvard U Pr, 1953.

Psathas, G.: Phase, movement and equilibrium tendencies in interaction process in psychotherapy groups. *Sociometry, 23:*177-194, 1960.

Rhodes, S. L.: Short-term groups of latency age children in a school setting. *International Journal of Group Psychotherapy, 23:*204-216, 1973.

Rickard, H. C.: Tailored criteria of change in psychotherapy. *Journal of General Psychology. 72:*63-68, 1965.

Rogers, C. R.: A tentative formulation of a general law of interpersonal relationships. In *On Becoming a Person.* Boston, HM, 1961.

Ryan, W.: Capacity for mutual dependencies and involvement in group psychotherapy. *Dissertation Abstracts, 19:*1119, 1958.

Schafer, R.: The termination of brief psychoanalytic psychotherapy. *International Journal of Psychoanalytic Psychotherapy, 2:*135-148, 1973.

Sethna, E. R., and Harrington, J. A.: A study of patients who lapsed from group psychotherapy. *British Journal of Psychiatry, 119:*59-69, 1971.

Spielberger, C. O., Weitz, H., and Denny, J. P.: Group counseling and academic performance of anxious college freshmen. *Journal of Counseling Psychology, 9:*195-204, 1962.

Stewart, H.: Six-months, fixed-term, once weekly psychotherapy: a report of twenty with follow-ups. *British Journal of Psychiatry, 121:*425-435, 1972.

Thelen, H. A., and Stock, D.: Basic problems in developing the mature and effective group. *National Education Association Journal, 44:*105-106, 1955.

Thomas, M. R.: An investigation of two different processes in short-term psychotherapy. *Dissertation Abstracts, 33:*5527, 1973.

Torre, J. De La: The therapist tells a story: a technique in brief psychotherapy. *Bulletin Menninger Clinic, 36:*609-616, 1972.

Weigel, R., Dinges, N., Dyer, R., and Straumfjoid, A. A.: Perceived self disclosure, mental health, and who is liked in group treatment. *Journal of Counseling Psychology, 19:*47-52, 1972.

Wolberg, L. R.: *Short-term Psychotherapy.* New York, Grune, 1965.

VI

GROUP-CENTERED COUNSELING

WALTER M. LIFTON

THIS CHAPTER is to be focused on a client-centered approach for working with groups. Actually, since effective therapy must always be centered on the needs and problems of the client, it would be more correct to label the philosophy to be presented as "group centered." A group-centered approach recognizes several important assumptions that are critical to current society. Any person desiring to use the approach described in this chapter will have to accept the validity of these assumptions, since no one can implement a theory which violates his or her basic beliefs. A brief discussion of the eleven assumptions basic to this approach is presented below.

1. Individuals and groups, when freed of threat, strive toward healthier, more adaptive kinds of behavior. There is a drive in everyone toward homeostasis.

2. Each individual lives in a world of his or her own, bound by the uniqueness of personal perceptions and past experiences. No one can share past experiences of perceptions with another. People can only be helped to experience and clarify their own perceptions. Each group member checks his or her perceptions of reality by comparing them with significant "others." The most important "others" tend to be the member's peers.

3. Even when individuals are convinced of the correctness of their perceptions, if their behavior, based upon these perceptions, does not cause others to respond to them in the desired fashion, from a purely pragmatic point of view they will have to revise their behavior if they seek a different response from others.

4. Because everyone needs ways of defending himself or herself and avoiding unacceptable pressures, everyone has defenses which may cause behavior inconsistent with the verbalized goals

he or she states to others. These defenses are necessary to existence and cannot be removed until a substitute is found.

5. People react to each other based upon what they feel the other person's behavior implies. Because of the incongruity between a person's communications to others (on a feeling versus a content level), breakdown in communication occurs. One assumes people respond to what he/she says, rather than to the feelings his/her words convey.

6. By providing acceptance and support to individuals and groups, they may be less constricted in their perceptions of their behavior, feeling safe enough to let themselves face feelings they know exist but could not before afford to acknowledge.

7. Since most people tend to move in their thinking from the concrete to the abstract, members dealing with their here-and-now problems in the group are more likely to see the relevance of the group's activity and, given the security of the group, are likely to be able to generalize from their current experiences to past ones, which then have new meaning. Put in another way, by dealing with the here-and-now one also alters the meaning and import of the past.

8. The group leader, to be effective, must be able either to live out a variety of group roles or, at the very least, to ensure that other group members can serve as role models. Members then learn not only the many types of roles needed in our society, but they also can learn to emulate these roles and thereby increase their ability to cope with society.

9. Society is not something external to the lives of the group members. The group members by their behavior have a vital role in setting the limits and mores which individual members learn to understanding and live with.

10. In a democratic society the ultimate source of authority is not vested in a single individual, but remains the responsibility of the entire group.

11. The group provides all the elements needed to assist change. It offers support, feedback of perceived behavior, information about alternatives which could be considered, reinforcement of positive behavior and rejection of unacceptable beha-

vior, and new experiences designed to broaden the repertoire of experiences and skills needed to cope with society (the group).

A simple summing-up of these assumptions would suggest that group-centered counseling is a humanistic, existential approach where the source of support for the individual rests upon people's perceived dependence on their peers and their willingness to help others, since in the process they help themselves. The leader's role is basically one of facilitating group interaction, so that the group develops ways of functioning which will increase communication between group members, while providing a setting for ongoing reality testing.

THE RELATIONSHIP OF GROUP-CENTERED COUNSELING TO EDUCATIONAL PHILOSOPHIES

Many people find differentiating between learning, counseling, and therapy difficult. Much of the difference found in definition arises from philosophical differences in the role of the teacher or counselor, or differences in theories about how personality is formed or reformed.

Group counseling in schools inescapably reflects the values of the schools and their belief about ways to achieve effective learning. The effectiveness of any group approach is intimately dependent upon the acceptability of the approach to the school policy makers. There are three prevalent attitudes encountered by group leaders in school settings.

1. "You can do in your group only that which you have described prior to the group initiation." This approach reflects a "lesson plan" mentality and reflects fear that group content or process might cause the school problems. Also, it supports the belief that learning is best achieved by following logical steps in sequential order.

2. "It is all right to give students freedom to choose topics and process but you are expected to see that they arrive at societally approved decisions." This stance recognizes that learning should be student-centered and reflect student needs but also takes for granted society's answers. In this setting group leaders may find themselves serving as ombudsmen to help the group and society communicate and come to terms.

3. "The students know where they are hurting or are curious and it is our job to help them come to answers they can live with and understand." This approach also reflects the philosophy which became clearly defined in the development of the Economic Opportunity Program. It states that institutions are the servants, not the masters, of their clients and therefore their shape and function should be defined by those they plan to serve.

The continuum presented runs from seeing the mission of the school as the transmission of society's cultural values and heritage, to the opposite extreme where schools are viewed as the servants of the pupils. In the latter view the school is seen as an agency designed to help individuals secure the help and information they need as they try to solve the problems of immediate concern to them.

The first theoretical position cited sees the role of the school as indoctrinating values that society holds to be true and unquestioned. Given that value system, the authoritarian and fundamentalist values implied tend also to be reflected in the way their groups are organized and run. Leader control is important, the information or values to be learned must be imparted, and a system of rewards and punishments need to be developed to shape individual and group behavior in the desired direction. In years gone by, group guidance typically reflected a school's attempt to present organized information to large numbers of pupils on the assumption that all needed the same information, at the same point in time, and could be taught the logic which would help them come to the approved answers.

The author believes that learning in schools takes place most effectively when:

1. The skills or knowledge to be learned is related to what each person already knows and can do;
2. The learning setting provides for two simultaneous conditions: security for the student in the setting where learning takes place, but anxiety, curiosity, and unease within the student because of his or her needs to secure answers to resolve an unmet need, tension, or a seeking for solutions;

3. All persons have the chance to digest and incorporate learnings at their *own* rate and in their *own* way;
4. The setting provides a chance to practice skills or clarify ideas with no fear of failure.

The author also believes that learning will persist when the rewards for learning are intrinsic to the individual. A learning setting which has incorporated the private needs of the person assures that the behavior learned will continue because the rewards will remain as long as the person's needs persist. The educational philosophy being presented here is currently found in the open classroom, individualized learning, and in society pressures toward consumer control of education.

For the reader who is unfamiliar with the impact of philosophical values and psychological theories on education, the author would urge him/her to read Barclay's book entitled *Foundations of Counseling Strategies* (John Wiley, 1971). Following is a brief review of the philosophical heritage upon which the group-centered approach being described is based.

PHILOSOPHICAL HERITAGE

Certainly the philosophy being presented is not original. It owes its heritage to Rousseau, Bergson, Rank, Taft, Rogers, and many who have assumed a positive drive within individuals directed toward health and homeostasis. It owes an allegiance to Snygg and Combs for their contributions on the relevance of phenomenological theory to approaches seeking to reeducate the individual. Notice the word *reeducate*. This word does not demand a difference between learning, counseling, and psychotherapy. It assumes that any change in individual's perceptions will alter his or her attitudes, behavior, and ultimately, what might be called his or her personality. No change is insignificant, since any change of a part causes a new gestalt to result for the total configuration. This philosophic concept is important because it does not limit the effectiveness of the approach to those who are seen as severely disturbed. It has equal meaning for normal individuals who seek a more effective means of achieving satisfaction in life. Because the group in reality reflects a microcosm of life, heterogeneity of group membership is desirable. Although all initial group members need to see the group as offering a specific form of help for them personally, the divergent personalities with their unique strengths and weaknesses offer a testing ground that reflects the many facets of their own society.

No discussion of an approach has much meaning unless it recognizes the concerns and experiences of those evaluating the presentation. There can be little doubt this is an age which emphasizes materialistic values, a pragmatic approach, and is object rather than person-oriented. The current popularity of learning theory approaches which lend themselves to manipulation of others to achieve desired ends can be exemplified by brainwashing on one end (Lifton, 1963) and programmed instruction on the other.

Readers of this text will be faced by quite different concepts of the way to work with groups, with different theories about appropriate group goals, and ultimately, with the pragmatic issue of which approach seems most effective.

Few research studies are available which can demonstrate completely positive results. Eysenck (1961) in his survey of the effectiveness of all types of psychotherapy felt that the positive results achieved were no more than could be expected by chance. Much of the research he reported suffered from lack of instruments sensitive enough to measure the types of change to be expected.

There is an interesting instrument which was designed by Hill (1965) to categorize the content and processes found in group therapy sessions along two continua, one dealing with the levels and style of content (four categories), and the other dealing with the level and style of therapeutic work (five categories). These form a matrix and provide an analysis of where the group appears to be functioning. The approach apparently has been useful in describing the effect of group composition, leadership and philosophy upon group behavior.

According to the format of the matrix, the least therapeutically effective group is one where the content is nonmember centered and where the group member is not even responsive to discussion on conventional topics. The most effective therapeutic group is one where the discussion is based upon member-centered concern about interpersonal relationships and where the content confronts the members with their behavior, rather than permitting any hiding or maintenance of facade.

Confrontation involves "pinning members to the mat" with material and behavior they have presented, and which they cannot therefore deny or evade. The process of confrontation, although part of all therapies, is handled in quite different ways by each approach and most readily reflects the underlying concept the philosophy embodies about the nature of personality structure and the rights of the individual in controlling the process.

The whole process underlying confrontation rests upon a concept developed by Rogers (1957).

> The greater the congruence of experience, awareness, and communication on the part of one individual, the more the ensuing relationship will involve a tendency toward mutually accurate understanding of the communications; improved psychological adjustment and functioning in both parties; mutual satisfaction in the relationship (p. 5).

Behind this concept is an important psychological assumption that individuals cannot be honest and open in their relationships, giving up their normal defensive facades unless they can be sure that they will receive support to face the anxiety involved in giving up their customary behavior, and that the rewards that they will receive in the new mode at least equal the payoff they are now receiving.

In group-centered therapy this needed support to enable the group member to deal with anxiety-producing confrontations comes from several sources, which are listed below:

1. The security provided by the limits set for and by the group ("I know what the score is, how to play the game, and what is going to happen."),

2. The nonpunitive, accepting, warm understanding offered initially by the leader and later by the group ("Even if I have some faults, the leader likes me and nothing I can do

will make him/her think I am less worthy." "Even if he/she doesn't like what I'm doing, he/she seems still to like me."),

3. The opportunity to try out new behavior in a setting where possible results of failure are less severe, where feedback will help the person develop a new approach, and where the alternate new behavior is not used consistently until it provides rewards equal to those of the old behavior. This occurs when the old behavior seems not so effective as the person originally assumed.

As indicated earlier, the act of confrontation largely reflects the values and philosophy operating in the group.

Many of the current reality-oriented therapies insist on members providing others with their perceptions about others' behavior. They are implying that what group members see is correct and, therefore, what the individual sees is wrong. They tend to emphasize the need for the individual to be "honest," "frank," and "open"; but they tend to evaluate the person's statements in terms of their congruence with the group members' frame of reference. This approach differs little from the brainwashing techniques of the Communists, except that in a democracy one is unable to control the person's complete environment, or to destroy all "inappropriate responses." This makes it difficult to be equally as effective in the use of this approach as that achieved by totalitarian states.

It is vital to evaluate group-centered therapy by examining the means-ends controversy as it applies to the techniques of confrontation. Group members are learning as much through the process as they are about reaching the group's objective. Because the "conditioning approaches" start out with a value judgment about what is best, the individuals quickly learn that they are subservient to the group. There is literally no way in which their behavior, in this approach, can change societal values or the process itself.

Even agreeing that operant conditioning and associated behavioral techniques work, one is still left with the problem of assessing their effect on a society that is presumably dedicated to a concept of democracy which implies the right of all individuals to their uniqueness, as long as their actions do not infringe on the rights of others. Democracy also includes the idea that there are some rights individuals may be willing to give up as the price of achieving group support in other areas are of greater importance to them. The role of confrontation and its use, therefore, becomes an important consideration in assessing the impact of any approach towards maintenance of the status quo in society or providing means for change.

GROUP COUNSELING AND SOCIAL CHANGE

On every front people are being forcefully made aware of the major changes taking place in this society. Alienation from society is becoming an increasingly popular symptom affecting significant segments of our culture. Psychiatrists, psychologists, and other mental health workers find their services needed by people who appear quite conscious of the reality situation they face, but see societally approved techniques seemingly ineffective in producing a satisfying situation for them. The role of group leaders working with this type of group requires that they help group members learn not only about themselves, but also learn some of the skills needed to cope with society. Of greater relevance is the freedom within the approach for groups to reject the status quo and seek to define alternate societal goals as well as their role in the emerging society. They also need to discover how to move from the here-and-now to their desired Utopian society.

One of the maturational tasks faced by youngsters in school is that of defining who they are and what they believe in. They are painfully aware of the defects of society and want to create a new and better world. It is normal for them to reject what adults define as reality because they wish to be sure that what they come to accept as reality is something they really believe in and understand. They need to discover truth in their own way so they can be sure that what they stand for represents their own convictions, not those adopted from others. In this emancipating process they reject the authority of the adult and may replace it with the conformity pressures coming from their peers. It is for this reason, among others, that helping students learn how to develop helpful peer groups is most important to the students and society. If group members can be helped to clarify goals and examine the ways they seek to obtain support and understanding from others, a society can truly develop which respects individual differences and teaches people responsibility for their behavior. The application of these concepts to work with young people about problems related to drug use, sexual behavior, achievement motivation, etc., should be clear.

Leader's Role

Each of the preceding paragraphs emphasizing the autonomy and responsibility of the group may easily create confusion about the role of the leader and where the therapeutic elements necessary for change come from in group-centered counseling. Stated simply, the leader's role is to induct the group members into the kinds of relationships, roles, and skills that will permit them ultimately to carry on with decreasing dependence on the initial leader. The leader accomplishes this goal by the way in which, serving as a mirror, he or she focuses the group's attention on group process and the problems it needs to face and solve to become an effective group.

The leader's attention is on process, not product, since as insights occur, and as the group matures, it may redefine its original goal. By his/her behavior, which demonstrates respect for the worth and perceptions of each member, the leader provides a role model of the way group members too can help their peers in the group setting. Depending upon the leader's perceptions of the initial needs of group, he or she may find himself/herself playing such diverse roles as therapist, client, resource person, reactor, and the like.

Note the inclusion of the client role. Although the purpose of the group is not to provide therapy for the leader, when the leader can appropriately seek assistance, it conveys a symbolic message of great meaning to group members. On the surface level it helps people who are fearful of the helping process to see that the leader is not demanding a protected and judgmental position different from the others. For some group members, who start with feelings that place the leader in an exalted position, to see the leader acknowledge that there are points where he/she too needs help is translated into, "If he or she can afford to be vulnerable, why can't I who have less to lose in status?" It is also symbolically saying that the leader is "of" the group, not in charge of it.

There is a direct parallel between the leader's described role and that of the teacher who serves as a consultant rather than evaluator.

Not knowing ahead of time the ways in which a group will interact and letting each group evolve at its own pace and in its own desired direction, the leader must first help group members learn the housekeeping functions that are necessary to group life. The leader may seek the group's help in establishing ground rules covering confidentiality, time, limits, requirements of group members, and the ways in which such a setting can be used to clarify each member's perceptions of himself/herself, in addition to establishing ideas in which he/she believes. As the group begins to consider these problems, the leader may actively reflect the feelings behind a group member's statement, thereby alerting the group to the different levels of communication.

More often the leader will serve as a catalyst by showing how different members of the group seem to be agreeing or disagreeing with each other. Through this process the leader points up the nature of peer group support, along with the subtle differences in perceptions that may make two statements which sound similar actually represent different feelings in different group members. Of most vital significance is the leader's activity in reflecting total group atmosphere: "We all seem to be angry with each other." The group members then can recognize the ways in which group climate affects group behavior. Also, through this labeling process the group is made consciously aware of feelings or problems they need to cope with and solve.

The author is taking the position that the expertise of the leader is felt by the group as they recognize his or her ability to provide support, understand and accept feelings, accept hostility, clarify issues needing group discussion, and be sensitive to group interaction, even on the nonverbal level.

A Person Is Important

For too long, therapies operating from a medical model have approached the client from a frame of reference of pathology. The emphasis on diagnosis, prognosis, and appropriate treatment is well within the experience of most readers. By its nature this frame of reference focuses on weaknesses, problems, and a biased classification of the meaning of symptoms derived from the class or caste of the patient. Even action-oriented approaches, such as sensitivity training, tend to emphasize behaviors or attitudes of group members which are disturbing to others. Few approaches seem by their behavior to be concerned with the whole person.

If group-centered counseling is to truly reflect the mirror qualities needed for reality testing it must be sure to help members see their strengths, too. It is interesting to see whole new groups or approaches developing based upon the need to maximize the person's awareness of his or her strengths so he or she feels able to cope with areas in which he or she feels incompetent (Otto, 1946). When the mores of the group demand that members be sensitive to the needs of their peers, top priority has to be given to those acts which convey a real feeling that each person is worthwhile and has important contributions to make to the group. In early stages, before group members are secure enough to reveal their affection for each other, it may be most important for the leader to call the group's attention to statements, actions, or decisions that reflect awareness of a person's or the group's strengths. It may also be helpful to assist the group in exploring the effect of these positive statements on subsequent behavior.

This society embodies many elements that reflect its Puritan heritage. When its people talk about self-acceptance, they tend most often to mean that they want each person to accept humbly his or her weaknesses and to be responsible for his or her sins. They reject those who "blow their own horn," and in the process, fail to realize that each feels others will value him/her by his/her achievements. Needing to be accepted by others, people find themselves in conflict since it is hard to believe their weaknesses, which they feel everyone else can see, can compensate for the strengths they doubt others can see and which they are expected to keep well hidden.

With so many influences in this society accentuating the negative and eliminating the positive, one of the most dramatic ways a group organized for counseling can demonstrate the manner in which this setting departs from typical day-to-day experience is by making clearly evident that this setting is one where positive strengths are valued and made visible. Here persons are accepted completely not only for what they are, but for what all feel they can become (Maslow, 1962; Rogers, 1961).

FOR WHOM IS GROUP-CENTERED COUNSELING INDICATED?

No one can grow up in this world without blocking out unacceptable stimuli from his or her perceptual field. Similarly, the sheer stress of everyday living tends to cause people to conserve their energy by attending to only those needs which are most visible and pressing. Although some people need to restrict themselves to fewer elements in life, all have potentialities for achievement and enjoyment of life beyond their present functioning. Few will change their present functioning unless some agency intervenes and helps them take the time to assess their satisfaction with what is, as contrasted with what could be.

The paradigm presented does not demand a medical model of illness. It does not have relevance to only special kinds of behavior. The beneficial effects possible through group counseling should be the birthright for every segment of our society.

Because the counseling group serves as a miniature testing ground, the more closely it resembles the total society, the greater the possibilities for reality testing. Society includes men and women, rich and poor, bright and dull, as well as numerous other categories. All need to get along with each other and learn to see the other person's strengths. It follows, then, that heterogeneity of members, along with common agreement about the issue that causes them to want to work together, represents the screening criteria to be applied in determining eligibility for group membership.

Many authors have pointed out that certain kinds of people cause groups considerable trouble. Those who will not abide by group rules, psychopaths, those who cannot possibly share group time with others, monopolists, those whose behavior so scares others that they cannot see the strengths of the individual behind the behavior, sexual deviates—these are but a few of the categories of people who make the moment-to-moment movement of the group more difficult. Although the author has seen each of these types of people improve behavior in group settings, he can readily recognize that most groups do not possess enough security and patience to meet the exorbitant demands typically made by people like those described.

In many school settings it is the very people who do not fit easily into a group who find themselves in trouble in school. This is especially true where the school sees its function as shaping behavior toward the model behavior that is defined as normal.

Partially because of their rejection by society, groups composed of students showing unusual or societally disturbing behavior particularly appreciate a setting where they need not feel inadequate or guilty for their current behavior. Groups designed for truants, dropouts, overweight people, as well as those in other problem areas, have been successful in improving group members' adjustment to themselves and others.

Group Size

The criteria for group membership that focus on range of experience and ease of intergroup communication also determine the optimal size of the group. The larger the group, the less chance each person has to participate and receive group feedback. The larger the group, the less possible it becomes to physically see, hear, or be aware of intragroup interaction. There is no magic number for maximum group size. People who are hard of hearing or visually limited obviously need a tighter circle for communication to continue. Groups where several members identify with each other may be able to be larger, since the help received by one member may be applied and incorporated by another member who recognizes what is happening. The normal optimal group size is between five and fifteen. Most groups seem to prefer eight to ten members.

IMPLEMENTING THE GROUP-CENTERED POINT OF VIEW

The initial session of any group tends to reflect quite clearly the philosophy of the leader and the mores by which the group will live. It is in the first session that the group discovers the limits within which they will have to work, and the responsibilities they and the leader are willing to accept. This initial structuring is done on at least two levels: by actual words used to define the situation, and by each person's behavior, which gives a more accurate cue as to what the person really believes.

Although it is desirable for members of a group to have had a chance to understand the purpose and method of operation of the group before they become involved, few referrals provide all of the insights a person needs to be comfortable in a new setting. In many groups it may be well for the leaders to assume that little prior orientation has taken place. The leader may also have to bridge the difference between the school's or student's expectations from the group and what could be possible in the setting. Below is a typical example of a group set up initially because of the administrator's, not the student's concern.

"Selling" a Group—A Protocol Involving Resistant Clients[1]

Every school has a group of youngsters labeled underachievers. Sometimes they function at such a low level that they fail class after class. Many become convinced that they cannot achieve and fear to try, desiring to avoid another unpleasant experience.

❋   ❋   ❋

One summer, while serving as Coordinator of Pupil Person-

---

1. The following section comes from Lifton, W.: *Groups: Facilitating Individual Growth and Societal Change.* New York, Wiley, 1972, pp. 151-157. Courtesy John Wiley & Sons, Inc.

nel Services in Rochester, I was talking with the Principal of a high school about his plans for summer session. He expressed deep concern over a group of boys and girls who planned to attend summer school, but who he felt were doomed to fail unless something different was tried. Recognizing that changing teachers or the curriculum did not appear likely *in the immediate future,* the question was whether anything could be done to help this group of students develop attitudes and skills which would improve their chances of success in that setting. The school counselors saw each student and offered him or her a chance to join a group, prior to summer session, which might help them in school. It is hard to know how much arm-twisting occurred, but on a hot summer day I met a group of six students in a dingy school basement to see if somehow I could help them (1) feel someone cared, (2) express their feelings so they could deal with their anger and permit themselves to recognize their strengths, and (3) help provide study skills, if or when the group saw a need for them.

The reader will note that as leader, I played an active role. It is of interest to read that Rogers in his book *Freedom To Learn* (p. 73) now feels that, in school settings, providing initial limits or requirements may supply the group with enough structure so that they can feel secure enough to start work. It is then possible to help the group face the freedom the leader would have preferred to offer initially.

It is suggested that the reader try to identify with the leader. Place yourself in a small dark room with six scared and angry students, and guess what you might have done during the segment of the first session recorded below.

The session started with an introduction of myself and a request for each student to identify himself or herself. We then moved off almost immediately into their feelings about how teachers rejected them. Notice the leader's attempt to help the group discover the many answers and resources they already possess.

Protocol

Dr. Lifton: Teachers are more comfortable with people who can understand what they're saying than with those that don't. Is that what you're trying to say?

Girl: Yeah, and they more or less, I mean, don't ignore, but they don't really pay too much attention to people who don't.

Dr. Lifton: So you kind of feel that if you don't master the stuff, they don't give you the attention. You don't feel that they care and you don't care. And so it sort of goes on like that.

Same Girl: I guess so.

Dr. Lifton: Well, we're saying some things about teachers that are very real, and I'm sure you have some teachers that click and others that don't. The chances are that you're going to have some more teachers that you're not going to click with. What then? Are you doomed? (pause) How do you cope with it? Suppose you have a teacher who doesn't seem to really act toward you the way you'd like him or her to act toward you. He really isn't warm, interested. Is there anything you can do about it?

Karen: Pay attention.

Dr. Lifton: Paying attention will change his attitude?

Karen: Well, if you just work up to your ability and show him what you can do.

Dr. Lifton: Yes, but you know, Karen, it's kind of a booby trap. If I understand what Gail is saying, she is saying, "If you don't care about me, I say 'the hell with you.'" And so it's sort of, you know, a cycle, and I'm not sure that I'm on the track.

Boy: If you don't like the teacher, you're not going to be able to do very well in the work.

Dr. Lifton: Bill's saying something interesting. He's saying if you don't like the teacher, why should you try.

Girl: (Inaudible comment.)

Boy: Well, the teacher's not the one who's got to get along.

Dr. Lifton: (Noticing a boy's attempt to contribute, but hesitant to talk) You seem to want to say something, Bill.

Bill: I don't know.

Boy: The teacher's got to be interested in the class. . . . If the teacher don't like you, he's going to make it hard for you.

Girl: Not always.

Boy: But one of my teachers did.

Girl: Who are you referring to? (giggling)

Dr. Lifton: (recognizing concern over confidentiality) Don't worry about mentioning names. We can wipe this tape. So don't worry about it. But I think the question is an important one because no matter who the person is, you're likely from here on in to get other teachers, or bosses, that you may not like and so the real question is what do you do about these characters? Are you just stuck or, of course, one way of doing it, is to do as Bill suggested, to say "Go peddle your papers. I don't want anything to do with you." You can't always do that.

Boy: Try to get them to like you. Show interest.

Karen: It happened to my brother last year. He just worked up to his ability to show the teacher what he could do. And that helped.

Dr. Lifton: So this would be one way to prove the teacher was wrong, by being something different than what he thought. Suppose you had a friend that you'd like to have with you. How would you get this person to see you in a way that she would want to be your friend? What would you do about it? (pause)

Girl: Nothing.

Gail: If a person doesn't like you, you can't make them.

Dr. Lifton: There's no way of helping people see you differently than they see you at first? You're stuck with the first impression?

Girl: Oh, no.

Dr. Lifton: How do you change people's ideas about you?

Gail: Well, you can't just be perfect when you're near them, be different. You are what you are. You can't put on fronts in front of people because I think that would make them like you least.

Dr. Lifton: So you've got to be true; you can't be false to them. But do we act the same—are you the same person to Diane as you are to your mother or as you might be to Tom?

Girl: No.

Dr. Lifton: So that there's more than one "you" too. (laughter) That's kind of a funny idea, isn't it—that there really isn't one you. There are several different "you's."

Girl: Well, I think people are like her, she . . . I mean I'd show my personality to her. When I'm home, I'd be showing my—there's a word for it but I can't think of it—

Dr. Lifton: Just try.

Girl: Myself.

Boy: Another character. In other words, you have a different front.

Girl: Yes, everybody does. I mean you're different when you're home. You're more relaxed and. . . .

Boy: You wouldn't treat your mother like a girl friend, in other words.

Girl: That's right—I'd be uncomfortable. (laughter)

Dr. Lifton: We're also saying that the people that we feel very com-

fortable with, we're able to let them see more of us than others;
that the more we feel comfortable in letting a person know who
we really are, the easier it is for us to talk to them and to begin
to work with them.

Girl: That's why you really never know a person until you see them
in their home. . . .

Dr. Lifton: You see, that's one of the problems that we've really got
to understand. For this group to be most helpful, we have to find
a place where we can be comfortable with each other because
until we feel able to say what we really feel, we're just playing
games. We have to begin to say under what conditions would we
be willing to share things with each other. How can we help each
other feel that the other guy cares, or that he won't misuse what
we're saying, or won't think less of us. That's the real problem
that we've got to face. If we could have with this group, what you
have with some of your girl friends, except that here you have
different kinds of people, you might have a chance to think
through some ideas that you wished you had a chance to talk to
somebody about, but don't know if they could manage it. This is
really what the problem of this group is. This is why I was trying
to have us see ways in which we could get comfortable with one
another. (long pause)

Dr. Lifton: Kind of scares you, huh? Not always sure that you do
want to share things with other people. Some things that maybe
you don't feel you want to talk about. (long pause)

Gail: We all don't want to talk. When we do we get in trouble.

Dr. Lifton: Interesting, isn't it, Gail? Have you any idea why we got
caught up? I have an idea. I said something that I think some
people didn't like and they pulled away in a hurry. They're letting
me know that they're not sure that they like this and so the best
way of getting away from me is just being quiet because that's
safest. Isn't that somewhat like the classroom then? I don't like
the teacher; so I'm just going to keep my mouth shut and then
she can't know what I'm thinking and I can't get into trouble.
That doesn't quite solve it though, does it?

Tom: (inaudible reply).

Dr. Lifton: Can't hear you, Tom.

Tom: Keep your mouth shut and they give you a bad mark because
you don't do anything in class.

Dr. Lifton: It's a funny thing, isn't it? If you do something, then
they hear what you're saying. If you don't say something, then
you're in trouble anyway. So that it sort of ways that (interruption by boy)—

Boy: That you're doing something.

Dr. Lifton: For the public?

Boy: Yeah.

Dr. Lifton: Kind of odd though, isn't it? No matter what we do, if we keep our mouth shut or if we open it, we still are doing something. Gail pointed this out very nicely. You're bound to do something. (long pause)

Dr. Lifton: You know it's an interesting thing. Part of what we're saying is that sometimes the exams don't measure what we study. We're saying some of the teachers don't teach what we're being tested on. We're saying some of the teachers don't like us—what's the use of trying—We're saying some of the courses, we wish we weren't in them in the first place. And all these answers are real, and there's no question that for many of you this is one of the problems involved. But is this going to solve it for you if we come up with this as answers? Is it going to solve it? Is this going to make it easier? For example, this summer, is this going to make it easier for you this summer when you go to school if we come up with these answers?

Girl: Yes, I believe so.

Boy: Maybe.

Girl: Because if you walk into a room with the right attitude, then . . . I don't know.

Girl: Then you can do better. If you walk in with the wrong attitude, then you hate it. (pause)

Karen: Oh, I know why I worked the way I work in school, I mean, why I'm working for a goal. Well, I'm planning to go to college. I think if you have a goal set, I think you work harder.

Dr. Lifton: I'm wondering, would any of the rest of you be willing to share with us what it is you see as your purpose in school. Karen has suggested that she sees a goal that seems to be very clear to her. What about some of the rest of you? Can you see any purpose in returning.

Gail: We have no choice.

Dr. Lifton: Beg your pardon.

Gail: We haven't got any choice.

Dr. Lifton: You have no choice?

Gail: You have to go to school. It's compulsory. I think if you didn't have to, I think more people would take an interest in it. There might not be as many going to school but there would be a better attitude in school.

Dr. Lifton: In a sense, I think what you're saying is that you're kind of not liking it because you have to.

Girl: It's true.

Dr. Lifton: So you'll prove to them they can't make you do something, huh? (pause)

Boy: If you could pick your own subjects, that would be better.

Dr. Lifton: Just for kicks, what would you take if you had your own way?

Boy: Math.

Dr. Lifton: You would take only math? (inaudible comments and laughter)

Dr. Lifton: Do you want to tell us about it? Why math?

Boy: I just like math. I don't know why. It just came to me easy. I like numbers better than I do words. (pause)

Girl: I'd take all English.

Dr. Lifton: You'd take all English.

Boy: Science.

Dr. Lifton: You'd take all science.

Girl/Boy: Science.

Dr. Lifton: You'd take science too.

End of Segment of Session One

❁　　❁　　❁

The group-centered approach is useful in many settings, not the least of which is the typical classroom. In the protocol which follows a group is going through the first stages of defining their societally approved reasons for the group's existence, their own hidden agenda and their need to test other group members to see how much personal acceptance of their ideas exists. The protocol is a transcript of a tape recording made during an institute held at Utah State University, designed to train state employment service counselors in the use of group techniques. The participants came from states west of the Mississippi, were from different levels of administrative responsibility and were all involved in the operation of Youth Opportunity Centers. Their selection to participate did not always represent their own choice.

During the first few hours of the program, time was spent on administrative details and some lecturing. The cues the group received suggested a passive role, rather than the introspective group concern that was desired by the leaders of the institute. Accordingly, six participants were asked to volunteer for a session in which they would try to explore how the group might use this setting more effectively. It was also suggested that the larger group, serving as observers, needed also to consider problems of group process being faced in the smaller group. The institute therefore had a dual purpose: first, to give meaning on a personal level to institute activities; second, to provide didactic material to which all could relate on a feeling level.

Protocol	*Underlying Dynamics*
Man 1: Do we all get an "A"?	
Lady 1: There are too many men.	
Leader: There are too many men?	Reflection of content as a way of encouraging further definition of meaning.
Man 1: Women can outtalk men anyway.	
Leader: You think the composition of the sexes is relevant?	Seeking to determine if group composition itself was a source of threat.
Lady 1: No.	
Man 1: It doesn't make any difference.	
Leader: Part of the reason for wanting to get us together in this group, and it's obviously an artificial group, is that as I listened to you this morning your major concern was how you could help people "stick" in your YOC groups. It's true that Logan is pretty far from home for many of you, but you can escape in many ways. You don't have to escape physically. You can escape in other ways too. I think if this session and this institute are to be of value, we need to take a look together, from the very beginning, about how you feel about the whole setting and some of the things you'd like to have happen, and the ways in which you feel we can get moving more effectively.	Verbal structuring. Attempts to relate present group to reasons for their selection and participation in the current setting. Leader points up idea that verbal participation does not equate to involvement and that talk can also be used to avoid issues. Indicates group's responsibility for what occurs and their need to take action to set limits.

Lady 1: Well, it seems to me that the thing of "sticking" is basic particularly with the clients we deal with, because most of them haven't stuck to anything and if you can get them to stick to a group counseling session, well then maybe it will rub off on something else too.

Talks about "clients" as a way of maintaining distance.
Actually suggests her awareness that content is the vehicle for more significant interaction.

Leader: So you see their behavior *here* as symptomatic of their behavior in all other settings.

Leader relates feeling to the current setting. By this approach, suggests this group shares common concerns with their clients in other settings.

Man 2: I see it in the same way, but when the kids come in they want something and I've been talking with some of the counselors on what is called the carrot theory of group counseling. You've got to dangle something or give them some specific meaning or reason of why they are in that group . . . and to dangle this in front of them to get people together to discuss specifically how to get a job for themselves and for the rest of the people in the group. Try to get them to work together so if one can't get a job he may find prospects for another. In other words, the group is a resource for each other person in the group.

He seems to be asking, "What do we want?" "What's in it for us?" He also is seeking to define the limits of rewards or punishment present in the current group. He is also asking if motivation will come from leader activity, or is it the responsibility of the group.

Maybe one source of support can come from intragroup interaction.

Leader: If I'm hearing you correctly, I think you are saying quite different things. (Lady 1) seems to be saying that people's departure from a group is because they don't know how to stick to a task, and I think I'm hearing you say that they don't stick to it because the carrot isn't good enough. It's a little different.

Shows the difference in ideas of two group members, focusing on their interrelationship. Also pinpointing different rewards obtainable from a group.

Man 2: Well, first of all I think

Member shows awareness of a basis

you've got to make them want the carrot. I've run into this problem and I assume all the others have too. There's the kid who doesn't want to work and before you can really accomplish anything, you've got to make him really want the carrot and then you go about finding how you can accomplish this.

Man 3: And also what kind of a carrot will entice him, because we're all motivated by different things. But I've wondered from my own experience if we've found the carrot which will really have value for him.

Lady 2: I've found that in some groups that if the people come once or twice, they'll probably come back after that and they'll find the motivation in simply just having a forum, you know, in that here they are treated with respect, and they can speak out, and it's kind of a fun experience that they enjoy. So that the problem of getting them to stick can be worked out if you can just get them to come just the first few times, then it's no longer a problem.

Man 1: Well, in your group they have some particular reason, some particular subject that means something to everyone there. Ah, this is where I think that in groups, at least in the vocational aspect of it, part of what we have to learn to do is to select individuals for a group rather than just tossing in anyone at any time.

Lady 1: Isn't that what you do in

for group common concern. He also pinpoints his own problems as a group leader. He tends to require a status role where he controls others.

"Do we all need to get the same reward from the group?"

"Just being recognized as a person is important enough."

"How compatible are we? Can we get along together? If we aren't similar, can we get along?"

"Don't we need to find a common

group counseling, that you get people who have a common problem, I mean you just can't throw in just this one or that one or the other one in, can you?

Leader: There is something I find a little bothersome here. Are you saying that people having a common problem see the problem the same way?

Chorus: No, not necessarily.

Leader: Maybe you can help me. I guess I didn't understand you. What do you mean by a common problem?

Man 1: Maybe I can clarify what I was thinking of. This might be a group of people interested in one specific vocation. How do you go about getting into it? What's necessary for each one of them?

Leader: May I interrupt for just a moment? How do you know that this is what they are interested in?

Man 1: Well, possibly from a verbal expression, or they may have said this before they came in, ah, expressing an interest in a particular field. After involvement in a group, they may find this isn't it and they may branch off into other things.

Leader: Are you saying then that your group is comprised of people who in individual interviews said to you, "I want to find out how to be a plumber," and you said, "I've got five other people who are interested in this. Would you like to talk this over with others who have the same kind of interest?" Is that it?

basis on which we can all interact?"

Tries to pinpoint the group's concern over a commonly shared goal versus individual agendas.

"You aren't getting through. I need help to help you."

Leader goofed! Attempt to move group too rapidly away from facade. Also interruption violates right of group member.

"Are we committed to what we say now or can we change direction?"

Man 1: Yup.

Man 3: I think a more illustrative problem is a person who is an older person. They all have the problem of going to an employer, and they're fifty years of age, and they can't get employed because it's against company rules. Now then, they *have* a common problem. You bet they do! How do they overcome this problem?

What forms the basis for common concern? How general does it have to be?"

Lady 1: What about kids in the Job Corps? They want to, for some reason, get away from their home environment so you would think. . . .

Man 3: . . . a common problem.

"I'm with you."

Leader: So from one point of view these people ought to feel the same way about these problems, or at least see a common kinship with the others.

Man 3: Right.

Leader: From one point of view.

Attempts to help group see if this is the only answer.

Man 3: From one point of view, yes!

Leader: So we think *this* ought to make a group because they seem to be people who are similar, but somehow when we get them together they don't click, and you sometimes wonder why.

Man 4: I wonder if we set them up for the group properly. In other words, do we just get a group together and do they fully understand why they are there? It's my feeling that it takes a certain amount of individual counseling prior to a group session in most cases.

"If a group fails, it's because the counselor hasn't done his job well."

"All of us aren't convinced this is the place we want to be."

Man 3: And I think that's what we should be learning in this Institute, the techniques for determin-

Returns group to the fact that they are really talking about themselves.

ing which ones will make up the best groups.

Leader: And yet (Lady 2) said something quite different. She seems to be taking a position which is quite different from any of the rest of you. She said that if I have people in a group, *people*, not necessarily a problem-centered group that has been organized that way, but people, that in this meeting I give them some sense of acceptance as a person, then their original reason for coming into the group may have less meaning. Am I picking up what you are saying correctly? (to Lady 2)

Attempt to support individual perceptions while pointing up problems to be worked on by the group.

Tries to help group see that all group members have hidden agendas that may need to be recognized and met before they become task oriented.

Lady 2: M-hm.

Man 3: Fundamental.

Man 2: It appears from what I'm hearing as if people who are trying to get a group together may be trying to be too specific on a problem; like, for example, wanting to be a plumber. You have to have your problem more general. If you get too specific you can get the answers out of a book, or you can ditto it on a sheet and hand it to them.

Picks up cue from leader and directs comments to group concern. Sees maybe the focus is not just information giving that applies to all, but rather that some kind of personal feedback that must come from others may be the real purpose.

Lady 1: Then you would say that they are youth and out of a job, and that is enough.

Man 2: And can't find work.

Lady 1: Yup.

Man 3: You say that's too specific?

Man 2: No, no, that would be a good example.

Man 3: All right.

Leader: With one other ingredient that I think we've suggested, but haven't stated, that they are also ready to come to a group because

Introduces another possible way to use the group. Also, attempts to verbalize the idea that was implied but not stated.

here's a place they think that maybe they can get some answers they haven't gotten before.

Man 4: This seems the most serious because if you haven't got the group to start, holding them isn't a problem. Orienting them, or in a sense selling them, holding a carrot out to them, trying to get them to feel that this kind of a meeting has a value. . . . Most of them shy away from group activity and they don't verbalize very well.

"Can we offer anything to nonverbal, shy people?"

Lady 1: But they verbalize better with their peers than they do with us. I think if the group gets off to a real swinging start, that then they'll probably be back.

"Is the nature of the relationship affecting ability to communicate?"

Leader: So, maybe we're getting in the way?

Lady 1: Could be.

Man 3: Yes.

Man 2: This is a real good point because there are times when you as a counselor in this group are an authority figure or whatever it is. This is some of my anxiety in a group situation. Ah, trying to act as a group leader; ah, what do I say; what do I do to get started; and when do I get started? Do I interrupt or do I interject at the wrong times; do I stick my snout in and cut things off?

Note repeat of content in thirteenth response in group. Man 2 again brings up his own cause for concern.

In later sessions the group pinpointed this, saying he always needed to be a leader, and couldn't treat them as peers.

(This session continues as the group works out their own readiness to get involved and their feelings of threat about being evaluated.)

It is fascinating to see how group members provided clues to their own personal concerns in the first session, which did not become clearly apparent until many sessions later. Note that the leader focused activities on providing group support through linking group members together, by clarifying problems the group needed to solve, by playing different roles, and by reflecting the feelings of participants, feelings which provided the keys to their major concerns. It is these concerns, of course, which are the primary source for motivating each individual's participation in the group.

Many of the cues the group members responded to were nonverbal. This protocol therefore gives no evidence of intragroup interaction seen through head shaking, smiles, closed eyes, or agitated movement. Hopefully, this protocol does demonstrate that even in groups convened without prior notice, in what might be considered as a minimal therapeutic setting, the actions and feelings of participants permit the group to move from a superficial discussion of conventional topics to those loaded with personal meaning and dealing with intragroup relationships.

This protocol should also demonstrate that a group does not just happen. If one assembles a group of people at a movie, he/she does not necessarily have a supportive kind of group as a result. It is a crowd, not a therapeutic group. There are things one has to do, overtly do, to help people learn how to provide support to each other. This is one of the reasons why, when earlier publications described client-centered therapy as extremely permissive, they were right in one way and wrong in another. They were correct in assuming that individuals had the freedom to make decisions about their own behavior, but were wrong in suggesting that there are no limits. There *are* limits.

The limits most immediately imposed are the limits that come from what peer group members will permit an individual group member to do. When he or she acts, he/she is doing something to them, and they may respond with the feeling that it is an act they will not let anyone get away with. One of the things that people learn in a group where open communication is possible is that their freedom ends where the rights of others begin. They learn this very overtly through the process of confrontation described earlier in this chapter.

Obviously no short segment of a group's life can convey the whole story. Readers interested in learning more about this approach may care to read a more complete presentation available in the author's text, *Groups: Facilitating Individual Growth and Societal Change* (Lifton, 1972).

QUALIFICATIONS OF THE LEADER

This section is probably the most difficult to write. It is easy to set criteria that are so demanding that the individual obviously would be all-knowing and have the warm, empathic characteristics needed in a therapeutic relationship. To follow this route would be talking about graduate training which probably would include the following:

1. Courses covering personality theory and the dynamics of human behavior.
2. Courses covering semantics and effective verbal communication.
3. Courses providing background of an anthropological or sociological nature which will assist the student in recognizing the meaning or symbolic significance of various roles or acts in our culture.
4. Courses training a person in specific counseling skills.
5. Courses providing supervised practicum experiences where the students are helped to discover the ways in which their needs are affecting their behavior.
6. Experiences as a group leader or member to sensitize the person to typical experiences in the life of a group.

However, research by Hereford (1963) has provided concrete evidence that laymen working with their peers to explore feelings and attitudes can, with minimal training, learn how to help members of a group use each other as a source of support. Recent programs using the indigenous population as case aides or nursery school aides have also demonstrated that the absence of class bias, the ability to communicate in ways easily understood by clients, and the warm concern of these relatively unskilled people have resulted in movement within the groups they have led that is significant and therapeutic for the group members. Equal success has come from training students to serve as peer counselors.

It would appear obvious that despite the status needs of "the establishment," there may be many people who can function effectively who have not come up the traditional graduate study route. Few would deny that more background would enable these people to become more effective group leaders, but this author is not prepared at this time to bar from the helping process any segment of the population because of the absence of an appropriate professional label. It is easy to justify the status quo, but courage is needed to see if alternate ways of securing personnel and training them can be equally effective (Carkhuff, 1966).

OTHER READINGS

The most complete presentation of the point of view expressed in this chapter can be found in the works of two authors, Gordon (1955) and Lifton (1972). Both texts provide philosophical as well as pragmatic material. Specific crises in the life of the group are covered. Also available is an exposition of techniques considered suitable for use within this frame of reference.

The reader seeking to compare various approaches based upon sample protocols will find Corsini's (1957) text quite helpful. For those with an interest in research, review of a text by Gorlow, Hoch, and Telschow (1952) based upon three doctoral dissertations analyzing group nondirective counseling will prove useful.

One of the earliest writers in this area is Hobbs (1949). The publication cited provides an illustration of group-centered counseling in a university setting.

Although it is possible to list other books carrying a similar orientation, no true understanding of working with groups can be achieved solely through reading. The absence of many of the cues, both auditory and visual, to which the leader responds makes a printed protocol a sterile replica of what actually occurs.

SUMMARY

This chapter has attempted to describe an approach which was labeled *group centered* because the major concern of the leader was in helping the group learn its responsibility for assisting each group member in developing himself or herself. It has departed from the traditional nondirective approaches described by Hobbs (1951), Corsini (1957), Gordon (1955), and others in that the leader has been given a more active role both in teaching the needed group roles and also in the use of labeling to help provide group members with cues to use when they take over the leadership role.

With the emphasis on the role of the group as a miniature society, this chapter tried to reflect the focus toward social change and toward client social action which is shaping increasing community rejection of the medical model as a basis for therapy groups. Both for philosophical reasons and in terms of the desire by large segments of the population for concrete, here-and-now attacks on problems, the approach has incorporated some of the concepts found in ego psychology (emphasis on strengths), reality therapy (need to be honest and share feelings), as well as the translation of these concepts as found in the open classroom and alternate schools.

Social change sometimes demands that the leader take initiative in calling the group's attention to values commonly held but not overtly voiced. Since peer-group pressures restrict the initiative of the individual, the hidden value shared by group members needs to be clearly perceived by all before each member may be secure enough to act.

The lack of congruence between feelings and overt verbal behavior limits the potential happiness of everyone. Good mental health in society suggests the need for therapy groups at all levels of society. This is particularly so for youngsters, since a prophylactic approach is the only answer to the rapid growth in numbers of people alienated from society.

The most important message of this chapter should be that the final evaluation of any theory or approach to group counseling ought to be in terms of the values of the user, and an awareness that means do determine ends. If and when that fact is forgotten, democracy will have lost all hope for survival.

REFERENCES

Barclay, J.: *Foundations of Counseling Strategies.* New York, Wiley, 1971.

Carkhuff, R. R.: Training in the counseling and therapeutic practices: Requiem or reveille? *Journal of Counseling Psychology, 13:*360, 1966.

Cohn, B. (Ed.): *Guidelines for Future Research on Group Counseling in the Public School Setting.* Bedford Hills (Board of Cooperative Educational Services—Coop. Research Project No. F-029), 1964.

Corsini, R. J.: *Methods of Group Psychotherapy.* Chicago, William James, 1957.

Eysenck, H. J. (Ed.): *Handbook of Abnormal Psychology: An Experimental Approach.* New York, Basic, 1961.

Gordon, T.: *Group-Centered Leadership.* Boston, HM, 1955.

Gordon, T.: The functioning of the group leader. In Kemp, C. G. (Ed.): *Perspectives on the Group Process.* Boston, HM, 1964.

Gorlow, L., Hock, E. L., and Telschow, E.: *The Nature of Nondirective Group Psychotherapy.* New York, Tchrs Coll, 1952.

Hereford, F.: *Changing Parental Attitudes through Group Discussion.* Austin, U. of Tex Pr, 1963.

Hill, W.: *Hill Interaction Matrix.* Los Angeles, U. of Southern California Youth Study Center, 1965.

Hobbs, N.: Nondirective group therapy. *Journal of the National Association of Women Deans and Counselors, 12:*114, 1949.

Hobbs, N.: Group-centered psychotherapy. In Rogers, C. R.: *Client-Centered Therapy.* Boston, HM, 1951.

Lifton, R. J.: *Thought Reform and the Psychology of Totalism: A Study of "Brainwashing" in China.* New York, Norton, 1963.

Lifton, W.: *Groups: Facilitating Individual Growth and Societal Change.* New York, Wiley, 1972.

Maslow, A. H.: *Toward a Psychology of Being.* New York, An Insight Book, 1962.

Otto, H.: Toward a holistic treatment program—some concepts and methods, *Mental Hygiene, 48:*439, 1964.

Rogers, C. R.: *A Tentative Formulation of a General Law of Interpersonal Relationships.* U of Chicago Pr, July, 1957.

Rogers, C. R.: *On Becoming a Person.* Boston, HM, 1961.

Rogers, C. R.: *Freedom to Learn.* Columbus, Merrill, 1969.

VII

BEHAVIORAL GROUP COUNSELING

Barbara B. Varenhorst

BEHAVIORAL GROUP COUNSELING has experienced considerable recognition, maturity, use, and modification since the first edition of this text appeared in 1968. Behavioral counseling theory was labeled unique and revolutionary at that time (Krumboltz, 1966) because knowledge of the learning process was leading to the development of specific counseling techniques and procedures for changing behavior. However, as the author concluded her chapter in the earlier edition by saying that with more knowledge about factors affecting behavioral group processes, the field of guidance would see greater use of this type of counseling, so, with greater use and acceptance has come a loss of uniqueness and revolutionary shock. Greater utilization has been witnessed not only in the field of guidance, but in the entire field of education, psychology, business, and industry over this period of time. Parents are also being introduced to the theoretical principles of behavioral counseling and are attempting to use them in child-rearing practices (Krumboltz and Krumboltz, 1972).

Witness to this claim are the waves of interest and involvement in learning specific skills and behaviors via the group process. The popularity among all age groups of courses on parent effectiveness, time management, value clarification, risk taking, transactional analysis, and most recently, assertiveness training indicate the widespread use of behavioral counseling concepts. It is of particular interest to note the interest in assertiveness training as this was one of the original techniques developed by behavior modification theorists. Those who enroll in such courses are committing themselves to a group goal of learning specific behaviors to extend, modify, or eliminate certain personal behaviors in their lives. Individuals are joining with others to

215

reach a stated group goal as they help themselves. Both teaching and learning takes place and this in essence is behavioral group counseling.

The basic objective of all counseling, education, and teaching is to change people's behavior in terms of how they think, feel, and act with themselves and others. The only evidence of learning is a change in behavior. In this sense there is no such thing as "nonbehavioral" guidance, counseling, or teaching. Vriend and Dyer (1973a) acknowledge this when speaking of group counseling: "It seeks to develop people, to aid any and all individuals in adding to their repertoire of *behaviors* mustered to work in their behalf, to help them cope better or to develop mastery over their own mental, emotional, social, and physical *behaving*" (p. 50, italics added).

There are some specific characteristics of behavioral group counseling, however, that distinguish it from other theoretical models of group counseling. Counselors may assume these "requirements" are either too technical or too difficult to follow, and are therefore hesitant to attempt behavioral group counseling. Others may still have a philosophical bias against this approach, feeling it is too mechanical and lacks the warmth and caring of other approaches. It is the intent of this chapter to clarify some of these assumptions, to illustrate the concepts through a description of a peer counseling model of group counseling, and to identify the potentials of this approach as contrasted with other traditional approaches to group work.

RATIONALE FOR GROUP COUNSELING

Group counseling has demonstrated its effectiveness in helping individuals with problems, particularly those related to social and interpersonal relationships. It is a counseling method which draws on a variety of resources to help members of a group to change behaviors and learn others, to eliminate conflicts in their lives, and to increase personal satisfaction. A group provides the presence of others who share common concerns, who exhibit multiple behaviors and, therefore, can serve as models to others, and who also can institute peer influence both to reinforce behaviors as well as to provide constructive feedback to an individual. The group situation makes it possible to simulate a real life social situation, which is a rich environment in which group members can try out new behaviors in preparation of applying them to the situations where individuals experience difficulty. As Thoresen and Potter (1975) have indicated, "the group serves as a laboratory for learning, a time and place to consider, observe, try out and receive information on certain actions."

Most groups are focused around a common purpose to which members of the group are voluntarily committed. The counselor attempts to engage all group members in working towards the agreed-upon goal and to utilize members of the group to help one another. The usual technique employed is group discussion. Vriend and Dyer (1973b) speak of effective group counseling as "the process of unequivocally identifying self-defeating behaviors, actively working at understanding the maintenance system and psychological motivation for such behaviors, and establishing workable alternatives to them in a group setting—a crucible employing the powerful peer influence resources so vital to human development . . ." (p. 3).

ILLUSTRATION OF BEHAVIORAL GROUP COUNSELING: PEER COUNSELING TRAINING

Several years ago the author became aware of the increasing number of students who expressed a feeling of loneliness and isolation in school. They felt they had few, if any friends, and no adult in the school knew them, other than perhaps their names. They did not exhibit any severe behavioral problems to merit individual attention from counselors, nor were they so outstanding they obtained recognition through achievements. According to common definition, they were "normal" kids.

From this identification of a "problem" emerged the idea of training students to be friends to peers—to reach out to other lonely students, helping them to learn new skills, to try new alternatives in handling the concerns in their lives. Students, when asked about this idea, seemed enthusiastic.

Preparation for beginning such a program included consulting with the superintendent, principals, psychologists, counselors, and parents, asking them for ideas, their reactions, and their support. Based on their response a peer group counseling training program was developed. The plan and procedure was the following:

Students would be informed of this training by visits to classrooms, through announcements, and by recommendation from teachers and counselors. Students would meet in small groups of approximately ten to twelve for a period of twelve weeks. The sessions would be held after school or in the evening and would meet for one and a half hours. The members of the groups would be a mixture of junior and senior high students and from all six secondary schools. No screening would be done before taking the training if a student was willing to commit the eighteen hours of time to complete the training. This would allow for students to come to get help for themselves in learning how to make more friends, be more comfortable in social situations, or to get help for particular problems.

Students recruited for the program were interviewed in small groups so that they could be given a more complete definition of the purpose and the activities of the session. If they were still interested following the small group session, they were asked to come to a large group orientation for additional explanation of the goals for the training. Those still interested were asked to complete registration forms indicating their interests in the training and additional data.

Planning the Sequence of Sessions

Administrators, parents, and students had been told the purpose of this training was to reach out to the lonely and isolated students in the schools. Therefore, the activities of the group were designed for particular tasks students would need to be able to do if the purpose was to be achieved. In learning these skills, individual trainees would be learning new behaviors, practicing them in their own lives, and trying out new alternatives for their own problems.

The skills identified for attention through the twelve weeks were the following:

1. Ability to approach a stranger and engage in constructive conversation,
2. Ability to listen to another, including nonverbal communication,
3. Ability to observe and evaluate the behaviors of others,
4. Ability to talk with another about personal problems and feelings,
5. Ability to utilize decision-making counseling in dealing with personal problems, family problems, health problems, school planning, and peer relations,
6. Ability to develop alternative actions when faced with a problem,
7. Ability to apply interpersonal skills to the initiation of a first meeting with a student needing help,
8. Ability to develop observational skills in order to distinguish abnormal from normal behavior, and identify behaviors related to differences among drug problems, feelings of isolation, and extreme nervous habits,
9. Ability to utilize referral resources as a source of help to students, and
10. Ability to demonstrate an awareness of the ethics and strategies of counseling.

These behaviors were grouped around three major areas, viz. communication skills, problem-solving skills, and ethics and strategies of counseling. Four sessions would be spent on each of the areas.

Each session would attempt to deal with a new behavior and students in the group were asked to practice the skills throughout the week between sessions. If members of a group indicated they needed more work on some of the skills, additional time was devoted to this. As the group moved into the problem-solving areas, after trust had been developed within the group, members would be using their own problems and would be practicing helping one another in dealing with these concerns.

The training developed involved using a variety of techniques. Each session began with some group discussion about the behaviors, and this was followed by some activity. Students worked in dyads, in groups of three or groups of six. They role-played talking to a student about a family problem, attempting to talk to a student about a sensitive issue, and meeting a stranger for the first time. The counselor modeled some of the behaviors and students were frequently asked to model behaviors. Group members were continually cued to reinforce the progress individuals made in their attempts.

Certain tasks appeared to be harder for students than others. When this was observed, additional activities were tried. For example, students demonstrated that they tended to "interrogate" a stranger on the first meeting, shooting one question after another at the person. To overcome this the group was asked to brainstorm the kinds of questions they liked being asked and why, and the difference between open-ended questions and those that could be answered with a yes or no response.

Assignments and Practicums

Many students completing the twelve weeks revealed in their self-evaluations that they had learned and used new interpersonal skills and problem-solving alternatives. Many said they had achieved what they had desired through the training. Some said they did not yet feel confident to take an assignment to help their peers. The vast majority were eager to put into practice in a more formal way what they had learned.

The adult evaluations indicated that students were at differing levels of competency and therefore discrimination was necessary in assigning students to work with certain types of problems. Further supervision and training were needed for many of the peer counselors.

To provide for this, weekly practicum groups were formed. Students again were assigned to a particular group of ten to twelve students to obtain assignments, to get help in completing assignments, and to learn additional skills that might be needed. The continuing work within the group reinforced their using the skills they had learned in training and provided ongoing support and reinforcement from the group. Some students did not take assignments, but used the practicum as their counseling group for continued help with their problems.

Since that beginning in 1970, the program has expanded and approximately 1,000 students have taken the training providing evaluation data on changes of behavior, what techniques are successful, and what modifications still need to be done. For a more complete description of the program see Varenhorst (1973, 1974, and in press).

SPECIFICS OF BEHAVIORAL GROUP COUNSELING

The description of an innovative use of behavioral group counseling illustrates the critical distinctions of this method of counseling. In delineating these distinct characteristics, support is given for the assertion that "teaching" groups are in fact behavioral groups if group dynamics are utilized and individual members of the group are "counseled" in the behaviors and alternatives they desire for a more self-enhancing life.

Major Features of Behavioral Counseling

A summary of the process used (see Table VII-1) in establishing the peer counselor training illustrates the key features of behavioral group counseling. These concepts will be developed in greater depth throughout the remaining portion of the chapter.

Comparisons With Traditional Group Counseling

Behavioral approaches to group counseling do not differ from the basic description of the group process, yet they go further to define specifically some procedures and to add some particulars to provide for greater potential of success.

Behavioral counseling developed from a variety of theoretical positions. It was first closely identified with behavior modification concepts pioneered by such researchers and therapists as Ullmann and Krasner (1965), Wolpe (1969), Lazarus (1971), and Krumboltz (1966, 1968). For a detailed description of the theory and counseling techniques involved in behavior modifications see Varenhorst (1969). As the use of behavioral counseling

TABLE VII-1

SUMMARY OF BEHAVORIAL COUNSELING PROCESS

Distinct Features of Behavioral Counseling	*Peer Counseling Model*
I. Identifying the problem and stating a goal	The awareness of loneliness and isolation leading to the goal of training students to help themselves and others
II. Arranging the environment and eliciting support	The key decision-makers in the school community were contacted regarding the idea and their support was sought
III. Determining the content, sequence, methods, and procedures of training	Identifying the tasks to be done, the skills to be learned and planning the learning activities to accomplish this
IV. Recruiting of members	Meeting with students in classes, informing by announcements, meeting for individual interviews, and conducting the large group orientation
V. Conducting group sessions	Reviewing the goals for the training, identifying individual member's objectives, establishing group trust and cohesiveness, and directing learning activities
VI. Ongoing monitoring and evaluation of progress	Observations made each session of skill development, obtaining feedback from group members, practicing skills outside of the group
VII. Terminating groups	Completing the training, assessing outcomes and planning for follow-up assignments and supervision
VIII. Providing for follow-up contacts and maintenance of behaviors	Developing weekly practicum groups

has grown, more therapists have based their theoretical framework on social learning theory as presented by Bandura (1969). Eysenck (1971) and Thoresen and Potter (1975) advocate a "technically eclectic" approach which leads therapists to experiment with empirically useful methods, using techniques which work with different individuals under different conditions. These people suggest letting the questions of "why" follow, rather than precede, answers to "what" helps people change. Krumboltz and Thoresen (1969) look forward to the time when there no longer will be a label of "behavioral" counseling but rather all would refer merely to the profession of *counseling*. The field of group counseling may be closer to this point than many may realize.

Basically, behavioral counseling is founded on the principles of how people learn—recognizing that all behavior is learned and the ways in which people learn behavior can also systematically be used to change behavior or help individuals learn new behaviors they desire. Based on this, one could restate Vriend and Dyer's definition of group counseling, in behavioral group counseling terms, by saying effective group counseling is the process of clearly identifying behaviors a person wants to eliminate, i.e. setting clear goals for counseling, actively working at understanding what rewards and reinforcements are maintaining these behaviors which are to be changed, and helping the individual develop workable alternatives through a group setting by teaching them the behaviors which are desired and how to eliminate those that are not.

Some people assume the difference between behavioral group counseling and other approaches is the use of certain prescribed techniques. Some counselors feel these techniques are mechanical, perhaps contrived, uncaring, and artificial. It is therefore important to point out that behavioral counseling is not identified by the *methods* or *techniques* used by a counselor, but rather by the steps that are taken and by assuring that certain criteria are met in setting up groups and evaluating the ongoing progress of the group. These essential steps and criteria have been illustrated in the peer counseling model and will be elaborated on later.

Behavioral counselors use a variety of techniques, experimenting with what works best for helping individuals achieve counseling goals. Counselors have available and use a wide repertoire of techniques for counseling, such as modeling, behavioral rehearsal, social reinforcement, cueing-shaping, extinction, group discussion, and direct verbal instruction. As Thoresen and Potter

(1975) have pointed out, techniques advocated by Gestalt therapy, client-centered counseling, and other theoretical approaches may be used in behavioral counseling if they seem appropriate for the situation to better assist a client in his or her development. In fact, a significant uniqueness of this approach is that a counselor *does* experiment with all kinds of methods, continually monitoring the success of the method, and adjusting such methods as they prove ineffective or as goals are reached. In this way great flexibility is employed rather than rigidity, providing for more opportunities for successful outcomes. The continuing evaluation process *is* critical and why this is so will be discussed in greater detail later in this chapter.

Essential Characteristics of Behavioral Groups

Krumboltz and Thoresen (1969) have stated what they believe to be the essential features of behavioral counseling. These are:

1. Formulating clear goals and objectives in performance terms, i.e. stating what actions, under what circumstances, and to what extent the counselee will do these at the conclusion of counseling;
2. Tailoring techniques to help a counselee accomplish particular goals;
3. Experimenting with procedures to assess those which are best suited for helping various kinds of counselees with various problems;
4. Conducting continuous and systematic evaluations of progress of counseling to modify or improve the procedures being used in counseling.

These criteria apply not only to individual counseling but to group counseling as well. In group situations, particular attention to certain issues is important because of multiple counselees participating in the group.

Setting Goals

Group counseling begins with the identification of a clear behavioral group goal to which each member joining the group agrees. Group members are identified or recruited on the basis of need, desire, involvement and commitment to this prescribed goal. This differs dramatically from the practice of bringing together students who have "problems" for group counseling as a method of reaching more students at one time. The behavioral counselor starts with a goal and recruits members based on that goal.

The importance of this criterion has been pointed out by Gazda and Larsen (1968) who found on the basis of a comprehensive review of group counseling research of over 100 studies from 1938 to 1968, that goal setting was a major weakness. They found that outcome variables were too global to be tied down to treatment; specific goals were not stated in measureable terms; and specific outcome goals for each member of the group were lacking. True behavioral group counseling is not being practiced if any of these limitations are evident. Treatment must be tailored to the group goal; each member must have a specific subgoal, which also dictates techniques of treatment; and the goals must be ones which are measurable and observable.

Ryan (1973) has stated that goal setting is one of the most critical elements in group counseling, bearing either directly or indirectly on every other element in the system. She has found in two studies, where the effectiveness of group counseling was demonstrated for improving decision-making behaviors and increasing study behaviors, that the success of the process was attributed in part to the fact that clearly defined objectives had been set in advance (Ryan, 1968, 1969b).

The goal of a group can be to remedy particular problems, to prevent certain problems from developing or to learn specified skills to be used by members of the group in many aspects of their lives. In this way there perhaps is little distinction between "counseling" groups and "teaching" groups. For example, Johnson (1964) demonstrated the effectiveness of behavioral group counseling in helping fourth, fifth, and sixth graders learn how to increase their verbal participation in class. Laemmle and Thoresen (1968) used groups to help individuals reduce examination anxiety. Beach (1967) worked with junior high underachieving students and demonstrated that groups listening to a taped model where reinforcement was used to change under-achieving behaviors showed significant improvement in their GPA following the experiment.

Many of the early behavior modification studies done by Krumboltz and his students at Stanford have demonstrated the use of groups to prevent problems from developing, as well as remedying problems. The early studies by Krumboltz and Thoresen (1964), Thoresen, Krumboltz, and Varenhorst (1967), and Thoresen and Stewart (1967) were designed to help students with their career planning and vocational information seeking. Thoresen and Potter (1975) refer to a teachers' group with a goal of learning how to manage stress and tension. Varenhorst (in press) has demonstrated that groups can be used to teach secondary school students peer counseling skills; and as has been pointed out earlier, courses such as assertiveness training illustrate how the group process is used to remedy unsatisfying conditions of life by learning behaviors to correct them.

These studies illustrate examples of behavioral outcomes around which groups were formed for counseling. The identification of a group goal can emerge from a counselor's observation of students with similar problems; or it could be one a counselor thinks is important, such as the loneliness and isolation of students previously described, or similar problems around which the counselor actively recruits group members. For example, a counselor may have talked with ten students over the past month who have expressed concern about their future decisions. The counselor may decide that a decision-making group would be helpful to these students and begin the process of setting up a group around this concern.

In establishing group counseling goals, careful attention needs to be given to the following critical areas:

1. *The outcome group goal is defined in specific, clear behavioral terms.* Each person joining a group should understand the purpose of the group, basically what they will be doing in the group and how they will know if the group is successful when finished. Critical observers, i.e. faculty, administrators, parents, and other students also should understand the purpose,

eliminating some of the anxiety attached to vagueness of group activity and discussions.

The decision-making group stated as its goal: learning the skills of decision making, i.e. clarifying values, setting objectives, examining alternatives, etc., as opposed to the nonspecific goal of group counseling such as meeting to learn more about themselves as individuals or to reduce personal confusions about the future. The peer counseling group had as its group goal learning the skills to talk with lonely, isolated students, considering alternatives and actions to take when faced with physical problems, peer relationship concerns, family concerns, et cetera.

2. *The group goal must be broader than the goals of individual members but one that provides for the achievement of individual goals.* A group may have the goal of learning assertiveness, but an individual member may want to learn how to be assertive with his or her peers; another may want to learn the difference between assertiveness and aggression. Both would be possible within the broader group goal.

3. *The group and individual members' goals must be agreed on before the group begins.* To achieve this, individual interviews must be conducted with prospective group members. If the goal is one that emerged from repeated evidence of a problem area, the counselor would contact each person considered for the group and possibly might say, "You have talked with me about your desire to be less wishy-washy when you are with your friends. I wonder if you would like to join a group of students who want to learn how to be more assertive. We would be doing some talking, role playing and other activities to learn how to do this." The student would have a chance to ask questions; the counselor would explain further the plan for the group and what the students and counselor would expect would be the outcome from the group. The counselor might indicate other possible members of the group. The conclusion of the interview would be the student either consenting or declining the invitation.

Thoresen and Potter (1975) suggest having the student submit a written contract, stating the purpose of the group and the student's goal and agreement to work to achieve both. Many groups began with only a verbal agreement. However, in establishing the peer counseling groups, students were asked to think about their commitment, then to send a note of intent to participate. This was followed by a group orientation meeting and eventually with individual students and parents signing a consent form. All of these methods provide suggestions of how to obtain this agreement on the part of group members. Throughout the process students are led to understand clearly what they are attempting to accomplish through this experience. With such understanding and clarification, students also have been found (Raven and Rietsema, 1957) to like their own task and group task more, to be less hostile, and to be more responsive to group influence than those in groups in which goals are unclear.

4. *The identified goal should be one that can best be achieved through a group experience.* This factor relates to the ultimate achievement of individual goals. A powerful technique for changing behavior is creating the group social environment itself, with a variety of role models and peer influences who act as "teachers" and "counselors." Not all counseling concerns are appropriate to such a setting, nor are all most effectively handled in groups. Group counselors must determine *before* beginning a group if the identified problem is one that suits the dynamics and activities of groups. If not, other methods should be employed for helping a student.

Tailoring the Techniques and Activities to Help Individuals

As has been mentioned earlier, a behavioral group counselor uses a variety of techniques to help individuals and the group achieve their goals. The clear setting of goals initially determines to some extent the techniques and activities a counselor will use, as well as determining that a group environment is appropriate.

However, a group counselor not only has the responsibility for planning and implementing techniques, monitoring progress, and evaluating according to progress (known as *task* responsibilities), but also the responsibility for weaving a group together and establishing the trust and cohesiveness that is a necessary ingredient for effective group work. This is "climate" responsibility and perhaps is more demanding of a counselor's skill than the utilization of the techniques themselves.

CLIMATE RESPONSIBILITIES. Individual group members have agreed to participate in a group to achieve stated goals. They have some clear expectations of what will happen in the group meetings. However, they do not know other group members— know them to trust them if they should open up in a group or reveal personal behaviors and concerns they may have. They may not know what is expected of them to help others in the group nor how to help. They may be shy about participating in group activities. They particularly may not know if they can trust the adult counselor. The counselor's first responsibility is to deal with these fears, unknowns, and expectations, leading to a climate of trust and cohesiveness that makes possible the utilization of the group to accomplish the counseling tasks.

Krumboltz and Potter (1973) define these concepts in behavioral terms and point out that a behavioral counselor uses techniques to develop these necessary elements of a positive climate for a group. Liberman (1970) has demonstrated that the systematic use of social reinforcement can be used to increase group cohesiveness and also that once a specific observable category of behavior has been identified, behavioral techniques can be applied to either increase or decrease the frequency of that behavior.

The behaviors defining trust, openness, and cohesiveness, according to Krumboltz and Potter (1973), include such things as making here-and-now statements, making self-disclosing statements, spontaneous unprompted participation, members reinforcing each other, "we" statements referring to the whole group, statements expressing liking for the group, talk directed to the other group members, talk relevant to previous members' statements and cooperative statements.

The counselor works at achieving high frequency of such behaviors through such behavioral techniques as modeling the desired behavior, reinforcing such behavior when it occurs, asking questions or making comments to elicit small steps which can be reinforced towards the desired behavior, extinguishing by ignoring or cutting off inappropriate talk and behavior, setting explicit and implicit norms for the group, confronting by calling attention to inappropriate behavior, reflecting, restating harsh and negative statements to point out positive implications, and redirecting statements from leader to other members.

The modeling by the counselor is critical and must be done initially to start a group. Explicit and implicit norms must be established early. Many of the other techniques must be used as activities in the group proceed, gradually building the trust and cohesiveness desired.

In peer counseling groups the author begins the group by having each person introduce him or herself by talking about his or her name. Each person is asked to give his/her full name, saying something about where the name originated, its nationality, and meaning, nicknames they have had, good and bad experiences they have had with the name, and their feelings about it. The adult counselor "models" this procedure, beginning with an introduction of his or her name, sharing personal experiences and anecdotes connected with the name.

This activity serves to move the group quickly to desired behaviors. Individuals immediately begin sharing personal things, giving here-and-now statements as well as making self-disclosing statements. Usually individuals will refer to something someone else has said, and there often is pleasure expressed over what some have said. The counselor has modeled that it is "safe" to be personal; and individuals express they feel closer to the group and seem to know each other better after such sharing.

Despite the warm feeling which emerges from this initial warm up, personal matters such as family problems, interpersonal problems with the opposite sex, and feelings about self in relationship to peers are reserved for later sessions of the group when greater trust has been established. Individuals need to "try out" the group in less threatening topics before trusting on the "risky" topics.

TASK RESPONSIBILITIES. The task responsibilities are the heart of the group counseling process and form the content of what is done in each session. Two major tasks have been completed at the time of the beginning of group sessions, i.e. the setting of clear group and individual behavioral goals.

The next important task is helping to define behavioral objectives for individual members to be accomplished from session to session and between sessions. Evidence of meeting these objectives determines progress towards reaching outcome goals. The counselor must also have clear objectives for the entire group. One such objective would be to establish the trust and cohesiveness mentioned earlier. This must be achieved before the group may proceed to work on other objectives.

Krumboltz and Thoresen (1969) indicate three criteria of an adequate objective. First, a behavioral objective specifies the behavior to be performed to an extent that it may be reliably observed. Tom will go up to the new boy in his class and engage him in conversation, learning one personal piece of information about him. Second, a behavioral objective indicates how much of the behavior is required to meet the objective. Tom has already specified he will learn one piece of information, which partially meets this second criteria. However, it would be more specific for the objective to state that Tom will approach the new boy in his class twice a week and each time obtain one new piece of information about him. Third, a behavioral objective specifies under what conditions or circumstances the behavior will occur. For Tom's objective, approaching the new boy in his class, before class begins, or at the conclusion of class, or even during the lunch hour in the lunch room would meet this third criterion.

The value of clear objectives lies in the guidelines they provide for the necessary actions that are to be taken to change behavior and to reach goals. Clear objectives also lead to greater commitment on the part of the person, followed by self-reinforcement as the person does something he/she had desired. And there is also the potential reinforcement from the group. Clear objectives assist individuals in looking at goal accomplishment in smaller units of risk. Approaching a stranger in a fairly safe environment such as a classroom seems a much smaller step to learn initially than learning to be confident and comfortable in a large group social situation outside of school. Attempting the approaching of one stranger, feeling pleased to be able to do it, and being able to report it to the group leads to greater confidence to approach two strangers in a group. Progressively one takes greater risks, such as walking into a large room where one is a stranger, and eventually reaching the goal of becoming a part of a social group with poise and confidence.

The identification of clear objectives for each member of the group assists the counselor in tailoring the tasks to be done in the group sessions and in determining the techniques that seem to be appropriate to the learning desired.

TECHNIQUES. It is further emphasized that the behavioral group counselor is not limited to one or two techniques dictated by a theoretical model. The behavioral counselor uses a wide variety and combinations of techniques to counsel with groups, including nonverbal messages and reinforcements such as a nod or smile, role playing, tape or video models, practicing, group discussion, and even written exercises. The continual evaluation of feedback by observing what is learned as a result of anything that is done guides the counselor in choosing and modifying subsequent techniques.

In a peer counseling training group, students were to practice what they could do to welcome a stranger into a group. The initial technique used was to discuss what a person feels like when he moves into a neighborhood or goes to a youth group for the first time. What did people do that made them feel comfortable? What are additional things a person could say or do that might make a stranger feel welcome?

This was followed by dividing the group into four smaller groups. Each group was to choose someone who would be the stranger and that person was to leave the room. While gone, the small group decided the setting and the strategy they would use to welcome the stranger. When this was done each group brought the stranger in and proceeded to role-play what had been

planned. After an appropriate amount of time everyone was re-
convened to discuss what happened.

Part of the discussion centered on how the "stranger" felt
when sent from the room and what seemed to make him or her
more nervous or more comfortable when he or she joined the
group. Other points discussed included what actually happened,
and how individuals sometimes do not behave the way they had
planned to behave when in a group situation.

In one experience, a group was actually verbally cruel to the
"stranger." Students made remarks about not wanting the stranger (a boy) there. The group was stopped and the counselor confronted the individuals with what was happening, including
having them hear exactly how the boy felt during the experience. Possible alternative responses were discussed, followed by
individuals practicing in pairs how to say some friendly and nice
things to each other. Then the "welcoming a stranger activity"
was repeated. In the concluding discussion a member of the
group said, "It's really *hard* to be nice to someone." The girl was
expressing the pains of learning a new behavior—a behavior the
adult counselor assumed everyone knew. When the evidence revealed this not to be true, other methods were needed to achieve
the objective for that particular session.

Experimenting With Procedures to Identify Those Most Suitable to Helping Members Reach Their Goals and Objectives

As Thoresen and Potter (1975) have pointed out, behavioral
group counseling is experimental, drawing in large part on social
learning theory as a basis for techniques (Bandura, 1969). It is
known, for example, that positive reinforcement and modeling
are effective because of research data. However, a behavioral
counselor should and does try other techniques which may not
have research support, testing them out for their effectiveness with
a particular group or student under particular circumstances. For
example, one group was having a difficult time establishing cohesiveness. Individuals did not seem to show interest in other
members of the group. The author decided to ask members to

take turns at "share and tell," bringing to each session of the group something of which they were proud, or sharing an experience or accomplishment which pleased them. The member having his or her turn would spend five minutes telling about it and then the rest of the group was allowed to ask questions or make positive comments.

The group members seemed to enjoy the activity, looking forward to individual turns, but the group as a whole was having a hard time knowing what to say, or how to give compliments. This led to a vocabulary "lesson." The group brain stormed different words that one could use to compliment or say something positive to another person. These were written on the board and discussed with respect to their meaning and when they might be appropriately used. Following this exercise certain words were chosen to be used to compliment the "sharer" in each "share and tell" session of the day.

The author had never read about the use of these techniques, nor did she know how they might work, but she decided to try them. The failure of the group to be able to compliment led to trying the second "teaching" technique, which did produce the outcomes she desired.

The author has used other so-called "teaching" methods effectively in group counseling. The Life Career Game (Varenhorst, 1968, 1969), a simulation technique for teaching problems of decision making, vocational and educational planning, as well as social interactions and problem solving, has proven to be effective in counseling groups. Exercises from *Deciding* (Gelatt, Varenhorst, and Carey, 1972) and *Decisions and Outcomes* (Gelatt, Varenhorst, Carey, and Miller, 1973) have been used by the author in teaching alternatives for problem solving, and in using peers to counsel their fellow group members.

Many techniques used in individual counseling settings also are effective in group situations, although not extensively researched. Krumboltz and Thoresen (1969) present a wide variety of examples of behavioral techniques supported by evidence of their use with counseling cases that could be tried in the group setting. The counselor may need to risk a little, chancing that the technique chosen may not work, but perhaps in most cases the counselor may learn how to use the technique more effectively another time with a different situation.

Continuous and Systematic Evaluation

Continuous monitoring of progress and evaluating outcomes is an essential ingredient of behavioral counseling. If systematic collecting of data is not possible, then behavioral counseling is not being employed. The fact that the goals are defined in behavioral terms that can be observed, that progress objectives are defined by observable benchmarks, and techniques are modified when desired behaviors are not demonstrated ensures clear evidence of success or failure.

This monitoring characteristic of behavioral counseling seems to be one of the significant differences compared to other types of group counseling. Often in other types of counseling a counselor is vague about the progress of the group, based on *subjective* rather than objective evaluations.

The particular strength of the requirement of specificity in behavioral counseling is defining the termination of counseling. Nonbehavioral groups very often determine termination by the school year, i.e. the end of the semester, or the end of the year. Such termination points may even influence the degree of involvement of a group. For example, it has been the author's experience that nonbehavioral groups tend to wait until the final sessions to deal with serious issues, not leaving sufficient time to resolve such issues. Often on this basis, the counselor and/or the group finish with little satisfaction in what has been accomplished.

The behavioral group has a clear guideline for completion—when the goal has been reached. If the goal is reached in fewer sessions than had originally been determined, the group can be dissolved, with satisfaction in what happened.

Inadequately controlled empirical research on behavioral group counseling as a method remains a prime concern of those who support this approach to counseling. Very little has been done to systematically evaluate certain techniques related to specific outcomes with differing populations. As Thoresen and Potter (1975) point out, many of the assumed requirements and procedures, such as the pregroup interview, self-monitoring and charting of progress, and maintaining behavior change after the group has terminated, need investigation on a much broader basis, with replicated studies done on varied populations.

The author has attempted to study the outcomes of behaviors of students in peer counseling training (Varenhorst, in press). Baseline data were collected on behaviors of trainees before training, following training, before supervised practicums, and at the conclusion of the practicum year. Overall changes were significant, yet no data were collected to identify which technique, composition of group, group counselor, or length of training contributed differentially, if at all, to these outcomes. Certainly these kinds of unanswered questions represent the most serious limitation of the behavioral approach.

OPERATIONAL CONCERNS OF GROUPS

Consideration of particulars in setting up groups such as setting, composition of groups, group size, and frequency of meetings are necessary details requiring attention. However, behavioral group counseling differs very little in these areas from other theoretical approaches, with the exception of group composition and duration of sessions.

Group Setting

Whenever a group is being composed for counseling, the significant decision makers in that environment should be consulted and informed with respect to the purpose of the group. Most group counseling probably takes place within a school environment and this requires the knowledge and support of administrators, faculty, and parents if success is to be achieved. There still remains a sense of fear or mystery regarding group counseling activity on the part of some. Concern over what is being discussed, who is being discussed, and what is being done to individuals in groups is the basis of resistance when proper efforts are not made to inform these constituents.

Behavioral groups seem to have an advantage when it comes to informing the public because the counselor can be precise as to the purpose and intent, and even possible activities employed. The purpose is stated in terms that should be easily understood by those who question the procedure, and if the purpose is legitimate and ethical, support is usually obtained. In the peer counseling groups, the district administrators, psychological staff, counselors, and parents were consulted *before* any students were contacted or groups set up. These people were told that the groups were *task* and *time* oriented and the "curriculum" was available for study. Parents were asked to sign consent forms. As a result this program has received solid support throughout the school district.

Composition of Group

It is a basic assumption that behavioral counseling groups are composed of individuals who share a similar goal and have acknowledged this goal through a personal commitment. Such groups may include individuals of the same sex, differing sexes, differing ages and personalities. The overriding interwoven thread is the defined goal. This may differ significantly from so-called traditional counseling groups where the basic principle for selecting group membership may be diversity of individuals, including diversity of communication ability.

Even starting with the commonality of goals, a group may represent a wide range of ages, personalities, and abilities. A counselor may in fact seek to structure the composition of a group on the similarity of goals, but include variety of ages and sexes, knowing that older students can be influential models for younger students and sex differences can provide a potential environment for trying out behavioral skills in interpersonal relationships.

When a counselor has the opportunity to select from a number of candidates for a group, several key factors might be considered. For example, Schachter, Ellertson, McBride, and Gregory (1960) found that the more attractive the group appeared to a potential member of the group, the more likely he or she would work for the cohesiveness of the group if he/she eventually became a member of the group. Aronson and Mills (1960) found that if students went through a great deal of trouble or pain to attain membership in a group, they tended to value it more highly than a person who attained membership with a minimum of effort. Although some studies have shown that elementary aged children do respond to group counseling (Johnson, 1964), if the prime activity for counseling is to be verbal discussion, younger children have a more limited verbal repertoire and therefore less ability to benefit from such a group. On the other hand, if the group counseling is primarily focused on experiential learning activities, younger children can become involved as fully as older group members.

Members for the peer counseling groups are recruited and no screening is done on those who indicate an interest, after individuals are fully aware of the purpose of the groups. Those who request training in groups are placed in groups to vary the age, sex, and perhaps social abilities to the degree that this is possible. This permits a rich mixture for trying out different behavior with group members.

Group Size

No experimental evidence seems to be available on optimal group size for behavioral counseling. Goldstein, Heller, and Sechrest (1966) indicate some guidelines from their work in group dynamics. They found as a group size increases the group leader talks more, and the average member talks less. Individuals report feelings of threat and inhibition in participation in a large group, and there seems to be more information giving and less sharing and asking of opinions. Cohesiveness is more difficult to achieve and subgroups and cliques increase. All of these factors would affect the success of a traditional counseling group.

In behavioral group counseling, the larger the group the more varied are the models, and the potential for simulating a realistic social environment. Less individual attention from the leader and more opportunities for "practicing" behaviors would also result with the increase of size.

A group that is less than eight in number can also be inhibited by a feeling of exposure on the part of group members. Group discussion may be more limited with a very small group.

It has been the author's experience and preference to work with groups of twelve to fourteen. Such a number is manageable inasmuch as the leader is able to monitor each individual's progress and to provide a sufficient mixture of personalities to utilize varied activities and achieve sufficient verbal interaction in group discussion.

Frequency, Length, and Duration of Meetings

No evidence seems to exist related to these factors of group counseling. The most common practice is for groups to meet once a week. In behavioral group counseling the duration would depend on the time needed to achieve the stated goal.

Experience has demonstrated that meeting every day for six to seven weeks is too intense and does not provide for opportunities to try out behaviors to any great degree outside the counseling setting. Too much concentration on self day-by-day may be too intense for many individuals, including the counselor. Some time to think, reflect, and absorb what is being covered in the group may be a necessary part of the process.

The work with peer group counseling has indicated that a minimum of an hour and half is needed to try out activities and to discuss what has or has not been learned from each. Such a time block may not be possible if the counseling is to take place within the school day. Whenever possible, a minimum of an hour and half should be considered. Some groups meet once a week for a three-hour period with a short break in the middle. This has proven to be satisfying in terms of in-depth rehearsal of behaviors being taught and practiced combined with sufficient time for group discussion.

Counselor Qualifications

The counselor doing *any* type of group work needs certain skills over and beyond individual counseling skills. For example, in peer counseling training a counselor needs to have the confidence of successful past experience with the age group with whom he or she is working. Group work can be threatening. The presence of a group of individuals exposes the counselor in a more demanding way than individual work. The counselor who feels comfortable working with certain populations one-to-one is more able to handle what may unexpectedly occur in group situations.

Group counselors need to be skilled in handling group dynamics and in establishing trust and cohesiveness. Without this skill, individuals meeting together regularly will never develop into a true group. Counselors also need to be flexible. The dynamics arising from the varied individuals in groups create unexpected events and situations that may not have been previously programmed. Those counselors who can utilize these unprogrammed situations and unexpected events for teaching strengthen the counseling experience. Those who counsel by rote miss valuable teaching and learning possibilities and their groups reflect this by poor attendance, unfocused activity, and lack of cohesiveness.

The *behavioral* group counselors must have other qualifications, because they differ somewhat in what they do from traditional group counselors. These unique qualifications are the following:

1. The behavioral counselor must take an active role in all the counseling sessions. The counselor frequently serves as the model of behavior to be learned. Often the counselor takes the position of a teacher, reviewing principles of what someone in the group is attempting to learn. The counselor directs activities and assumes a directive position in group discussions.

2. The behavioral counselor must be knowledgeable in and have experience with a wide variety of techniques for use in assisting individuals in the group. The experience with such techniques may be as important as understanding the principles of the techniques. This understanding may help a counselor to sense what will be effective. For example, understanding the importance of modeling, the counselor may quickly do this to demonstrate something he or she observes is needed.

3. An essential knowledge and ability for behavioral counselors is the ability to define behavioral goals and objectives. It

is easier to say what a behavioral goal should be than actually identify and describe one for groups and to help individuals define one for themselves. Preparation for this skill almost requires that counselors have done some defining of goals and objectives for themselves and have gone through the experiences needed to achieve them.

4. A behavioral counselor must be research oriented if he or she is to be observant and sensitive to small changes in individual behaviors. The need to experiment with what he/she does throughout the sessions also relates to the researcher's inclination. The approach of "define-assess-intervene-assess-modify-assess-and-try-again" describes this counselor-researcher capability.

5. Finally, a successful behavioral counselor is one who can establish a warm relationship with a group and individually with members of the group, establishing himself or herself as a respected model and reinforcer of the behaviors of all within the group. At the same time the counselor must be aware and sensitive to the times when warmth and acceptance may not be conducive to the process of change. As Thoresen (1968) has suggested, in the complex social-psychological phenomenon where the behavior of counselor and student is being influenced, a variety of counselor-student relationships may be demanded. A counselor, in his or her role, must be able to draw upon a different kind of relationship with different students in the same group at the same time, and different kinds of relationships with the same student at different times. What results from using of different modes of relating is the criterion against which the "goodness" or "badness" of the relationship is evaluated.

POSSIBLE LIMITATIONS OF THE PROCESS

It is difficult to analyze limitations of the behavioral counseling process. There are limitations in all counseling methods, yet one weighs the potentials for effectiveness over such limitations. All group work has the limitation of being more demanding than individual counseling and less appropriate for certain counseling problems.

It has already been mentioned that the lack of research knowledge about techniques and procedures of behavioral group counseling is a serious limitation. Much more needs to be done to answer questions people legitimately raise about the significance of variables included in the process and the relative effectiveness of certain techniques used. Other fields of counseling and psychology suffer from the same limitations.

The factor of time deserves serious consideration. The preliminaries of setting up a behavioral group requires sufficient time for informing the adult support group in the school, conducting personal interviews with possible members, and planning the intervention program. Working with individuals to set clear objectives also may demand additional time of a counselor. However, if the goal is meaningful, and the group counseling has purpose, it should deserve the priority of time needed to complete these procedures.

As has been mentioned frequently, behavioral counseling requires a broad spectrum of skills and knowledge on the part of the counselor. To be effective as a behavioral group counselor a person may have to get additional special training, perhaps some experience, and be alert to innovative practices in counseling.

Finally, time is a critical factor. Even with specified goals and objectives, a tailored program of intervention, and the utilization of principles for changing behavior, often there is not enough time to change behavior within the group environment. Factors in the environment outside the group may work to tear down the achievements within the group. A counselor can not control these unknown events. No one knows how much time is needed to help everyone learn completely the behaviors they desire. More time and research is needed to deal with this limitation.

CONCLUSION

At a time when accountability is the key word in the entire field of education, when counseling and guidance in particular is under the hard scrutiny of budget-cutters, administrators, and critics, behavioral counseling deserves careful consideration. The entire process of behavioral group counseling is linked with accountability—declaring intentions before starting, choosing procedures, monitoring progress, and providing observable evidence after the termination of the group.

Counselors are unique in that they are among the few in education who never get a report card—evaluative feedback as to how successful they are. Without such criteria to guide them, the behavioral approach, nevertheless, provides some self-monitoring. This can be self-reinforcing and should lead to increased counseling efforts.

SUMMARY

Group counseling is an effective method for dealing with a wide range of human problems resulting from the social and physical environment. The presence of a variety of role models, counselors, and teachers helps to make group counseling an effective model. Behavioral group counseling is unique from other approaches in several ways:

1. Group goals are specifically defined in behavioral outcomes before the group begins.
2. Each member of a group is helped to define behavioral subgoals and objectives within the broader group goal.
3. A variety of techniques based in part on social learning theory can be used to assist individuals and the group to reach their goals and objectives.
4. Continuous monitoring of progress is made throughout the process, leading to necessary modifications in the intervention program.
5. Data in terms of behavioral outcomes are available to measure the degree of success at the conclusion of the group.

The behavioral group counselor must take an active role in all counseling sessions, be knowledgeable and skilled in social learning techniques as well as other methods of counseling, have the ability to define behavioral goals and objectives, have some skill in assessing progress and collecting data on changes each individual demonstrates, and have the capacity to establish a warm relationship with a group, varying that relationship when needed to assist the group towards the achievement of its goal.

REFERENCES

Aronson, E., and Mills, J.: The affect of severity of initiation on liking for a group. In Cartwright, D., and Zander, A. (Eds.): *Group Dynamics.* Evanston, Row, Peterson, pp. 95-104, 1960.

Bandura, A.: *Principles of Behavior Modification.* New York, HR&W, 1969.

Beach, A. I.: *The Effect of Group Model-Reinforcement Counseling on Achievement Behavior of Seventh and Eighth Grade Students.* Unpublished doctoral dissertation, Stanford University, 1967.

Eysenck, H. J.: Behavior therapy as a scientific discipline. *Journal of Consulting and Clinical Psychology, 36:*314-319, 1971.

Gazda, G. M., and Larsen, M. J.: A comprehensive appraisal of group and multiple counseling. *Journal of Research and Development in Education, 1:*57-132, 1968.

Gelatt, H. B., Varenhorst, B. B., and Carey, R.: *Deciding.* New York, College Ent Exam, 1972.

Gelatt, H. B., Varenhorst, B. B., Carey, R., and Miller, G. P.: *Decisions and Outcomes.* New York, College Ent Exam, 1973.

Goldstein, A. P., Heller, K., and Sechrest, L. B.: *Psychotherapy and the Psychology of Behavior Change.* New York, Wiley, 1966.

Johnson, C. J.: *Reinforcing Verbal Participation in Treatment Groups of Varying Composition.* Unpublished doctoral dissertation, Stanford University, 1964.

Krumboltz, J. D.: Promoting adaptive behavior: new answers to familiar questions. In Krumboltz, J. D. (Ed.): *Revolution in Counseling.* New York, HM, pp. 3-27, 1966.

Krumboltz, J. D.: A behavioral approach to group counseling and therapy. *Journal of Research and Development in Education, 1:*3-19, 1968.

Krumboltz, J. D., and Potter, B.: Behavioral techniques for developing trust, cohesiveness and goal accomplishment. In Vriend, J., and Dyer, W. (Eds.): *Counseling Effectively in Groups.* Englewood Cliffs, Ed Technology, pp. 71-80, 1973.

Krumboltz, J. D., and Thoresen, C. E.: The effects of behavioral counseling in group and individual settings on information-seeking behavior. *Journal of Counseling Psychology, 11:*324-333, 1964.

Krumboltz, J. D., and Thoresen, C. E. (Eds.): *Behavioral Counseling: Cases and Techniques.* New York, HR&W, 1969.

Krumboltz, J. D., and Krumboltz, H. B.: *Changing Children's Behavior.* Englewood Cliffs, P-H, 1972.

Laemmle, P. E., and Thoresen, C. E.: *Physiological Measures as Outcome*

Criteria in Group Desensitization. Paper presented at the American Educational Research Association Convention, Chicago, February 1968.

Lazarus, A. A.: *Behavior Therapy and Beyond.* New York, McGraw, 1971.

Liberman, R.: A behavioral approach to group dynamics. I. Reinforcement and prompting of cohesivenss in group therapy. *Behavior Therapy, 1:* 141-175, 1970.

Raven, B. H., and Reitsema, J.: The effects of varied clarity of group goal and group path upon the individual and his relation to his group. *Human Relations, 10:*29-45, 1957.

Ryan, T. A.: *Effect of an Integrated Instructional-Counseling Program to Improve Vocational Decision-making of Community College Youth.* Final report, OE 413-65-5-0154-6-85-065, Corvallis, Oregon State University, 1968.

Ryan, T. A.: Formulating Educational Goals. In Krumboltz, J. D., and Thoresen, C. E. (Eds.): *Behavioral Counseling: Cases and Techniques.* New York, HR&W, pp. 70-73, 1969.

Ryan, T. A.: Goal-setting in group counseling. In Vriend, J., and Dyer, W. (Eds.): *Counseling Effectively in Groups.* Englewood Cliffs, Ed Technology, pp. 56-70, 1973.

Schacter, S., Ellerston, N., McBride, D., and Gregory, D.: An experimental study of cohesiveness and productivity. In Cartwright, D., and Zander, A. (Eds.): *Group Dynamics.* Evanston, Row, Peterson, pp. 152-162, 1960.

Thoresen, C. E.: "Counselor as an Applied Behavioral Scientist." Invited Address, Third Annual Research in Guidance Institute, University of Wisconsin, June 1968.

Thoresen, C. E., Krumboltz, J. D., and Varenhorst, B. B.: Sex of counselors and models: effect on client career exploration. *Journal of Counseling Psychology, 14:*503-509, 1967.

Thoresen, C. E., and Potter, B.: Behavioral group counseling. In Gazda, G. M. (Ed.): *Basic Approaches to Group Psychotherapy and Group Counseling,* rev ed. Springfield, Thomas, 1975.

Thoresen, C. E., and Stewart, N. R.: *Counseling in Groups: Using Group Social Models.* Paper presented at the American Educational Research Association Convention, New York, February 1967.

Ullmann, L. P., and Krasner, L. (Eds.): *Case Studies in Behavior Modification.* New York, HR&W, 1965.

Varenhorst, B. B.: Innovative tool for group counseling: the Life Career Game. *School Counselor, 15:*357-363, 1968.

Varenhorst, B. B.: Behavioral group counseling. In Gazda, G. M. (Ed.): *Theories and Methods of Group Counseling in the Schools.* Springfield, Thomas, pp. 119-156, 1969.

Varenhorst, B.: Hello me—Hello you! Peer counseling interventions. In Mitchell, A. M., and Johnson, C. D. (Eds.): *Therapeutic Techniques: Working Models for the Helping Professional.* Fullerton, California Personnel and Guidance Association, pp. 185-203, 1973.

Varenhorst, B. B.: Training adolescents as peer counselors. *Personnel and Guidance Journal,* 53(4):271-275, 1974.

Varenhorst, B.: Peer counseling: a guidance program and a behavioral intervention. In Krumboltz, J. D., and Thoresen, C. E. (Eds.): *Counseling Methods.* New York, HR&W, 1976 (in press).

Vriend, J., and Dyer, W.: A case for a technology of group counseling and delineation of major group categories. In Vriend, J., and Dyer, W. (Eds.): *Counseling Effectively in Groups.* Englewood Cliffs, Ed Technology, pp. 41-55, 1973a.

Vriend, J., and Dyer, W.: Introduction: effectiveness is the name and technology the game. In Vriend, J., and Dyer, W. (Eds.): *Counseling Effectively in Groups.* Englewood Cliffs, Ed Technology, pp. 3-9, 1973b.

Wolfe, J.: *The Practice of Behavior Therapy.* New York, Pergamon, 1969.

VIII

ADLERIAN GROUP COUNSELING[1]

RICHARD A. GRANUM

DISCOURAGEMENT IS RAMPANT in society today. Crime, alcoholism, and drug abuse are just a few of the problem behaviors that tell of this discouragement. Feelings of helplessness and hopelessness accompany problem behavior. People are heard to say, "I just don't understand how it could happen." Parents, teachers, and school administrators are bewildered by Johnny who can not read, as well as by the wide variety of antisocial behavior. The concerned parent, teacher, and counselor express their ignorance and confusion: "We just don't know what to do; we've tried everything."

Adler's contributions to counseling, as much philosophical as psychological, are expressed in a series of statements about the nature of the human being, statements based upon observation and clinical experience. Adler (1870-1937) was a medical doctor, a contemporary of Freud (1856-1939), and a member of the Vienna Psycho-Analytical Society at Freud's invitation. Philosophical differences, however, carried these two men in different directions. Adler viewed the nature of man in terms of social interest, love, and usefulness, while Freud's views were more deterministic. Adler believed that behavior was socially motivated, whereas Freud theorized a drive psychology largely biological in origin. It is not the purpose of this chapter to contrast the differences between Freud and Adler, but rather to describe Adler's contribution to group procedures for school counselors.

Adler's contributions to modern psychology are known by various titles: individual, teleoanalytic, neo-Freudian, humanistic, or phenomenologic. Two of Adler's contributions were a system for understanding behavior and a model for intervention using

1. The author wishes to acknowledge and express appreciation for the assistance of Jo Anne Lowe in the preparation of this chapter.

group procedures. As early as 1919, Adler was operating a child guidance clinic which employed a group approach in learning to understand children's behavior. As a pioneer and foundation unit of modern psychology, Adlerian psychology is a dynamic theory that continues to change, grow, and is subject to personal interpretation. Adler's students, particularly Rudolph Dreikurs, have perpetuated and extended the theory to include concepts such as mistaken goal analysis. Adlerian psychology is therefore defined so as to include extensions by current practitioners. The reader may observe certain similarities between Adlerian psychology and the views of Ellis, Gordon, Glasser, Harris, and some behaviorists.

The delivery system for Adlerian counseling uses an educational model because behavior, appropriate and inappropriate, is learned and is directed at achieving a future goal. Furthermore, behavior is based on individual perceptions of responses to stimuli in an environmental setting. The counselor's role is largely one of teaching, because significant persons who are part of the environment, such as parents, teachers, and peers, learn to recognize goals of behavior and to respond in ways that build confidence, responsibility, independence, cooperation, and other socially useful behaviors. The counselor teaches rather than treats, working with the environment as well as the individual, and he fosters independence rather than dependence.

DEFINITION OF GROUP COUNSELING

Group counseling is learning that occurs in a setting where information can be shared, experiences structured, ideas expressed, and feedback received from other people. The counseling group may consist of students, teachers, or parents who are experiencing problem behavior; such counselees are not "sick" or in need of personality change. These group counselees simply need to (1) learn principles that aid in systematically understanding the goals of behaviors, (2) develop a repertoire of alternate responses, and (3) participate in a setting that encourages the practice of the learned principles.

Children or adolescents who are discouraged may seek to be

significant by academic failure, fighting, or behaving in other ways that frustrate adults. These children can learn that their perceptions are mistaken and that goals can be achieved through more useful means. This learning can best occur in a setting that allows the child to experience encouragement, success, and consequences.

Counselors in the school setting may work with natural groups or groups structured for specific learning tasks. Natural groups exist for a purpose apart from counseling and might include the family, peer groups, or play groups. Groups structured for specific learning have been formed as a part of the learning process and include classrooms, teams, and guidance groups. Parent study groups or teacher study groups that utilize materials based upon Adlerian principles are examples of structured groups.

How are Adlerian counseling groups different from classroom groups or from other counseling groups? The role of the leader is different and assumptions about the members are different, as well as the group process and content. The answers can be made more explicit by examining the theoretical foundation of Adlerian psychology.

BASIC ASSUMPTIONS OF ADLERIAN PSYCHOLOGY

The discouragement felt by many teachers and counselors grows from ignorance. Experts seldom explain problem behavior in terms that are understandable or terms that suggest appropriate intervention strategies. Counselor training programs have frequently failed to provide systematic theories with which counselors may understand problem behavior. The following basic assumptions of Adlerian psychology have been identified (Dinkmeyer, 1968; Dinkmeyer and McKay, 1973) and are the building blocks of Adlerian group procedures.

1. *Equality Is Basic to Effective Interpersonal Relations:* The generation gap, problems in the family, in love, and between nations, and all damaged relationships grow out of inequality in interpersonal relationships. The improvement of interpersonal relations requires the establishment of equality and mutual respect. In a democratic society, positions of superiority-inferi-

ority, master-servant, need to be replaced with a valuing of the unique contribution of each individual. An atmosphere of equality does not mean sameness, for the adult is different from the child; equality, however, does imply a climate of respecting the worth of each individual.

2. *Social Interest:* Men and women are social beings. The child's first cry and reaching out toward other beings is a signal of the desire to communicate and to be accepted. Social interest is an innate quality subject to conditions of development. The person who has developed social interest places the needs of the situation ahead of personal demands and is capable of cooperating, trusting, and seeking ways to be useful. The person who lacks confidence and lacks interest in others is experiencing an arrest in the development of social interest.

3. *Striving for Superiority:* All persons strive to be superior or significant. Everybody seeks to be recognized and to be respected for achieving something. Competition is a basic demonstration of this striving for superiority. Within the family unit children often seek opposite areas in which to excel. If the oldest child is serious, responsible, and gets good grades, many times the second child will be social, carefree, and athletic. All children find unique ways of being significant, and for some children, mischief appears to be the best or only way to be significant.

4. *Problem Behavior is a Symptom of Discouragement:* All problem behavior can be interpreted in terms of discouragement. Children who feel that they cannot compete or who cannot be significant in socially useful ways may seek to be significant in useless ways. Criminal acts, alcoholism, drug abuse, temper tantrums, bed wetting, and underachievement are all symptomatic of a discouraged individual.

5. *Behavior Is Perceptual, Patterned, and Learned:* The individual attaches a subjective, personalized, and creative meaning to each interpersonal transaction. The individual reacts selectively to stimuli received from the environment and develops a repertoire of response patterns based upon previous experiences. Diagramatically, behavior is S-O-R.

6. *Mistaken Goals:* All problem behavior could be viewed as

being directed toward one of four *mistaken* goals: attention, power, revenge, or a display of inadequacy. These goals are termed mistaken because they are based on an error or unique interpretation that the individual makes about the environment. The feelings and responses of significant adults are clues in determining the mistaken goals of behavior.

Attention is the first mistaken goal. Most problem behavior of children fits this category. The child's perception is that he or she only counts if he/she is being noticed. Such behavior may be socially acceptable, such as always being right, being first, being overly neat or overly polite. Attention-getting behavior may also be unacceptable; for example, being late, noisy, or provoking. When attention is the goal, the parent or teacher involved will feel annoyed. When attention is paid, the behavior will subside, at least momentarily. The child's motivation is that it is better to be punished than ignored.

Power is the second mistaken goal. When involved in a power struggle, the child's perception is that he or she is only significant when he or she is the boss or is in control. The child in effect says, "You can't make me," and the child is usually right. Adults seldom win power struggles with children because adults must fight by rules, whereas children have not acquired social norms for fighting. The activity may be the same in a power struggle as when seeking attention (being late, fighting, or refusing to do homework). The clue to the goal is the significant adult's feeling of anger. Intervention results in an escalation of the behavior.

Revenge is the third level of mistaken goal when a child perceives that he/she has been "wronged" and, therefore, has a right to get even. Revenge behavior is active and destructive. A clue to the goal is the significant other's feeling of being hurt. Interventions call for providing encouragement and maintaining order. Occasionally, doing the unexpected may also be corrective because a unique environment is created.

Display of inadequacy, the fourth mistaken goal, represents the ultimate discouragement because the child expects only failure and has learned to avoid failure by nonparticipation. Displays of inadequacy are characterized by passive destructive behaviors, such as the child who cannot read, who just sits and says and does nothing. At this level the significant other's feeling is that of helplessness. Encouragement is the only effective intervention.

APPLICATIONS OF ADLERIAN COUNSELING IN SCHOOL

Adlerian group counseling focuses upon interpersonal relations rather than intrapersonal relations, that is, what goes on between people rather than inside the person. Problems in interpersonal relations result, not because one or both parties to the relationship are ill and in need of treatment, but rather because one or both parties lack information or have attached erroneous meaning to the information possessed. Change occurs through a learning process when the counselees acquire new information, new insight, or attach new meaning to information at hand. Because the Adlerian approach to behavior change is a learning process, it is extremely appropriate for the educational setting. Four variations of the Adlerian group counseling model in a school setting will be described briefly and then illustrated with a counseling script. These four are the parent study group, the teacher study group, the parent/teacher counseling center, and the classroom discussion group. All four focus upon learning as the primary means of behavior change.

Parent Study Group

Parent study groups consist of persons who share common concerns about rearing their children. Typically they seek a better way of dealing with the normal problems of rearing children. Occasionally, they seek help in solving problems that are seriously disruptive of the family atmosphere. Regardless of the severity or degree of concern, all members seek to learn a systematic approach to democratic child rearing. Leaders of a parent study group do not function as experts in psychology or child rearing; instead, their primary role is to facilitate a learning climate. Books typical of those used for such study groups include *Children the Challenge* (Dreikurs, 1964), *Raising a Responsible Child* (Dinkmeyer and McKay, 1973), *Parent Effectiveness*

Training (Gordon, 1970), or *Between Parent and Child* (Ginnott, 1969). Group membership is achieved through the expression of a commitment to participate. Norms are established insofar as each member secures a book, identifies specific behaviors of concern, reads, contributes to the discussion, and carries out "homework assignments" between sessions. Membership is open during the initial session but then becomes closed, not to approved observers but to outside participants. Each group goes through an organizational stage and period of getting acquainted. Members may initially be reluctant to discuss problems that involve personal embarrassment such as temper tantrums, bed wetting, and drug abuse. As the group matures, members self-disclose and discover that other persons have similar concerns and that their feelings are treated with respect. The last session is frequently characterized by separation anxiety that takes the form of wanting to continue as a group. Some members join advanced groups or become group leaders in training.

Parent education groups have a syllabus or topic outline that includes specific reading assignments for each session, issues to be discussed during the session, and assignments to be implemented between sessions (Soltz, 1970).

Protocol From a Typical Parent Study Group

Leader: Are you ready to begin? (waits for members' attention) We covered a lot of material in our second session last week. I'm wondering what you learned?

Alice: I was surprised at how much alike our youngest children seem to be. The family constellation has really helped me.

Barbara: It's a lot easier to talk about encouragement than it is to do it.

Christene: I can't tell the difference between punishment and consequences.

Edward: I think they are the same. If Bobby picks on Ricky he's going to get sent to his room. That's the consequence of starting a fight.

Dorothy: I liked the mistaken goals idea, but I find so many things can be more than one goal—like fighting. I think it's usually 'attention' but sometimes I get really angry.

Alice: I know it; my middle child is always getting into a fight with the youngest or the oldest and then he comes to me and wants me to settle it.

Leader: You have picked out some of the important ideas from our first two sessions. It sounds like many of you are on the right track. Perhaps we can help one another concerning points of confusion. The differences between punishment and consequences is one point that a couple of you seem to be wrestling with. What is the difference?

Barbara: Well, one difference is that the situation determines the punishment.

Dorothy: With consequences we respect the child's right to make choices. With punishment we are insisting upon our right to dominate.

Edward: Yes, but like the example in the book, about the lost baseball glove. I just can't afford to keep buying him a new one and he needs it if he's going to play.

Leader: So what do you do?

Edward: Well, I check to see that he has everything before we leave, and if he forgets I talk to him about it. Or if I'm not there and he came home without the glove, I have to go back and get it and he has to do some extra work.

Leader: The book says that too much talk turns a consequence into a punishment.

Dorothy: It also seems that we deny our children the opportunity to be responsible for their own behavior. Children need to learn to care for their own things. Mother can't always look after everything.

Leader: That's a very good point. Your assignment was "action, not words." You were supposed to act rather than talk.

Barbara: I don't know what you mean, at home or in the group?

Leader: No, no, at home. I want you to talk here.

Edward: Can I give you a bad example?

Leader: Well, if we don't have a good example, we'll take a bad one.

Edward: Well, I had an experience last evening. Catherine was out and the two girls began fighting. Like the book says, I ignored it. Everything went along real well, each one was slapping the other one, racing through the house, and I sat very calmly. When they got louder, I just turned the stereo louder. Finally one of them slammed the door on the other one's head and left a real nice knot on her.

Members: (laughter)

Edward: I very quietly got up adjusted the stereo, got their pajamas on and sent them to bed. I had explained ahead of time that they would get sent to bed if they could not get along together.

Members: Why was that bad? That sounds good, that sounds like it worked perfectly.

Edward: Because when I said it was time for bed it was very obvious that they had better go.

Alice: That was better than nagging at them all evening.

Edward: I explained to them that I had sat there through their fights and that I was not going to take care of it until the time came when one really hurt the other one and that I wasn't going to permit that, so they were going to have to suffer the consequences, both of them were going to bed.

Leader: And what else did you do? Did you—

Edward: That was it!

Leader: You didn't make a fuss over the wounded head, or indicate how sorry you were.

Edward: Oh no, that was it, I spanked her, too.

Members: (Much laughter)

Dorothy: A' ha, you weren't going to tell us that.

Edward: I have a belt about this wide. They had their night gowns on, I tapped each one just about like this. It didn't even leave a red mark. It was just enough to let them know they had been spanked. I waited about fifteen minutes and then went in and kissed them both good night.

Leader: Let's talk about what you did do that was really good.

Alice: You didn't raise your voice.

Barbara: You didn't nag.

Christene: You gave them a certain leeway. You let them go until it reached a point where it was intolerable.

Dorothy: They really made the decision because they knew that when they get into a fight they were going to bed.

Alice: Maybe they were just testing you.

Edward: Ha Ha! You could say that (laughingly).

Leader: One of the chapters, I believe nineteen, talks about "don't shoo flies." How could you have done this?

Dorothy: (Mimicking) All right girls, you're getting too noisy. If you don't quiet down you'll have to go to bed, and on, and on, and on.

Leader: Could you remove yourself, go the neighbors for a cup of coffee?

Dorothy: Well, I'll go along with that. Particularly when I've had a busy day, I feel infringed upon. Their noise and their blabbering infringes upon my right to watch the news. We have a big house. They can go and play somewhere else and I cannot tolerate this in and out fighting under my nose. I would not have been as patient as you.

Christene: I'm with you. I have rights, too. My question is this, will a few nights of this unholy noise eventually stop? For me I can't wait that long. I've tried it and the noise seems to get worse, and worse, and worse.

Leader: That may be a sign that your training is working. If the child's goal is power, problem behavior will escalate just before it gets better, or one child may get worse as another child gets better.

Barbara: When Robby has a friend overnight I expect Robby to let the friend know the rules of our household, but Robby doesn't assume that responsibility. He says, "Well you didn't tell me that we couldn't do that." I know I talk too much but I have to tell him each time.

Catherine: I just tell them, "You know that, I don't have to tell you."

Barbara: But Robby just turns me off when I start doing that.

Leader: O.K., let's look at this for a minute. Who is responsible for reviewing the house rules? How can you turn this around so that you don't have to do the talking? If your kids want company they can review the rules for you. Kids react real well to the word responsibility. "Whose responsibility is it to review the house rules? Tell me what house rules we will be concerned with." Get them to tell you. And if they leave one out say, "I think there's one you have forgotten." That's what "time for training" is all about.

Edward: I took Jane aside, while her company was there, and very quietly told her that there was too much noise and too much going on and that if she wanted to continue to have her friends over she was going to have to set them straight.

Dorothy: You were setting up a power play, weren't you?

Edward: That may be.

Alice: But if you do have house rules and you don't follow through with them, what then? I can't get home until 5:30 PM, and by then every house rule is broken. I hear all these good things in the neighborhood about house rules, and I try but I can't get them to work. I can't get them structured.

Barbara: Think of the natural consequences and logical consequences these other people have used.

Leader: That's why we are here, to help each other. Perhaps before we go on to the use of consequences we can summarize some of the things about time for training. When is a good time?

Catherine: Every day.

Alice: When you're in a good mood. Not when you are angry.

Barbara: At a set time.

Dorothy: When the child is feeling responsible.

Leader: Our reading for today included chapters fifteen, sixteen, and seventeen, "Avoiding Undue Attention," "Side-Stepping Power," and "Withdrawing from Conflict." How does the constant attention-seeker perceive himself?

Dorothy: He needs constant reassurance that he is important.

Barbara: The child feels she counts only when she is the center of attention.

Leader: How do you know when a situation is a power struggle?

Dorothy: By your reaction; if the child's mistaken goal is power, chances are you are feeling angry.

Cahterine: Also by watching the behavior. When you do something, the behavior will disappear temporarily if the goal is attention; it will intensify if the goal is power.

Leader: What questions do you have on the readings for today? (Allow time to formulate thoughts; several questions will always emerge.)

Leader: For next week our assignment is to read chapters fourteen, thirty-one, thirty, and thirty-nine. For homework the assignment is to withdraw from conflict. Can you all recognize a power struggle?

Members: (Affirmative responses)

Leader: And do you all know what you will do? You have expressed a lot of good ideas today and been helpful to one another. I appreciate your helpfulness and we'll see you next week.

Teacher Study Groups

Teacher study groups and parent study groups are similar both in theory and in practice. The majority of teachers who leave the profession do so not from a lack of subject matter competence but rather because of frustration in dealing with problems of classroom management. Teacher education has traditionally focused upon content, what is to be taught, while relatively little teacher training time is devoted to understanding or changing children's behavior. The teacher study groups provide a systematic way for counselors to help teachers understand student behavior and practice alternate strategies.

Teacher study groups operate on the same principles as parent study groups. Books that have been used for teacher study groups include *Maintaining Sanity in the Classroom* (Dreikurs, Grunwall, and Pepper, 1971); *Psychology in the Classroom* (Dreikurs, 1968); *Children the Challenge* (Dreikurs, 1964); and *Schools without Failure* (Glasser, 1969).

The counselor in teacher study groups is a facilitator of group discussion, not an expert in psychology or teaching. Other similarities with parent study groups exist. Both types of study programs satisfy the conditions necessary for a group: Unity of purpose exists; communication among members is established; initiation rights are held; norms for participation are established; leadership emerges; and the duration of the group is set by the number of sessions.

The dynamics of the group may be more complex than a parent group, depending upon the staffing pattern and atmosphere of the school. Teachers may feel that their professional prestige is on the line and may be reluctant to share relevant experiences. Subgroups are likely to exist, such as grade level teams, subject matter units, or teachers and teacher-aides. These groups or cliques will probably bring outside agendas to the study group. In the teacher study group, the focus is on the principles, not the problem. The problem is a way of making the principle concrete and thereby facilitating learning.

A typical session would follow a sequence of:

1. The teacher reports on between-session tasks assigned the previous week. Typical assignments include:
   a. identifying mistaken goals of classroom behavior,
   b. using natural consequences,
   c. practicing encouragement,
   d. giving responsibility,
   e. conducting a classroom council.
2. There is a discussion of key questions from the assigned reading. Examples of key questions are:
   a. What is wrong with trying to be fair? (Emphasis is on getting rather than giving.)
   b. How does one establish mutual respect in the classroom? (Equality implies equal value, not sameness.)

(One should focus on ability rather than disability.)

(One should have self-respect and not be pressed into the service of others.)

    c. How are logical consequences different from punishment? (The underlying attitude will be different.)

3. Teachers report specific incidents of recent classroom behavior that illustrate the discussion topic. This is followed by a sharing and suggestions of ways to deal with the behavior that would be consistent with the Adlerian model.
4. Leader answers specific question about the assigned readings.
5. Leader assigns readings for next session.
6. Leader assigns homework to be implemented in the classroom. (Action, not words, is emphasized.)

It is important to provide encouragement throughout the discussion group. Teachers who are encouraged will implement principles and experience success. Teachers who are discouraged will seek reasons why change is impossible. Encouragement is a companion of optimism and it is contagious. Teachers who can encourage one another can also encourage children.

The Parent/Teacher Education Center

The third application of Adlerian Group Counseling is in a parent/teacher education center. The parent/teacher education center is perhaps the oldest application of Adlerian principles, being practiced by Adler himself in Vienna as early as 1922 (Ansbacher and Ansbacher, 1973). The parent/teacher education center also emphasizes learning as a means of understanding behavior. The focus is on interpersonal behavior rather than the intrapersonal aspect of personality. Two groups may be in focus simultaneously, the family and the participating audience.

The family is the counselor's first focus. The entire family is interviewed, first the parents together, then the children, and then the entire family. Each family member plays a role in the behavior of the identified problem child. The entire family is a part of the dynamic interaction. Many of the typical interactions will be missed if the counselor works only with the problem child. The interactions and the participants' perceptions of those interactions are more important than the reality of a specific problem, such as fighting, not doing homework, or stealing.

The audience is the counselor's second concern. In keeping with the education aspect of this model, the audience is learning along with the family. Each person in the audience will identify members of their family or students in their class who are similar to members in the family being counseled. The audience at a parent/teacher education center is an open group usually consisting of teachers, teacher aides, other school personnel, parents, and college students. Typically, parents have been a part of the audience before being counseled themselves before an audience. This orients the family to the process and accomplishes a process of self-selection. Many parent/teacher education centers provide family counseling in private for those families who would not be comfortable appearing before an audience; however, such families miss the benefit of ideas and information from the audience. Family members unwilling to be observed may also be expressing a need to be perfect or an arrest in the development of social interest as they seek to get help but are unable to see their situation as being helpful to others. A sample dialogue of a family being counseled before a group of parents and teachers follows:[2]

> Counselor: We have the Wilson family with us today. We appreciate your willingness to help us learn about families and the way they operate. You are to be commended for your cooperation in coming before an audience like this. Allow me to introduce my co-counselor today. This is Joanne. And as you know the audience is made up of other parents, teachers, and university students. Are you feeling quite comfortable? Shall we begin?
>
> Mother: (Clears throat) Yes!
>
> Counselor: Will you begin by giving us the names and ages of the children? (Joanne writes on board.)
>
> Mother: There is John, eight, and Jim, seven.

---

2. Adapted from an interview conducted by O. C. Christensen and reported in Gazda (1971).

Counselor: (To the audience) Now what are some of the speculations which you might make about these children?

Audience: John is probably the good student, particularly in math
and science.

Audience: John tries to please by doing things at home, helping with
chores.

Audience: John is more responsible.

Audience: John might have been overtaken (defeated) by a more
social younger child.

Audience: Jim is probably the easy going charmer.

Audience: Jim can't do anything for himself.

Counselor: All of these are possibilities. Shall we find out who was
closest? Would you describe the children.

Dad: John is the more aggressive or outgoing, is interested and does
a lot of things well: reading, friends, athletics.

Mother: John is more competitive, wants to be right.

Dad: Yes, John is very competitive.

Counselor: Where does that leave Jim?

Dad: Jim is more of a Mama's boy.

Counselor: Easy going?

Mother: Lovable, cute, small for his age, but also demanding.

Counselor: Demanding? How do you mean? Can you give us a specific example?

Dad: I haven't really thought about it. He demands more attention.

Counselor: Does he try to please by helping?

Parents: Yes.

Counselor: (To the audience) We are probably beginning to form a
picture of opposites. What place is left for Jim? If John is star
quarterback, valedictorian, and class president, Jim can be best at
helping Mom, teasing the neighbor's dog, and falling into the pig
pen. Now which child do you suppose is of greatest concern?

Audience: Well, it could be John. If he feels that he isn't perfect or
winning, he could be quite a problem.

Audience: I think it's Jim. If all he can do is carry out the garbage
and fall into the pig pen, he would be discouraged.

Counselor: Shall we find out?

Mother: Well, really I'm concerned about Jim. John really doesn't
have any problems. Jim is hard to get started in the morning: he
procrastinates at school; the teacher can't get him to finish his
work on time; he won't cooperate with John after school; he gets
in a lot of fights with John and usually comes out crying.

Counselor: (To the group) O.K., now we are getting a clearer picture of John and Jim and particularly the contrast between them.

(To the parents) Let's take just one of these. Say the fighting. What have you tried to do about it?

Mother: Well, I've tried just about everything! This usually happens after school before I get home. John will call me and tell me that Jim is kicking and pinching him or that he spilled the coke and won't wipe it up. I've tried talking to him, having him stay in his room, going to a friend's house, getting him interested in Cub Scouts, et cetera.

Counselor: You've tried a lot of things, then, and nothing has worked for very long. You really are looking for some specific help, then?

Mother: (Nods, yes)

Counselor: Maybe it would help us to take a look at a typical day. Start at the beginning and describe the morning routine. Who is up first?

Mother: I'm up first and then John. Actually we get up at pretty much the same time. I let the dog out, get the paper, start the coffee. Then John is there getting his cereal; he eats quietly and goes to wash and gets dressed for school. About this time Jim comes out and is cheerful but gets into everything rather then tending to business. He plays with the dog, wonders what he will wear today, complains that there is no coupon in the cereal box, and generally just keeps me going with questions all morning.

Counselor: And what do you do about this procrastinating?

Mother: I get very angry. Soon I am shouting, "Hurry up! You'll be late for the bus!" And all he can say is, "I can't find my library book." To which I reply, "You should have gotten that stuff together last night!"

Counselor: And so what do you do?

Mother: I help him find his book. (laughter)

Counselor: And what is Dad doing through all this?

Dad: I stay in bed and out of the way. (laughter) In ten minutes it'll all be gone, then I can get up to peace and quiet.

Counselor: I sort of have a vision of Mom being the crossing guard at a major intersection (the kitchen) with a whistle and white gloves, making noises, giving signals, making sure everyone gets to the right spot on time, and that nobody loses their lunch ticket.

Mom: That's right.

Counselor: (To the audience) Is Jimmie's teacher here? (no response). Well, if she were we would want her perceptions of what Jim is like when he gets to school. My guess is that he would be quite different. Jim's behavior is conditioned by Mom's response. He knows he can keep Mom involved, at his service, by being pleasantly irresponsible. We would also enlist the teacher's cooperation in not bugging Mom about Jim being late or about missed library books. Those are Jim's responsibilities and he is capable of managing them.

Audience: Are you saying that Mom should just ignore Jim in the morning?

Counselor: We are a bit ahead of schedule making recommendations before seeing the children, but my hypothesis is that John and Jim are both capable and can be responsible for getting themselves off to school. I am also a bit concerned about John. John is so good at getting his own breakfast, not having to be reminded, getting his own books, et cetera. This serves to point up Jim's inadequacy. John has to be practically perfect to keep ahead of Jim.

Additional conversation brought out the mother's feelings about the fairness of her working, the after school fights, Jim's picky eating habits, and the mother's preparation of a special menu to prevent malnutrition. Bedtime presented additional confusion and guilt. The initial hypothesis is that Jim's mistaken goal is primarily attention seeking, but it could also be tending toward power, showing Mom who is boss. The interview with the children began as follows:

Counselor: Hi, fellows!

John: Hi. (Jim eyes the counselor intensely with a large grin.)

Counselor: We sure want to thank you for coming here today and helping us to learn more about families. Are you feeling comfortable? (Both smile.) What are some of the things that go on at your house that resulted in Mom's wanting to come here today?

Jim: Our fighting. John picks on me and we get into fights.

John: And he is pokey getting ready for school. He can't find his library books.

Counselor: Can you really lose your books whenever you want to? (Jim gives a big smile.)

Counselor: Why can't you find your books in the morning?

Jim: Because I'm tired.

Counselor: Maybe you are tired. That's a possibility. I have some other ideas. Would you like to know what I think? (Jim gives an affirmative smile.) Could it be that that's a way of keeping Mom busy?

Jim: No. (slight smile)

Counselor: No? Could it be, then, that taking so much time getting ready for school is a way of showing Mom who's boss?

Jim: Yes. (large smile). (Even if Jim had said, "no," the eyes would have said, "yes.")

Counselor: Do you think you can be responsible for your own books?

Jim: **Yes.**

Counselor: Do you know what is going to happen tomorrow? (Silence) I'm going to make some recommendations to your mother in a little while. One of the recommendations will be that you be responsible for getting yourself and your books to school, without Mother's help. Do you think you can handle that?

After concluding the children's interview, the parents and the children are brought together. The counselor summarizes major points of both sessions. The audience is invited to ask any questions and one or two "homework" assignments are made. In this case the homework was for Jim to be responsible for getting himself to school and for Mother to stay out of fights. In a second session, John's need to be perfect was dealt with. The learning by the audience can be illustrated by the reader's reactions to the dialogue: Did you find yourself identifying with one of the parents or children? Does the situation describe your family or someone you know?

The parent/teacher education center follows the four-stage counseling process dealt with elsewhere in the chapter. Direct questioning is avoided. A lengthy case history is not necessary to provide helpful guidance. Predictions or hypotheses are formulated on minimal cues and validated later. Parents and teachers can in this way learn to understand behavior and respond more appropriately.

Classroom Discussion Groups

The classroom discussion group is a fourth application of Adlerian Group Counseling. Society is becoming less autocratic and more egalitarian. As this change occurs, enforcement by the power of adult domination is diminished and both parents and teachers must make greater use of mutual respect, responsibility, cooperation, and shared decision making. As children reach adulthood, the influence of parents and teachers diminishes and the peer group becomes more important in shaping the child. The primary task of early childhood is finding one's place in the family. During the school years the task becomes finding one's place in the classroom and the peer groups. Teachers and counselors, like parents, lack the power to change behavior of recalcitrant or deviant children. Counselors can help teachers study the dynamics of classroom groups and utilize group process to the benefit of children. Teachers cannot control the group, but they can understand and use the group.

> The use of the group to influence the child not only constitutes an effective way to teach and exert corrective influencing, but it becomes imperative in our democratic atmosphere where the authority of the individual has been replaced by the authority of the group. The group is the reality in which the child operates. It establishes and reinforces through a collective feedback his attitudes and behavior (Dreikurs, 1959, p. 2).

Children of preschool age develop no strong group feeling, but rather conform to adult standards. The five- to eight-year-old finds it difficult to attend large group tasks, and the friendship group consists of two or three persons. Adolescents find a somewhat larger peer group which provides a dominant influence with cliques possessing higher degrees of intimacy and loyalty than family (Lindgren, 1956). A group is not a collection of individuals but has a personality of its own. With the onset of adolescence, mistaken goals and logical and natural consequences are less useful in understanding behavior, while group norms and group consequences become more useful. The educator who wishes to use group dynamics needs to develop a cooperative classroom atmosphere. The classroom atmosphere, like the family atmosphere, influences behavior.

While unsuccessful striving for superiority results in discouragement, the cohesiveness of a group facilitates the development of social interest, responsibility, cooperation, and the encouragement processes. Group norms will affect the learning of individual members; for example, a norm of cynicism will foster a prevailing negative view toward learning, while a norm of acceptance will foster cooperation and teamwork. Group membership requires communication and a shared purpose; a lack of communication or shared purpose will parallel a lack of cohesiveness.

The teacher can use the group to his/her advantage, or the group may become an obstacle. Counselors can help teachers identify subgroups within the class and interpret behavior in terms of group interaction.

To illustrate, a fifth-grade teacher has been concerned with disruptive behavior, talking out loud, fighting, and pinching. The teacher who wishes to use Adlerian concepts will share responsibility for the classroom with the students, thereby building a common ground on a shared goal.

> Teacher: What happens on the playground when one of the players on the team is out of position and not watching the ball?
> Bill: He misses a catch.
> Jill: They get a run.
> Mike: We lose the game.
> Teacher: Who is affected on the team?
> Students: Everybody.
> Teacher: The classroom is like a team. We all try to do our job. We all work together. But what happens when the group gets off task, when one student disrupts others?
> Pam: The room is noisy.
> Freda: I like it better with a lot of noise.
> Teacher: It's hard to see benefits of a quiet room and you like to be different. What happens when the room is noisy?
> Pam: We can't get our work done.
> Sherry: We can't hear announcements on the loud speaker.
> Bill: We might not hear our call to lunch.
> Jill: We don't like to miss lunch.

The discussion is carried to the point where teacher or students reach an understanding of their common ground. Teacher and students are together for several hours each day for the entire year. Everybody wants this time to be pleasant and productive. Everybody wants to be respected and helpful.

The teacher provides encouragement in the group. Verbal interactions are one way of providing encouragement. Teacher-structured success experiences are another means of providing encouragement. Children will learn more in an atmosphere that is optimistic and they will develop a great sense of self-worth and belonging in an optimistic atmosphere.

The teacher allows the students to identify logical and natural consequences that result from the class working together to achieve common goals. The teacher emphasizes equality by respecting the worth and views of each child. The teacher avoids making moral judgments and actively works at overcoming the natural tendency of the class to dichotomize in two groups, right-wrong, good-bad, correct-incorrect.

Competition is minimized because competition prevents the integration of each individual into the group. It sets one child against another rather than against a common problem, such as noise or fighting. In such an atmosphere the position of each child is insecure, because his or her position is dependent upon the performance of other individuals rather than the group. Competition emphasizes getting rather than giving. Competition is a part of society and, as such, cannot be totally overcome, but the teacher can avoid the overemphasis on competition. As an alternative to competition, cooperation is fostered through group tasks in which children share a common purpose. The teacher is a group leader. The only real question is whether the teacher will utilize democratic or autocratic means of leadership.

In addition to the developmental aspects of group work, the teacher can also use group procedures for corrective purposes. To accomplish this, the teacher must be trained to recognize mistaken goals and thus avoid unknowing reinforcement of the child's negative behavior. In classroom group discussion, children can speculate on the *purpose*, not the *cause* of problem behavior. Children can also identify ways that they can help encourage other children who exhibit problem behavior. The classroom council, like the family council, gives students a forum in which they can air grievances and, more important, it provides a setting for the development of social interest.

The teacher may initiate a problem solving discussion by telling a story parallel to the problem. (The children are capable of making fairly abstract transferences.)

Teacher: Ralph was a very small boy in the fourth grade. He was capable of doing well in school because he did so on occasion. He liked to go to school and was there on time everyday. He liked to draw pictures of airplanes and liked to do arithmetic. He did not like to read unless it was about airplanes or automobiles. Ralph's greatest problem was that he was frequently out of his seat disturbing other children. Particularly during reading, he would hit or pinch other students. This upset his teacher and some of the other students. The teacher would get angry, scold, and punish Ralph by having him write reports. When a report was assigned the teacher would send a note home to inform Ralph's parents of his added responsibility. This made mother angry and Ralph would have to stay up later to write reports. Dad would help if Ralph needed it. What do you think of Ralph?

Child: Well, he didn't do right.

Teacher: What do you mean?

Child: He shouldn't be hitting other people.

Child: He should be quiet.

Child: He shouldn't pinch other people.

Teacher: Why do you think Ralph did these things?

Child: He should stay in his seat like the other children.

Teacher: Yes, but what would be a possible reason for Ralph's hitting and pinching?

Child: He wanted to get hit.

Child: He didn't know what else to do.

Child: He couldn't do the work as well as other children.

Teacher: He wanted to be good at something.

Child: Well, he was good at something but he didn't like what they were reading.

Teacher: How do you know?

Child: Well, the story said so.

Teacher: You are a very good listener. Does this mean Ralph was bad?

Child: Well, I wouldn't like it if he pinched me.

Child: He wasn't bad, but he was bothering the group.

Teacher: What could you have done to help Ralph?

Child: I would have told him I liked him but that I didn't like for him to hit me.

Child: I would have told him to quit it.

Child: I would have tried not to listen to him.

Child: That's kind of like Freddie in our class.

Teacher: Yes, well what can we do to help Freddie?

Freddie: I'm not like that.

Child: Sometimes you are.

Teacher: Freddie is uncomfortable right now so let's talk about what
we can do to help Ralph.
Child: We could make him monitor during reading.

Even if the children had not talked about Freddie, their understanding and desire to help would have been felt. The burden of the teacher would have been shared and the children would have been included as a part of the learning climate.

In large part, the success of using group procedures in the classroom will be dependent upon the ability of the teacher to trust the involvement of the students. It is no longer a question of whether it is wise to involve students in classroom decisions, because the teacher is in no position to force the unwilling to learn. Since the adult can no longer dominate the child, the teacher can only win the cooperation of the child as an equal partner in structuring a learning climate. The teacher who wishes to win the cooperation of students begins by involving students in planning activities important to the students. How should the room be arranged? By what rules can we operate? This sets the stage for resolving problems which will inevitably occur. The teacher should ask for suggestions only when prepared to give serious consideration to the children's offering.

RESEARCH ON ADLERIAN GROUP PROCEDURES

One test of the scientific adequacy of any theory is the extent to which it stimulates research. The Adlerian position has frequently been criticized by those who are more behavioristically oriented for the lack of vigorous research generated. Adlerians have countered that the ideographic nature of the theory and the perceptual uniqueness of behavior renders inappropriate traditional research methods that attempt to classify or quantify behavior. The future-oriented, goal-directed nature of behavior makes correlation studies equally inappropriate because they frequently infer a causal relationship. Adlerians have found comfort in the thousands of case studies that support the adequacy of the theory, as well as in the effectiveness of group counseling that is based on the Adlerian theory. Case studies are reported in detail by Kransnow (1971-1972) and Dreikurs (1972b).

In spite of this rather *anti*research bias, a considerable volume of literature has been generated. Much of it is historic or descriptive in nature. Studies that have utilized research designs have focused primarily on the evaluation of effectiveness of delivery methods. Two journals are devoted exclusively to reporting the Adlerian position, *The Journal of Individual Psychology,* published since 1940, and the *Individual Psychologist,* published since 1963. *A Bibliography of Adlerian Psychology* Mosak, 1975) is an encyclopedic work that indexes over 9,000 published works related to individual psychology. The American Society of Adlerian Psychology has a standing committee on research that maintains a list of persons engaged in scientific inquiry on issues related to individual psychology.

It is not realistic to attempt to review adequately the research generated by Adler's theory. Nevertheless, current investigative efforts in the areas of personality and social interest, birth order, and counseling techniques will be summarized.

Personality and Social Interest

Is social interest as used in Adlerian writings an independent personality variable? Research studies have found a positive but low correlation among the personality variables of locus of control, social consciousness, interpersonal relations, Machiavellianism (belief in the manipulability of others), and fascism (national, racial, or genetic chauvinism) in a sample of 916 high school students. Using these variables, directional predictions were made lending support to Adlerian theory (McClay, 1972).

Two scales for the measurement of social interest are being developed. Both are still regarded as experimental. The Social Interest Index (SII) (Greever, 1972) consists of thirty-two self-report, Likert-type items covering social interest in the four life roles. Correlations of SII with selected scales of the California Psychological Inventory (CPI) are low and positive. They account for only 16 percent of variance, thus the SII and the CPI appear to be measuring two different factors. The Sulliman Scale of Social Interest (SSSI) (Sulliman, 1974) is a dichotomous scale (True-False) consisting of fifty self-report statements. The instrument consists of two subscales; (a) confidence in oneself and optimism in one's view of the world, and (b) concern for and trust in others. A split-half reliability of $r = .81$ and $r = .90$ has been established for the two scales respectively. A test-retest reliability of $r = .79$ and $r = .93$, respectively, has also been determined. Both instruments have face and construct validity.

Several studies have attempted to use group process in the development of social interest but findings have been inconclusive because of the difficulty in defining social interest as a measurable concept. The effect upon social interest of attending a community college was measured in one such study. In general, girls showed higher social interest than boys. The social interest of boys increased over one semester while girls showed no change. Social interest was found to be age related; however, it was not related to academic achievement, class rank, American College Test scores, or socioeconomic status (Greever, 1972).

In a study of performance of marginal students at a commuter college, twenty weekly sessions of Adlerian group counseling resulted in significantly higher academic achievement ($p < .05$) of well-adjusted (high interest in school) students, but produced no difference in the academic achievement of students less interested in school. The voluntary withdrawal rate and academic dismissal rate was higher among the noncounseled control groups. More credits were earned by the well-adjusted counseled groups when compared with the well-adjusted noncounseled group. Counseling did not affect the credits earned by a group of poorly adjusted students (Garni, 1972). The findings support the benefits for developmental counseling with well-adjusted, capable students, and also suggest that anxiety, deficiency, or illness are not preconditioned for counseling. Inconclusive results were obtained in another study involving twenty-three ninth-grade students who participated in a one-semester Adlerian counseling group intended to increase social interest. Weakness of the measuring instrument was cited as the probable reason for nonsignificant results (Friendland, 1972).

Social interest has been developed in a therapeutic community. Action therapy (O'Connell, 1972) draws upon the work of Adler, Lewin, and Moreno. Mental patients *learn* social interest through lectures and a problem-centered human relations laboratory called a "d" (developmental) group. Eight to twelve patients build a miniature community in which they set goals and develop procedures for living together. The hospitalized patients spend a portion of the time in group without a staff member. The resourcefulness of group members has led to increased self-esteem and social interest.

Birth Order

Building upon the concept of social interest, finding one's place or "fitting in" is a basic task of life, and fitting into the family unit is essential since it is the most basic of all units. Family constellation is a concept that incorporates ordinal position, sex, and age span of siblings. Hundreds of studies have been performed investigating the concept of birth order. Birth order and family constellation data allow helpers to formulate hypotheses or make tentative generalizations about behavior. In direct observation of three and one-half-year-old boys and girls, McGurk and Lewis (1972) observed that second-born children sought more adult help and approval, spent more time in individual activity, were more talkative, and expressed more negative affect than other children. Boys were more aggressive toward peers and adults and spent more time in individual activities. Girls sought more adult help and were more obedient. Sex-role stereotyping was observed in role playing among both sexes. None of the sex-birth order interactions were significant.

Bradley (1968), in a study of the relationship between birth order and college matriculation, found that about 35 percent of the total population are firstborn but that the rate of firstborn in a college population ranges from 50 percent to 65 percent. Firstborn individuals are better at meeting teacher expectations,

are more susceptible to social pressure, exhibit more information-seeking behavior, are more sensitive to tension-producing
situations, and are more achievement oriented.

Terman (1925) found a disproportionate number of his
1,000 high-performance children were firstborn and in 1964
Nichols (cited in Bradley, 1968) found that 66 percent of National Merit finalist were firstborn. In a study that compared
firstborn children with secondborn children, Bartelt (1973)
found that firstborn children were most self-directed, less parent
oriented, and had more younger friends; that secondborn children were more academically oriented and had more older
friends. An interaction of social class and birth order was observed among blue collar families and adding social class information to birth order improved predictions regarding discipline,
academic orientation, and independence.

The contradictory nature of these research findings gives support to the ideas that birth order, per se, is not an explanation
but only a tool in understanding; it is the child's individual interpretation or perception of place in the social order that affects behavior (Hillman, 1972). Information about birth order
can be used to understand the role participation of individuals
in guidance or counseling groups.

Techniques

Only limited efforts have been directed at researching specific
techniques using an Adlerian focus. Allred (1974) has modified
the Flanders Scale to develop an instrument that he calls an Interaction Analysis for Counselors. The experimental scale requires the user to chart the frequency with which the counselor
as facilitator gathers information or educates, interprets, seeks
alternatives/recommends, and supports. The scale may also be
used to rate the frequency of counselor obstructive behaviors,
facilitative or obstructive counselee behaviors, and miscellaneous
items including audience talk, confusion, and silence.

Personality variables appear to be associated with the effectiveness of Adlerian discussion leaders. The same study contained
evidence that high school students could be trained as counselor

helpers (McKelvie, 1972). Groups seeded with a peer helper were significantly superior to conventional counseling groups or control groups in producing behavior changes (Kern and Kirby, 1971). In the seeded groups, peer counselors were specialty trained and added to counseling groups to provide insight and reorientation. This approach also supports the desirability of modeling as an aid in changing behavior. Kradel (1973) added role playing to traditional Adlerian groups, but it did not improve the group's effectiveness. Traditional Adlerian groups and modified (role playing added) groups were both found to be effective in modifying teacher perception of problem children. Sophomores showed greater change in empathy than did juniors, who in turn changed more than seniors.

Consultation with parents is a developmental strategy that goes beyond the annual parent/teacher conference. Several studies have demonstrated that working with parents on an ongoing basis had beneficial effects on the achievement level of students (Warner, 1974).

Evaluation of Adlerian Groups

Parent study groups have been found to be effective in reducing problem behavior among children (Runyan, 1973). Taylor and Hoedt (1974) found that an indirect approach, a ten-week parent study group using *Children the Challenge,* was more effective in reducing problem behavior than more direct or eclectic group counseling with children. Study groups have been found to result in attitude changes, that is, parents becoming less controlling or restrictive in child-rearing practices (Freeman, 1972; Runyan, 1973). Combinations of student groups, family counseling, and teacher consultation resulted in changes in ratings of student behavior while placebo and no-counseling control groups resulted in no change (Platt, 1971).

Teacher study groups produce desired changes in behavior ratings of problem students (Granum, 1975; Helton, 1973; Taylor and Hoedt, 1974). Study groups (parent or teacher) are as effective but not superior to direct counseling when the desired outcome is a change in behavior, and both are more effective than no counseling at all (Marchant, 1972).

Marital adjustment can be affected by Adlerian-oriented group counseling. Cookerly (1973) studied the records of marriage counseling clients in terms of six major forms of counseling: (a) individual interview, (b) individual in groups, (c) concurrent interview, (d) concurrent group, (e) conjoint interview, and (f) conjoint group. Possible outcomes of marriage counseling were (a) divorce, poorly adjusted, (b) divorce, moderately adjusted, (c) divorce, well adjusted, (d) marriage, poorly adjusted, (e) marriage, moderately adjusted, and (f) marriage, well adjusted. He found that a combination of conjoint interviews and concurrent group counseling was most often associated with well-adjusted status while concurrent interviews and individuals in groups were least effective. Adlerian principles were also found to be useful in predicting the adjustment of family members as outcomes of counseling (Essig, 1972, Steed, 1971). Sauber (1971) identified a shared view of problem behavior as the outcome of family counseling.

Adlerian principles have also been found effective in working with student groups. The self-concept of females was improved and the frequency of both male and female behavior problems was reduced through role playing and discussions (Kradel, 1973). Group discussions have also led to a more democratic classroom atmosphere and improved student teacher interactions (Helton, 1973). Social interest level of college males was raised (Greever, Tseng, and Freidland, 1973) and the academic performance of well-adjusted college students was enhanced by group counseling (Garni, 1972). In comparing the differential effects of Adlerian group counseling, a human relation model, and a placebo of career development discussion, all three types of treatment were found to be effective (Thompson and Randolph, 1973). The Adlerian concepts have generated much research; however, each subsequent study seems to produce more questions than answers.

GOALS OF TREATMENT

Adlerian counseling is a four-stage process (Dinkmeyer, 1968):

(1) establishing a relationship,

(2) diagnosing the goals of behavior,

(3) developing insight, and

(4) reorientation or planning action.

Parent study groups, teacher study groups, or classroom groups all incorporate these stages that are a guide to more effective interpersonal relationships. The primary goal of all Adlerian counseling is to provide encouragement and this usually requires the reestablishment of mutual respect. A lack of mutual respect accompanies interpersonal relations that have deteriorated. Reestablished mutual respect brings about an improved climate in the classroom or family. The identification of mistaken goals of problem behavior is an intermediate goal that allows the counselor or parent to "know what to do." The end goals are insight and reorientation, the latter especially directed toward the development of greater social interest.

GROUP COMPOSITION

Inasmuch as learning is the primary outcome of any Adlerian group, the preferred composition is that of individuals who have similar learning goals. Parent study groups function best if composed of persons with similar age children. Teacher study groups function best if participants have children of similar grade levels. Combining persons of perceived status differences such as teachers and teacher aides has a negative effect, particularly if the leader is unaware of or fails to deal with these perceived differences. Parent and teacher study groups are open for the first one or two sessions, but the addition of new members to established groups is not recommended.

Persons who are interested in a personal growth experience should be offered a separate experience from parents or teachers seeking to understand and change problem behavior of children. The egalitarian philosophy of Adlerian psychology suggests that persons elect to participate and choose to learn rather than being selected or coerced into participation. Student groups are typically intact classroom groups. Relatively little attention is paid to balancing student groups in terms of age, sex, race, or strengths.

Setting

Learning is a socially acceptable activity and people learn from one another as well as from the leader or printed material. Family counseling groups are often conducted in an "open" setting in which an audience participates by interacting with the family or study group members. In this way, audience participants learn along with group members. Parent study groups typically meet in homes, churches, schools, libraries. Teacher study groups are usually sponsored by a school and meet in a public area such as the library, cafeteria, or auditorium.

Size

Parent study groups and teacher study groups range in size from five to twelve participants with eight being an optimum group size. Larger groups tend to make it more difficult to contribute and/or to receive help with individual concerns. Parent-teacher-education centers include all members of the family and a cocounselor in the group while the audience may vary from three or four to a full house of two hundred. Classroom councils are conducted with classroom-size groups. The counselor working with subgroups from a classroom will probably find six to eight members an optimum size.

Frequency, Length, and Duration of Group Meetings

Parent study groups usually meet once per week with sessions lasting an hour and a half extending over a ten-week cycle. Teacher study groups follow a similar pattern with sessions probably being limited to one hour. Parent-teacher education groups usually meet one day per week. The family being counseled will usually be interviewed two to five times. Rarely will a family receive as many as ten counseling sessions. Counseling is of short duration because Adlerian principles foster independence rather than dependence. The parent/teacher education center usually operates only while school is in session. Since the audience has open membership, parents may come and go as they feel the need for encouragement or additional training.

Classroom meetings are usually held on a weekly basis for twenty or thirty minutes depending upon the age of the children, throughout the school year. Student subgroups usually meet weekly for one class period and a minimum of ten sessions. Few groups have been described which meet for more than twenty sessions.

Media, Materials, and Task

Parent and teacher study groups usually utilize a text book; examples have been mentioned earlier. A *Study Group Leaders Manual* (Soltz, 1967) is a guide that suggests how to get started, outlines a series of sessions and suggests questions for discussions. Most study group leaders make extensive use of hand-out materials. *Practical Parenting* is a five-session parent education program including a cassette training tape, leader's guide, and an individual parent package (Marlin, 1974). Films illustrating Adlerian counseling are available from the American Personnel and Guidance Association or the Alfred Adler Institute of Chicago.* *Developing Understanding of Self and Others* (DUSO) (Dinkmeyer, 1970) is an example of curriculum materials packaged to aid teachers in the development of self-awareness and interpersonal skills for elementary school students.

Tasking is used in all forms of Adlerian group counseling. Specific homework assignments are made after each session, for which members are accountable. Group members report success with their homework and are encouraged by their results; learning is reinforced and other members receive hope for finding solutions to their problems.

Counselor Qualifications

The requisite counselor qualifications vary with the type of Adlerian group. Parent study groups are often led by lay persons who have participated in a study group and are enthusiastic about the principles. Teacher study groups are led by guidance supervisors, school counselors or teachers who have been trained in Adlerian concepts. Leadership training is available for study

---

* Located at 110 S. Dearborn Street, Chicago, Ill. 60603.

groups leaders through Adlerian institutes, college, or parent-teacher education centers.*

Parent-teacher education centers are staffed by professionally trained counselors, psychologists, social workers, or medical personnel. Persons functioning in such capacities should be eligible for appropriate professional licensing or certification in their state.

Classroom councils are conducted by teachers who have received training in Adlerian principles. Students groups have been conducted by teachers, counselors, and student peer counselors who have received a brief training program.

Qualifications of the leader vary with the type of group but some universals are observed. The effective study group leader maintains a position of equality with other group members. The leader is a facilitator of group discussion , and is knowledgeable of Adlerian principles. The leader functions by creating a learning climate, keeping the group on task, modeling, summarizing, clarifying, and closing. In study groups and counseling groups, perhaps the personality of the leader is the most important variable. The leader also must be confident of his or her ability to help.

Ethical Considerations

The absence of a confidential relationship is perhaps one of the principle departures of Adlerian counseling from other counseling forms. Mutual respect takes the place of confidentiality as the means of protecting the client from harm or embarrassment. If people in need of counseling are viewed as lacking information, rather than being ill, and counseling is viewed as learning rather than psychological probing, and reported problem behavior is viewed as useful to insight rather than deviant or degrading, there is then less need for confidentiality. In fact the concept of confidentiality as maintaining secrets is counter to the open, shared, common learning that occurs in an Adlerian

---

* One such community center is the Individual Psychology Association of greater Washington, D.C., Box 11, Garrett Park, Md. 20766, where directories of counseling centers and training facilities are maintained.

counseling group. True confidentiality is, of course, impossible in any group setting.

The Adlerian counselor needs to take care to inform participants of the process to be used and outcomes that can be expected. Counseling in a parent-teacher education open center may be viewed as a public performance; however, it is important to distinguish common learning from public performance. The counselor's purpose or motive is what distinguishes the two. Another safeguard of the counselee's personal privacy lies in the question technique: the counselor does not ask probing questions. The counselee is in control and freely chooses the information that is shared in the group.

Adlerian concepts have been conveyed using the public media such as radio talk shows or television programs. Persons so using the media are enjoined to provide an educational function and not provide personal counseling through the public media.

Limitations

Adlerian counseling is a cognitive process and, not unlike other group approaches, works best with the well-adjusted verbal person who is capable of learning and skilled in cognitive processes. School counselors are cautioned to function within the limits of their training, and the educational function of their institution. Adlerian psychology assumes that persons are capable, can assume responsibility for themselves, and can act in ways consistent with their thoughts. School counselors' use of Adlerian group approaches should be limited to situations that call for the development of social interest or self-concept, and the improvement of interpersonal relationships, such as the family atmosphere or classroom climate.

Training Activities

Training in Adlerian Group Counseling is available at several universities as well as Adlerian institutes. Training includes didactic instruction of the principles and experiential skill development. Counselors should be trained to utilize data from the family constellation, to recognize goals of behavior, to identify natural consequences and structure logical consequences, and to bring about insight and reorientation. Counselors need to be able to lead parent or teacher study groups, to conduct classroom activities and lead student subgroups, and to provide conjoint family counseling. Life-style analysis should be a skill of secondary and post-secondary school counselors. These skills are acquired by reading, discussion of theoretical issues, observation, and supervised practice. The counselor educators' tasks include modeling, providing encouragement, didactic instruction in basic principles, and supervision.

SUMMARY

Adlerian counseling is a developmental, preventative, and learning approach to increasing human effectiveness. Adlerian group counseling has been provided in hundreds of communities throughout the country in the form of parent and teacher study groups, family counseling, and student groups. Basic assumptions are similar in all of the settings.

(1) Behavior is goal directed.

(2) Problem behavior is an indicator of discouragement.

(3) The behavior occurs in an environment and it is essential to work with that environment to affect change.

(4) Problem behaviors are largely interpersonal rather than intrapersonal.

(5) The counselors, teachers, and parents (as well as significant others) are powerless to change the child's behavior (the only person's behavior one can change is his own).

Ways in which significant others can change their own behavior include:

(1) providing encouragement,

(2) allowing children to experience natural and logical consequences,

(3) withdrawing from conflict,

(4) maintaining order, and

(5) doing the unexpected.

The personality of the counselor is perhaps the greatest single variable in counselor competence. But this variable cannot compensate for inadequate knowledge or insufficient confidence resulting from lack of experience.

Adlerian principles are useful in facilitating the development process and therefore should be available at the elementary school level. The acquisition of social interest is a developmental process; all levels of education should work toward the continuous development of self-confidence and trust in others. Problem behaviors reflect an arrest in the development of social interest and an absence of mutual respect; therefore at times the counseling will be providing a remedial service.

Adlerian principles are consistent with accountability. Each group and each individual can identify goals or expected counseling outcomes that are behavioral in nature.

The counselor who wishes to use an Adlerian approach is encouraged to secure training. Training centers are cited in the section entitled "Counselor Qualifications."

REFERENCES

Allred, G. H.: *Allred's Interaction Analysis for Counselors*. Working paper, unpublished manuscript. Brigham Young University, 1974.

Ansbacher, L., and Ansbacher, R. R.: *Superiority and Social Interest*. New York, Viking Pr, 1973.

Bartelt, W.: Birth order of siblings and differences in orientation toward parents. *Dissertation Abstracts International, 33:*4556A, 1973.

Bradley, R. W.: Birth order and school related behavior: a heuristic review. *Psychology Bulletin, 70:*45-51, 1968.

Cookerly, J.: The outcomes of the six major forms of marriage counseling compared: a pilot study. *Journal of Marriage and the Family, 35:*608-610, 1973.

Dinkmeyer, D.: Contributions of teleonalytic theory and techniques to school counseling. *Personnel and Guidance Journal, 46:*898-202, 1968.

Dinkmeyer, D.: *Developing Understanding of Self and Others* (multimedia). Circle Pines, American Guidance Service, 1970.

Dinkmeyer, D., and McKay, G.: *Raising a Responsible Child*. New York, S&S, 1973.

Dreikurs, R.: *Group Dynamics in the Classroom*. Paper presented at the meeting of the International Congress of Applied Psychology, Rome, Italy, April, 1959.

Dreikurs, R.: *Children: the Challenge*. New York, Hawthorn, 1964.

Dreikurs, R.: *Psychology in the Classroom*. New York, Har-Row, 1968.

Driekurs, R.: Family counseling: a demonstration. *Journal of Individual Psychology, 28:*207-222, 1972a.

Dreikurs, R.: Counseling a boy: a demonstration. *Journal of Individual Psychology,* 28:223-231, 1972b.

Dreikurs, R., Grunwall, B. B., and Pepper, F. C.: *Maintaining Sanity in the Classroom: Illustrated Teaching Techniques.* New York, Har-Row, 1971.

Essig, J.: Prediction accuracy as a method of evaluating the Adlerian approach to improving family adjustment. *Dissertation Abstracts International,* 32:4945A, 1972.

Freeman, C. W.: Adlerian mother study groups and traditional mother discussion groups: a comparison of effectiveness. *Dissertation Abstracts International,* 32:4913A-4914A, 1972.

Friedland, B.: Changes in problems of ninth grade students as an outcome of Adlerian group counseling. *Dissertation Abstracts International,* 33: 1151A-1512A, 1972.

Garni, K. F.: The effect of Adlerian group counseling on the academic performance of marginal commuter college students. *Dissertation Abstracts International,* 33:1434A, 1971.

Gazda, G. M. (Ed.): *Proceedings of a Symposium on Family Counseling and Therapy.* College of Education, University of Georgia, Athens, Georgia, January, 1971.

Ginnott, H.: *Between Parent and Child.* New York, Macmillan, 1969.

Glasser, W.: *Schools Without Failure.* New York, Har-Row, 1969.

Gordon, T.: *P.E.T. Parent Effectiveness Training.* New York, Peter H. Wyden, 1970.

Granum, R.: Teacher study groups: do they make a difference? *Elementary School Guidance and Counseling,* 9:210-217, 1975.

Greever, K. B.: An Adlerian approach to measuring changes in entering freshman after one semester in an open-door community college. *Dissertation Abstracts International,* 33:1513A, 1972.

Greever, K. B., Tseng, M. S., and Friedland, B. O.: Development of social interest. *Journal of Consulting and Clinical Psychology,* 41:459-461, 1973.

Helton, M.: The use of Adlerian methods to develop democracy in the classroom. *Dissertation Abstracts International,* 34:1751A, 1973.

Hillman, W.: The family constellation: a clue to the behavior of elementary school children. *Elementary School Guidance and Counseling,* 7:20-25, 1972.

Kern, R., and Kirby, J. H.: Utilizing peer helper influence in group counseling. *Elementary School Guidance and Counseling,* 6:70-75, 1971.

Kradel, P. F.: Adlerian role playing for the reorientation and redirection of high school students with behavior problems. *Dissertation Abstracts International,* 33:6092A, 1973.

Krasnow, A.: Adlerian approaches to the problems of school maladjustment. *Academic Therapy,* 7:171-183, 1971-72.

Lindgren, H. C.: *Educational Psychology in the Classroom.* New York, Wiley, 1956.

Marchant, W. C.: Counseling and/or consultation: a test of the educational model in the elementary school. *Elementary School Guidance and Counseling, 7:*4-8, 1972.

Marlin, K.: *Practical Parenting.* Columbia, Practical Parenting Pub, 1974.

McClay, J. D.: Interrelationship of internal vs. external control, social conscience, interpersonal relationships, machiavellianism, and facist attitudes among adolescents: an Adlerian oriented investigation. *Dissertation Abstracts International, 32:*3793A, 1972.

McGurk, H., and Lewis, M.: Birth order: a phenomenon in search of explanation. *Development Psychology, 7:*366, 1972.

McKelvie, W. H.: An evaluation of a model to train high school students as leaders of Adlerian guidance groups. *Dissertation Abstracts International, 32:*3694A, 1972.

Mosak, H., and Mosak, B.: *A Bibliography of Adlerian Psychology.* Washington, D.C., Hemisphere, 1975.

O'Connell, W. E.: Adlerian action therapy techniques. *Journal of Individual Psychology, 28:*184-191, 1972.

Platt, J. M.: Efficacy of the Adlerian model in elementary school counseling. *Elementary School Guidance & Counseling, 6:*86-91, 1971.

Runyan, A.: Parent education with families of children with extreme reading problems. *Dissertation Abstracts International, 33:*5499A-5500A, 1973.

Sauber, S. R.: Multiple-family group counseling. *Personnel and Guidance Journal, 49:*459-465, 1971.

Soltz, V.: *Study Group Leaders Manual.* Chicago, Alfred Adler Institute, 1967.

Soltz, V.: *Articles of Supplementary Readings for Parents.* Chicago, Alfred Adler Institute, 1970.

Steed, S.: The influence of Adlerian counseling on family adjustment. *Dissertation Abstracts International, 31:*5782A, 1971.

Sulliman, J. R.: Personal communication, November 8, 1974.

Taylor, W. F., and Hoedt, K. C.: Classroom-related behavior problems: Counseling parents, teachers or children. *Journal of Counseling Psychology, 21:*3-8, 1974.

Terman, L. (Ed.): *Mental and Physical Traits of a Thousand Gifted Children: Genetic Studies of Genius.* Stanford, Stanford U Pr, 1925.

Thompson, W. R., and Randolph, D. L.: A comparison of the relative effectiveness of two different group approaches to counseling with sixth grade pupils. *Southern Journal of Educational Research, 7:*66-79.

Warner, R. W.: Consulting with parents. *Personnel and Guidance Journal, 53:*68-70, 1974.

IX

FAMILY GROUP CONSULTATION

Daniel W. Fullmer

F AMILY GROUP CONSULTATION is a very personal business. Next to invading the privacy of an individual, the intervention into the family is the most intimate. Some fifteen years have been committed to the development of family group consultation (FGC) as a method for group counseling. The theory of human behavior the author developed from FGC has been tested by his students and others. The Family Bond Inventory (FBI) has been developed as an instrument to measure interpersonal relationship definitions in the family. The instrument can be used to measure interpersonal relationship definitions in any human group.

A diverse range of symptoms can be treated by the FGC method. For example, the author has treated behavior disorders, family conflict, crises, drug abuse, schizophrenia, depression, and assorted self-defeating behaviors. FGC can be used conjointly with other treatment methods, individual or group. A newer adaption of FGC includes self-help models for reparenting disadvantaged students. Two programs, the Trio Project at Leeward Community College, Pearl City, Hawaii, and the College Opportunities Program at the University of Hawaii, Manoa, have produced college graduates from disadvantaged Hawaiian students who had dropped out of school at grades eight, nine, or later.

DEFINITION OF GROUP COUNSELING

The definition of group is two or more persons linked with a network of significant others. The connections between persons, whether family bonds or new acquaintances in a newly contrived and convened group, are the relationships treated in group counseling. Therefore, the definitions of group counseling, group psychotherapy and group interpersonal skill training are essentially identical except for how long the treatment continues. Group counseling treats the relationship definitions each group member promotes, so redefinition of a given relationship is a method for conflict resolution. Conflict resolution is the most frequent purpose for FGC during the first three months of treatment.

Term of Treatment	*Purpose or Goal*
One to six sessions	Interpersonal skill development
Seven to twelve sessions	Conflict resolution within the family
Three months to six months	Major redefinition of relationship within the family
Seven months to three years	Massive redefinition of relationship within the family and the public

Redefinition of a relationship is the key to behavior change in human beings within a group, and happens whenever the role expectations change. The parent-child relationship, for example, changes with the age of the child. More subtle changes happen with parent expectation at any age. If the parent expects the child to behave differently, the parent behaves differently toward the child, creating a redefinition of relationship. Everyone has experienced this phenomenon several times. When one first leaves home for an extended time and returns to a new definition of old relationships, he/she has a direct experience with the concept of redefinition, and behaves in a different way. His or her own children grow to be adults and he or she gets the parents' redefinition of relationship with each child-adult.

The FGC method is designed to achieve redefinition of relationships between significant members of a family. There is no waiting beyond the redefinition for change in behavior; it happens immediately following redefinition. How redefinition of a relationship is achieved can be seen by analysis of the process set in motion by a formula which calls for each person to speak only for himself or herself. The dynamics of the process can be understood in terms of multiple families in a semipublic (group) setting. The milieu is such that the counselors are in a unique position to take the role of therapist, counselor, consultant, teacher, or friend.

THEORETICAL FOUNDATIONS OF THE PROCESS

Fullmer (1971) published the theory of human behavior developed from FGC. The theory has received considerable research attention by his students. The most recent finding at this writing is the one by Boggs (1974), that only the friend-self relationship (F-S) holds together (unredefined) no matter where the F-S is or who else is present. The robust relationship of friend-self maintains itself in places where lover-self dissolves out of existence. Compared to a friend-self, the lover-self relationship is very fickle. Friendship is the relationship that seems unsinkable.

Earlier research reports indicate the usefulness of Fullmer's theory derived from FGC in cross-cultural studies of behavior (Cade, 1971, Engebretson, 1969). The territorial imperatives of each culture studied (Japanese, Filipino, and American) had matching patterns but significantly different distances in personal spacing. The Family Bond Inventory was developed on the foundations of the earlier studies and the reports by E. T. Hall (1959).

Bates (1974) found a connection between family background and school achievement among disadvantaged community college students. The findings support Hodgson's (1973) idea that family and schooling control much of what anyone can become in an open society. The above lend strong support to the use of group counseling, especially FGC, in the school and community.

The theoretical foundations are anthropological, psychological, and educational. The anthropological contribution is in the model for cross-cultural study. Psychological contribution comes with the several theories and systems to supply specific behavior treatment techniques within the family system. Educational foundations provide a broad base for acceptance of the method in application because FGC fits the classroom group expectations. The experience is familiar to parents and children because of the similarity with instruction in groups. There seems to be little or no aversive stimuli for participants from the FGC format, but counselors usually need careful training in the conduct of FGC. The biggest step has been the initial convening of a group of families.

The statement of the theory says human behavior comes directly from the relationship definition perceived by the individual in the immediate moment of behaving, and is further influenced by the context (social and physical) in which it occurs (Fullmer, 1971). The person behaving probably learned his or her repertory of behaviors through imprinting, imitating, and modeling by others in his or her family, peer group, and community (including mass media). Because human behavior encompasses verbal, nonverbal, and contextual symbol input, the range and complexity of specific behavior is very great (Haley, 1971). However, the patterns and sets used in a given culture, community, group, and individual will follow the established cultural parameters (roles) that set limits in communication by what constitutes a familiar form of cues. When behavior makes sense, one sees familiar cues. When behavior is missed or makes no sense, the cues are unfamiliar. To make unfamiliar cues make sense requires learning about the cue and learning how to learn the appropriate emotional response to the cue. Learning how to learn requires being in a group where someone else behaves with the appropriate emotion. Verbal instruction helps only to the extent that language symbols provide a vehicle for communicating about a change in feelings.

One important assumption in the theory of human behavior is that the behavior expressed by action, by word, or by context is the *symbolic representation of the person's perceived relationship definition with a significant other person, at the moment in time that the behavior exists.* The subjective meaning of the behavior is articulated in the message the behavior has for the significant other. The idea is that behavior is a silent language that each person in counseling learns to read. The behavior contains a personal message which is the personal definition of a relationship, and there is in this the most powerful motivation principle. Behavior is observed as a symbol system (language) for nonverbal communication of the behaver's subjective meaning. (If you are my friend I will know by your behavior. You will not need to tell me.)

Antecedents to behavior are relationship definition, the behaver's basic identity, i.e., ego, self-concept, roles, and the individual's subjective meaning based on earlier conditioning. The behavior of any person is perceived by himself/herself (the behaver's intent) and the other person. The other person's expressed perception represents feedback. If the two perceptions (behaver and observer) match, there is a high level of agreement. If not, there is a high probability for conflict. Because of the dynamic nature of the interaction in a group, especially a family, the relationship definition is rarely static.

New behavior is rarely invented by the behaver. Usually, modeling has taken place and the new behavior is a replication of the behavior observed during a prior exposure. Lack of prior exposure will be a limiting consequence for the behavior repertories of most persons.

Each person learns to meet the expectations of the family group, and subsequently any group, through a long, intimate, and confidential interpersonal relationship beginning at birth with the mother-infant relationship, a relationship which is crucial for the first six months. Ages one to four cover a period when additional sibling-friend relationships usually develop. It is in the friend-self relationship over a time span of many years that a person learns the principle of reciprocal trust in the caring for another person. Reciprocal trust develops when a friend does not miss meeting expectations without just and sufficient cause. The experience begins with one other significant person, mother, and extends to father, siblings, and others. Competent parenting in the initial years should be an adequate safeguard in child-rearing practice.

Summary of Theoretical Foundation

The theory is based on principles from anthropology, sociology, psychology, and communications. The social system in a family responds in ways similar to concepts given in general systems theory. Combined in a unique method, the group counseling concepts apply to operations with a group of families.

The theory statement given earlier is simply stated: Behavior comes out of the relationship definition perceived by the behaver in the given moment of behaving. The observed behavior is a symbolic representation of the meanings the behaver is communicating. The context in which the behavior happens will influence the relationship definition and consequently the behavior observed will communicate accordingly.

Goals of the Treatment

The goal is to cure the symptom behavior in one family member by treating the network of significant others, which is the family. The presence of other families in the treatment milieu is part of the method of treatment. Extremely disturbed families may be seen alone. Individual family members may receive counseling from other counselors on a one-to-one basis.

The goal is achieved when the symptom behavior is changed to acceptable, appropriate, and competent behavior.

Limitation of the Treatment

The idea of entering a group of families, in the case of the FGC session, is a big step for most counselors. Students in training learn by doing in a setting where they become cocounselors. Once achieved, the confidence to lead FGC can be used in many other settings.

Long-term counseling and therapy or short-term crisis intervention are the most appropriate for the FGC method. Middle-term counseling, from thirteen to thirty-seven sessions, may be contraindicated. The counselor does not know when a family group will be long-term, which is a third limitation.

Selection and Group Composition

The original group consisted of families in a psychiatric clinic. They had children referred for diagnosis and no pathology was found. The selection was on the basis that traditional counseling/therapy had nothing to treat. There were four families, and one academic year was set aside to see them once a week on Saturday mornings. After nine months, three of the families asked to continue until they felt that they had completed (on their terms) their counseling. Three years from the initial session, termination was complete. Subsequent family groups were given a contract for a specified number of sessions, usually six to eight, after which renegotiation could be carried on. The families who participated for one year or more achieved major changes in behavior.

Composition of the group consists of all the parents, children, grandparents, aunts, uncles, or close friends—anyone who has major influence in the family home is invited to attend the sessions. Usually the immediate nuclear family is isolated from influential friends and comes alone. The two or three nuclear families create a community of support and friendship during the counseling.

Two or more (up to four or five) counselors may lead the group. The responsibility for leading the group under direct supervision may be passed from one counselor to another.

Group Setting

A classroom, an office, or any comfortable place where everyone can sit (one and one-half to two hours) with ease of hearing and with a minimum of interruptions may be used for the group setting. The author has used a film studio, videotape, and audiotape, without any adverse effect on the interaction. The feedback from film and videotape can be very helpful. Audiotape is good for keeping a record if one is needed.

The school, church school, college, or private practice setting may afford a neutral setting to meet the families. The author avoids home visits or any invasion of privacy or territory in order to support the sanctuary of the family. The setting for FGC is semipublic because so many others are there. The guideline for confidentiality is to not disclose information that cannot become public knowledge.

Group Size

Three families with four people, or a dozen people, make a good group size. With two or more counselors, the numbers can climb to near-saturation at fourteen or fifteen persons. The author has worked with four families and twenty-six persons in the room. When such a large group is convened, the recommended pattern is to divide the group into a small participating group and a large audience. One can do this "demonstration counseling," but student counselors may react negatively to the idea of open sessions. However, in such a setting pathology will be brought to the surface very quickly. This author always responds by removing the stressed family immediately, without interrupting the ongoing session. He prefers to work in private with one or two families and a cocounselor.

Frequency, Length, and Duration of Group Sessions

Except under emergency or crisis conditions, the sessions are held for two hours once a week. Crisis families are seen as frequently as necessary to resolve the conflict; most families in FGC begin under the crisis conditions. The sessions will follow the pattern described below.

Initial Session

The initial session consists of supplying information and helping the family get acquainted with the physical arrangements and the psychological procedures of FGC. Factual information such as ages, interests, occupations, concerns, and other identifying items and criteria can be collected. Second, information based on an interpretation of behavior is obtained. Interpretation consists of descriptions of events concerning the interpersonal life of members within a family and the occurrence of interaction between family members and external agents, such as persons from other families, or persons in work groups or play groups.

Although the initial session is used primarily to gather information, information gathering continues in all subsequent sessions. The family members observe that the counselors make use of the information on the spot. They also learn more about themselves and about the learning process. The incidental nature of information gathering following the first session emphasizes the importance of the initial session since the emphasis or concern with the nature of the information gathered in subsequent session shifts from factual (identifying information) to the interpretative-descriptive type.

Each family member is asked to respond to a question, "What issues are before this family?" In turn, each person reports how he or she sees himself/herself in the family and explains the role that he or she plays in each significant family situation. Closure is achieved in this line of questioning when each member of the family has responded to the qualitative question, "In what way are you important to your family?"

All family members need to attend the consultation sessions if the family is to be unified. In addition to family members, all other persons significant to individual members of the family are urged to attend the FGC sessions. However, it is not uncommon for only a few members to be present in the initial session. There are limits to how much can be accomplished with only part of a family, but each counselor needs to discern for himself or herself the benefits of working with a part of a family as compared with the entire family. Counselors may consult each other as team members during each session as well as following each session.

The counselors keep a careful record of the members present from the nuclear family. They also are careful to delineate the relationships that appear between the mother and father, between mother, father, and the individual child, between and/or among siblings, and all of the possible combinations of the above. These data supply the basis for the counselors in helping them determine who controls the family. The decision is based tentatively upon the apparent kinds of involvement each individual family member demonstrates, e.g. who talks for himself or herself and who talks for the family. The interaction sequence of who talks for the individual and who talks for the family is also observed. Who talks for whom becomes a criterion for making the assessment concerning the controlling member of a family. The absent member may also control by withholding his or her participation.

In addition to the verbal exchange in FGC, other cues such as facial expression, physical activity, autistic activity, body posture, and intonation of voice are interpreted by the counselors in conjunction with the verbal exchanges. This is the reason for maintaining that each counselor must be aware of his or her own bias in relation to the interpretations he or she makes of other people's behavior. Another way of stating this is that one must learn to read behavior as a language of messages and meanings.

In summary, from the initial session, the counselors achieve an estimate of the involvement of each individual in a family group. The estimate is based upon assessment of loyalty, alliances, and interpersonal contracts maintained within the family. It is necessary to form some hypotheses concerning the kind, amount, and influence of the involvement of each individual in relation to each of the other individuals in the family group. This is a considerable task but must be performed in the initial session.

The initial session and all subsequent sessions are divided into two separate forty-five to sixty-minute meetings. During the first meeting, all parents and youngsters meet together in the same room with the counselors. It is recommended that, for the second meeting, the group be divided into two parts. This division is for the purpose of separating the children from the parents thus freeing them to discuss their concerns. The parents also experience less difficulty discussing some topics when their children are not present. The counselors note the change in behavior and in relationships among the children in the absence of parents and vice versa. Some items such as physical freedom, the ability to verbalize, and the inclination to discuss topics not discussed in the presence of parents (or children) are all examples of items to be noted by the counselors. A goal of FGC is to get parents and children to learn to discuss together any and all concerns—*without* a mediator.

Session Two

In the second session, the systematic process of discussing the basic issues and concerns of family members is begun. Counselors become mediators who listen as family members interact.

This is a complete change of behavior on the counselors' part when contrasted with the initial session.

The second session should occur no more than one week following the first session. The counselor may open the session after initial greetings with, "How has it been going?" A brief lead and a general question allows family members to determine the topic for discussion. The initial response will be closely related to social protocol and may go something like this, "Well, we went over to see Aunt Mary last night." The counselor then leads into more productive material including interpretation of behavior which occurred while the family was visiting Aunt Mary. What sorts of things transpired between them and among family members, and how each felt about the experience, constitute a major focus of the second session.

The special significance of a life event on the part of each individual member of a family can be determined if the counselors will carefully check the following events including the elements of before and after. What happened just before the event occurred? What was the contribution made by each person in the event? Next, the counselors investigate what happened while the event was taking place. They ask each person, beginning with the one relating the story, the following questions: "What happened? What did you do? What did each person do during the event?" Finally, the counselors gather information on behavior following the event. They ask, "What happened? How did it go? Who did what? What did you do? What did each person do? What happened as a consequence of the event?"

Out of this material, the counselors begin to get a pattern of loyalties, alliances, and contracts existing within the family and with members significant to the family. The counselors continue to check out with each member of the family what the relationship patterns really are on the dimensions of loyalties, alliances, and personal contracts. The dialogue in the second session is such that counselors participate only in terms of checking out what is being said to be sure to sift out the relevant meaning concerning certain patterns of behavior. These behavioral patterns are determined from material put together in answering these questions: What goes on in this family? What is it like to be a member of this family? How would one feel if he or she were a member of this family? What would life be like? What meanings would one have in this relationship setting?

A further example of the kind of relationships counselors study is exemplified in the mother-son relationship. A mother may be observed as trying to meet her son on his terms and asking the son for his loyalty in the form of a symbiotic alliance. To further check this hunch, the counselors listen closely for any evidence that would indicate the mother had disqualified herself as his mother in the eyes of this son when she attempted such a bargain.

The counselors also carefully explore the possibility that the mother knows the nature of her relationship with her son. In one such case, in response to a counselor's query, "What would you do?" the mother pleaded "Please, tell me what I should do." *The counselor should always avoid a direct response to such questions for information and description.* The real purpose of the query has been served if the mother does not countermand the counselor's estimate of the nature of the relationship.

Validation of the suspected mother-son relationship can be established based on information obtained in answer to the following queries: Does the son actually defer to this relationship? How does the son utilize the power he has over his mother? Does the mother receive a pay-off from the relationship that she is reluctant to exchange or give up in response to some alternative plan that might be evolved in the counseling relationship?

A basic principle that is adhered to in all family counseling is this: First and foremost in all behavior, and therefore in all counseling, counselors must be extremely sensitive to the need for allowing each person the privilege as well as the responsibility for owning his or her own behavior. To have answered the mother's question would be tantamount to sharing ownership of her behavior. To respond to her behavior with the questions, "Who holds the title to your behavior?" and, "Whose behavior do you hold title to?" could focus attention upon the basic criterion, "Who owns the behavior?" *Responsibility must be left with the owner of the behavior.* Accountability must be left with the significant group—the family.

Rather than answering the mother's question, the counselors might proceed by asking her to talk about the alternatives available to her. They might ask her, "What other possible ways of behaving have you thought about?"; or "How do you think a mother should act?" If the mother were unable to respond to the counselors' queries, the group is then utilized and questions are directed to them for discussion. In this way, the mother listens to other persons making statements about what they think is possible, and thus they share with the mother ideas from other points of view which otherwise might be unavailable to her. This is the process of consultation. A person has established access to others. The person is able to select and use what he or she wishes.

The second session, as are subsequent sessions, is used to give the members of a family extensive practice in reporting the behavior of themselves and others in the life events of the family. (It has been found that learning to tell one's story is a significant skill.)

Session Three

During the first two sessions, the counselors have accepted second-hand reporting of events in the lives of the members of the family. At the beginning of the third session, it is essential that each individual utilize the pronoun "I," rather than he, she, or they, as an event is related or as the story is told. This effort allows for the principle that each person must become owner of his or her own behavior, the only behavior over which he or she has any direct control. Each one must be permitted to speak for himself or herself.

By using the pronoun "I," the focus of the report is kept upon the individual recounting the event. The counselors must be alert to discourage parents or siblings from correcting one another and adjusting the story that an individual wants to tell. With the focus on the person who is recounting the life event, that person is encouraged to assume title to his or her perceptions of events; the use of the first person singular is a constant here-and-now reminder. Descriptions of the identical life events by each member of the family permit the counselors to formulate hypotheses concerning the patterns of behavior within a given family.

As one family relates its story, other families listen. Each individual is given a way of validating his perception of a life event by listening to the varying reports from other persons concerning a similar event. Through a series of meetings, individuals within the different families acquire experience together. The experiences that they have together become another source of confirmation in the continuing trek toward a mutual concept of behavior validation. The perceptual content of the reports and the individual's verbal exposé of his or her experience allows for this kind of multiple level dialogue within FGC. It is one of the unique methods of modifying behavior. (The process of behavior validation is the method used to teach persons how to use help. How to get help from other persons is the second phase of treatment.)

During the third session, each individual within each family should begin a kind of evaluation of his or her own behavior. By the third session, there are multiple opportunities for an individual to express an awareness that other families also experience difficulties and problems and that the kind of problem he or she experiences is not necessarily unique to him/her. By the end of the third session, families are expected to have established a firm commitment to the idea of consultation as a method of learning and one which holds possibilities for the family as a group as well as for the individual members. They become aware that more work in FGC will need to be done in learning and perfecting the methods of feedback and perceptual modification as well as learning to tell the story of the family. Learning to tell the story becomes a central issue by the beginning of the fourth session.

Session Four

The most obvious behavior which demonstrates commitment to FGC is regular attendance. Due consideration must be given to members absent for legitimate reasons; however, it is generally understood that the persistently absent member of a family is usually closely connected to the basic problem under discussion. The counselors must assume the responsibility for exposing covert concerns, and this includes confronting directly any member of any family with his or her poor attendance record. These types of questions may be put directly to him or her: "Why do you come here? What is the purpose in your coming? What purposes are served by your coming? For whom do you come?" The answers to any one of these questions may provide some clarification of each family member's status of attendance.

Further evidence of commitment can be gained from the extent of active participation in the process of family consultation. If someone has maintained a position of listener without any apparent pathology or any apparent resistance, the counselors should reevaluate the nature of the member's condition for participation. They can do this by checking the adequacy of descriptions offered by individual family members and the estimates obtained from counselors' observations over the first three sessions.

The counselors then reflect to the family members any consistency or discrepancy they pick up so that it may be clarified by some kind of rebuttal from the member in question. This is handled by simply making the query, "I see you behaving this way; I wonder if that is the way anyone else sees you?" Also valid is the question, "How do you see your behavior?" The feedback that the counselors give to the participant forms the basis for another kind of dialogue that goes on in family consultation. The member of a family is free to agree, disagree, or clarify the perceptions of the counselors. At times when the counselor "owns his or her statement," the member of a family is helped to "assume title to his or her statement."

During the fourth session, individual members also are encouraged to focus upon themselves in relation to other members. This activity is the most complex expected in family consultation. The individual must state his or her concept, clarify the relationship between his or her input and the other person's input, and assess the output on the basis of a set of values and a way of valuing (a way of thinking). This complex kind of interaction is particularly difficult when the other persons concerned are present and are able to check the validity of the story. The highest level achieved in family consultation on this dimension is that point in time when the individual can accurately assess his or her input and the input of others, analyze the relative meaning for each person involved, and confront himself or herself with discrepancies in his or her own behavior. The person who achieves this level is considered able to learn by his or her own efforts. He or she has a basis for knowing what it is he or she knows. The confirmation and validation, as always, must come from others.

The lack of commitment to the FGC process may be characterized by individual members who tend to wander from one topic to another without focusing for any extended period of time or any depth on a given issue. The wandering should become the issue so far as counselors are concerned, and the member should be confronted with the question focusing upon this observation. The nature of the question might be in the form of a statement of the observations, such as, "We don't seem to be able to focus on any one subject today; I wonder what is happening." The counselor's interjection of this observation allows for some further assessment of the commitment from individual members within the families. By the end of session four, each person should have the process of consultation learned and operating—namely, an internal reference to self in relations with others, rather than external problems about self and others.

Session Five

By the time the fifth session is underway, the members of the family groups will be able to use some of the counseling skills they have learned in Family Group Consultation. The idea of owning the perceptions of behavior through the use of first person singular, "I," helps to establish the possibility that individuals will have learned to focus upon the outcomes resulting from their relationships with other people. Focusing upon these consequences with due regard for the feedback from other persons constitutes the significant force operating in a learning-how-to-learn situation. Making self-conscious the process of learning concerning the informal culture, as described by Hall (1959), constitutes a major step in the direction of establishing successful conditions in family consultation.

A principle, which sometimes begins operating as early as session four, is concerned with meaningful communication. It is exemplified by the stated principle: "I cannot understand the communications of another person until I understand his meanings." The essential aspect of this concept relates to what happens without it. If the counselors interpret the meaning of a life event of another person in the terms of the counselors' own perceptions, values, and meanings, it will be at variance with the meanings experienced by the other person.

The concept of communication between the sender and the receiver of messages constitutes the major emphasis in the evaluation and feedback system utilized in family consultation. The attempts at clarification of meaning between the signal sender and the receiver continue as a check and balance system throughout all sessions of family consultation. Some attempts to clarify are, "What did you say? What did it mean to you? What did it mean to the other person? How does the other person respond to these meanings? Does he or she agree or does he or she contest the interpretation given by the other person?"

Specific life events, such as incidents happening within the group of families during consultation, serve as the proving ground for the validation of accurate communication. Because counselors and family members experience the incidents together, their consensual validation provides the beginning for an accurate assessment of perception and meaning. The process of clarification of this meaning is basic to the communication system in FGC. Family members learn how to do this without the mediation of the counselors. The behavior transfer of this kind of interaction becomes paramount to the success of family consultation.

Family Group Consultation is not complete until the family members can actually interact with one another apart from the counselors. This means that an individual within a family has learned to give feedback to each person in the family setting and also to evaluate and validate behavior and meaning of each person in the family setting. Once this has happened to the satisfaction of the significant other persons in the family, it is a signal to terminate family consultation.

Individuals will have been asked to look at their own behavior and then to look at behavior of others in the situation in response to their signals and their output. Sessions should continue for six to twelve meetings following the procedure outlined above. If after twelve meetings, people are not ready to terminate, they should be encouraged to take a furlough from family consultation. In the school setting, it is not desirable to extend sessions indefinitely. Because of limited time and the press of other business, it is essential to utilize the concept of a terminal group, six weeks or eight weeks is enough to commit to one group of families. In order to hold to this formula, the counselors should contract with the parent groups to meet with them regularly for five, six, seven, or even eight sessions, after which there will be a termination of the group. Contracting also is suggested as an antecedent condition to consultation in order to avoid the open-ended continuation of a desirable relationship.

Further Sessions

The sessions from the fifth to the terminal session constitute essentially the same procedure. In these sessions, the identification, description, and clarification of problems confronting the individual families continue as a central theme. The principle that all families encounter problems at all times is assumed in FGC. The concern is whether the problem confronted by the family actually handicaps the family in its operation in other areas. The healthy family has been described as one which can function in all other areas even though the members have a drastic conflict occurring in a specific area. By contrast, the unhealthy family or sick family is incapacitated in all areas until the conflict in a single area has been removed.

In terms of a dynamic society, such as the American western culture with its urban industrial complex, the possibilities for producing persons who are capable of productive behavior are enhanced by the healthy family. The postindustrial society is an assumption with some merit in terms of our educational system. Productivity is a goal. Productivity is defined as any and all behavior enhancing to self and/or others. Idea production is closely associated with the goals of education. The healthy individual can think and act.

A focus upon possible alternative ways of behaving is central in the procedures and the processes of family consultation. The sources of these alternatives range from individual member to members of other families and counselors. Individuals and families are encouraged to practice, on a tryout or experimental basis, new alternatives, i.e., new to their setting. They are then asked to report back to the group what happened. Again, the "event analysis" procedure—what happened before, during, and following, and who did what, when, and to whom—is used. The final evaluation questions are always, "How did it turn out? What will you modify next time?"

The group is helped to learn how to summarize what has been going on, how it has been proceeding. The family in this way learns to use the summary as a way of evaluating progress and a way of establishing the criteria for planning the next steps in their procedures to learn more.

The final session is concluded with the recommendation that the family seek further discussion either by phone or in person if they perceive that the situation requires it. Certain key questions are included as a method of helping to keep a communication process open and operating in the family. Before termination, it is established whether or not the family is practicing talking things over at home within the family in ways similar to those used in family consultation. They are asked whether they can use similar tactics outside their family in resolving conflicts and differences and gaining information and validation for their behavior in other groups. Each family is in consultation with every other family. As a result of this, each family is asked to suggest things to other families in circumstances similar to their own. The counselors are always concerned with the strategies that each family has learned to employ in order to maintain its more healthy functioning relationships (Watzlawick, Beavin, and Jackson, 1967).

MEDIA EMPLOYED IN FAMILY GROUP CONSULTATION

Film making, videotaping, and magnetic sound taping have all been used in FGC. Initially, the use of magnetic tape gave counselors a record and a system for selected feedback to the participating families. A family can gain significant self-awareness by hearing itself interact. Robert Burns' principle, "to see ourselves as others see us," helps to orient a family to the image it gives to others. Listening to reruns of taped sessions can be lengthy and labored unless the tape is carefully edited to reveal through brief clips the significant disclosure pattern.

Film is the least useful because it is expensive in time, material, and manpower. Film clips are useful as a visual record of behavior change in one or more persons in the family. Filmmaking introduces some very rigid formats because of lighting, camera angles, and equipment bulk—it is not recommended in FGC.

Videotaping is extremely useful and much less cumbersome. The usual stimulus has some very useful impact on family members. However, caution is advised to prevent a parent or sibling from harsh and intimidating criticism of how some one family member appears on the video screen. Video clips can be edited and held for periods of time to show changes in behavior as an evaluation process. The evaluation process can become very supportive and confirming for family members.

Over the years, the author and his colleagues have experimented with other materials and media. The use of food in a family group can be the medium for learning. One example is the story of a fourteen-year-old boy who was given the chore to prepare dinner for his family each evening. Many complaints came to FGC sessions from his efforts. Finally, one counselor from New York City who had been a caterer suggested preparing a meal for the group. The facilities included a kitchen, and a date was set. The discoveries were legion. The boy did not know how to peel a potato. He knew next to nothing about food preparation because he had received no instruction. The use of food to help families relate in FGC who come from different ethnic, racial, cultural, and social classes has been very useful. The food vehicle serves as a communion or common uniting force in cross-cultural counseling.

Music and dance are used to share with others a unique cultural heritage. A native American, Samoan, Hawaiian, Filipino, Japanese, Chinese, Korean, each can share these for purposes of pride in origin and as a celebration of talent. Hawaii's Community College counselors use music, dance, and art as vehicles in their FGC programs.

COUNSELOR QUALIFICATIONS FOR FAMILY GROUP CONSULTATION

The sheer power of natural groups like a family, even disorganized families, makes FGC a group procedure with many pitfalls for the neophyte counselor. It is not a diagnostic and clinical method for the school counselor, but it is a treatment-learning method. Clinical skills are useful in FGC, but it requires approximately two years for otherwise fully qualified school counselors to learn these skills from an expert under usual FGC conditions. The chief limitation, then, of this treatment-learning method, is reflected in the counselors' lack of clinical expertise in working with small groups and the length of time through tutorial methods that it takes counselors to become educated in the method.

ETHICAL CONSIDERATIONS IN FAMILY GROUP CONSULTATION

Group counseling shares a major concern for ethical practice. The professional associations only recently have shown interest. The American Personnel and Guidance Association formed the new division for Group Counseling (Association for Specialists in Group Work). A new journal and other publications should help counselors and educators keep abreast of the ethical issues in the field. Students of group counseling should also read the 1973 American Psychological Association publication on ethical considerations for human subjects.

Family Group Consultation has some unique ethical concerns because of the sanctions surrounding the family in American society. In addition, FGC enjoys all the usual ethical considerations for any other method of group counseling.

1. Counselors engaged in FGC must not cause the father, mother, or any other significant role incumbent to be downgraded, intimidated, or otherwise blamed for the family's plight or condition. The guideline this author uses is: Do not take away anything from the family that cannot be replaced immediately. Support the father and mother because the group is an ongoing, dynamic institution with a history and a future. The counselors practicing FGC will be well advised to remember their task is to help the family see its pattern of behavior, not to decide for the family what their behavior should be.

2. The counselors must not take sides. The family is very powerful and seductive in consultation sessions. Constant vigilance is the guideline to follow during and between sessions. A telephone call from one family member may give the counselor information in confidence that he or she cannot share in the group. If this happens, the counselor should disqualify himself or herself and get some other counselor to take his/her place, because the secret shared with the one family member puts the counselor in that person's corner. The counselor has taken sides innocently enough, but in family counseling that is a violation. One should always tell the family about the sharing policy: No information should be shared unless it can be shared in the group sessions.

3. When FGC is being used as a counselor training model, the ethical guideline is *prior permission*. Practice has taught that counselors should be aware that permission given on beginning FGC is not necessarily for every circumstance nor for the duration of the sessions. The counselor is accountable for maintaining the contract granted by permission. If a change takes place, the counselor must renegotiate the permission contract on the spot, even if it is during a session. Counselor training sessions include the counselors and the families, plus those counselors in training. The number of counselors in training may vary from

one to ten depending upon the setting. Larger numbers may attend if the staging permits. Demonstrations for more than ten counselors must be limited to introducing the method, or using the method as a family education model. If the conditions change, the permission contract should be renegotiated and the counselor should follow the families' decision.

4. Because counselors sometimes work as a team, when individual family members are seen for additional sessions (tutoring, counseling, therapy), it is important for the head counselor to know all that is happening and to staff the team before every FGC session. The open (no secrets) communications rule holds. When working with a family or families on a long-term basis, the ethical consideration becomes critical. The counselors must maintain their professional role and not become merely surrogate members of an extended family system. As mentioned earlier, families can be very seductive and powerful. That is the central reason for using at least one cocounselor in every session. The reality check each counselor performs for the other is one built-in safeguard against ethical violation.

PROTOCOL ILLUSTRATING THE PROCESS OF FAMILY GROUP CONSULTATION

The verbatim protocol of FGC is so diverse that selected statements are less representative of process than the illustrative table of forces identified as operating in the process. For comparison of what appear to be parallel systems of treatment, this author has selected that ancient Hawaiian method of family conflict resolution called *Ho'oponopono,* Family Group Consultation, and Mowrer's Integrity Group Therapy.

Ho'oponopono is being rediscovered by Hawaiians to use whenever a conflict troubles a family. The method of treatment requires the attendance of the entire family. The extended family system used by Hawaiians generates twenty to twenty-five persons from the eldest *(kupuna)* senior person to the youngest *(keiki)* child. All must come together in a group and remain throughout the process of resolving the conflict. The conflict is resolved whenever each partner to the conflict asks the other per-

TABLE IX-1

COMPARISON OF THREE METHODS OF GROUP
PSYCHOTHERAPY-COUNSELING

	Ho'oponopono	Family Group Consultation	Integrity Therapy
Method:	Group	Group	Group
Leader:	Kupuna	Counselor/ Consultants	Psychologist (Mowrer)
Qualification:	Senior person	Special training	Professor-prepared
Members:	Family member	Member of family(s)	Member of group (must want to be present)
Purpose:	Conflict resolution	Conflict resolution	Reestablish community
Time:	Original marathon or series of sessions	Marathon or series of sessions	Marathon or series of sessions
Process:	Define problem	Define issues & concerns	Self-disclosure before significant others
Kukulukumuhana: (Koo-koo-loo-koo-moo-haw-naw)	Reach out to the other person(s) in dispute	Identify conflict	Identify problem
Pule: (Poo-lay)	Prayer to re-define the statement of the problem	Problem re-de-fined & restated by continuous re-phrasing	Understand problem statement in process of disclosure
Hala: (Haw-law)	Disagreement may lead to a grudge	Conflict identi-fication among-between family members	Conflict between public-private image of self. Disclosure leads to radical honesty
Ho'omauhala: (ho-o-mow-haw-law)	Carry a grudge—the person may lose control, act out	Unresolved con-flict—may escalate under intense emotion	Conflict generated by separation from significant other because of sin (secret) violation of trust
Ho'omalu: (Ho-o-mau-lau)	A time to medi-tate; a cool-ing-off period (may come any time)	Quiet time meditate; cool off emotionally (may come any time)	Rest & recuperate; meditate; Cool down emotionally (may come anytime)
Hihia: (He-he-uh)	Fish net of troubles— once untied is long continuous string—a unit.	Troubles are resolved by being defined: 1. What I want 2. No big thing	Troubles are personal definition

	Ho'oponopono	Family Group Consultation	Integrity Therapy
	Dispute requires two	3. Reality is the trouble I seek 4. I am defined by my troubles	
Mahiki: (Maw-he-ke)	Speak for your-self only; Speak to the Kupuna	Each person speaks for himself or herself	Each member self-discloses to the group & leader
Mihi: (Me-he)	To forgive one another	Forgiveness is the essence of humility	Violater makes restitution to the violated one (significant other)
Kala: (Kaw-law)	To let go, each is free to go own way	The family members are to achieve individual free-dom and have autonomous rights within the family's system of rules. Each is responsible for keeping the rules. (Ac-countability comes with an-other con-sultation session)	When time passes following self-disclosure by the person, he or she has the obligation to make restitution and set right whatever was violated in the trust—contract be-tween himself/herself and the community. Radical honesty—hearing yourself speak the truth—is what counts. Self-respect is rein-stated intact; this is the magic
Oki: (Oh-key)	To sever or cut—ultimately a termination	Termination comes in two ways: 1. A contract for 6 to 8 or 12 sessions expires with the last session 2. Resolution is reached following one or more sessions	
Pani: (Pau-nee)	[Communion] have food to-gether	Closure may in-volve a cele-bration	Closure may in-volve a social celebration of life

son for forgiveness. The method of treatment must have been the original family marathon model. This author developed Family Group Consultation some twelve years before learning of the obviously parallel treatment system developed generations earlier by the ancient Hawaiians. O. H. Mowrer's Integrity Group Therapy seems to be strikingly parallel with both FGC and *Ho'oponopono*. The following table may help display the similarities.

Family Group Consultation process in the treatment model utilizes many of the same forces, dynamics, and principles used in other methods of group counseling and psychotherapy. The encounter process is similar to the encounter and confrontation process of encounter groups. The principle of forgiveness is best modeled in Hawaiian *Ho'oponopono*. Apologizing by saying, "I'm sorry," has much less powerful consequences. "Please forgive me for the injury (psychological) I gave to you" has much more humility in it. *Ho'oponopono* requires each participant of a dispute to ask the other for forgiveness. This author suggests adoption of, "Please forgive me . . ." as standard operating procedure in FGC.

Mowrer's Integrity Group Therapy model has a process this author adopted long ago in FGC. The act of self-disclosure is most effective when the transgressor can "confess" directly to the victim. The healing principle of "Hearing myself speak the truth . . ." (radical honesty) has been used successfully in FGC for many years. The concept of community can be achieved with several families together in FGC. The concept of community came from Mowrer's earlier writing. The goal of FGC is to reestablish community and thereby eliminate alienation, conflict, insecurity, and depression. Ideally, FGC establishes a sense of unity, security, safety, and a feeling of well-being in the behavior of each family member.

RESEARCH RESULTS OF THE PROCESS

Research has focused on the theory of behavior developed by the author out of the practice of FGC. Several doctoral dissertations have been completed to test one or more of the assumptions in the theory. The theory claims that individual behavior is an expression of the meaning the person has at a given moment because of the relationship definition between self and significant other. To investigate the relationship definition variable, an interpersonal distance measure was developed based on proxemics given by E. T. Hall (1959). At this writing there is the Family Bond Inventory (FBI) which is sensitive to subtle changes in relationship definitions within the primary family and other interpersonal relationships (Fullmer, 1971).

A significant use of the FBI is to analyze the conflicts in a family. If any given relationship, like father-mother, is seen by one member as close and a second member as distant, a conflict exists and cannot be resolved between the two. Resolution comes only after the relationship is redefined and the individual perceptions on the FBI record agreement.

Boggs (1974) has discovered the evidence to support a proposition about which relationship among the most common human bonds holds the most potential influence. Her findings about the self-friend relationship claim that relationship is the most stable of all those studied (self-lover, self-stranger, self-enemy). The search for the one type of relationship in parenting, counseling, therapy, teaching, and leadership common to all healing influence may have been found in the long-time behavior of a friend.

SUMMARY

Based upon theory from psychology, anthropology, and education, FGC theory states that behavior comes directly from the relationship definition perceived by the individual in the immediate moment of behaving, and is further influenced by the context (social and physical) in which it happens (Fullmer, 1971). Prime evidence is supplied when the same relationship is perceived as different by two or more family members. The source of conflict is frequently found between the members with discrepant perceptions.

The FBI has many practical uses. It may tell the counselor whether the family bonds have any substance left in them. For married couples the FBI will tell the counselor whether the relationship is broken or intact.

Family Group Consultation is a versatile method for group counseling with families. The method has shown success in treating a wide range of behavior disorders and adapts well to self-help group teaching models for helping persons learn new cultural rules.

Nearly any classroom in a school or church could be used to house FGC. No special effects are needed. The idea that family background and school achievement are closely linked signals the importance of having a group counseling method that includes family and school (Hodgson, 1973).

Like Henry Miller's "Smile," FGC reflects the individual's attempt to be his or herself—the family is permitted to be itself. The ladder leads not to eternity as in the "Smile," but to conflict resolution and new self-knowledge.

REFERENCES

Bates, E.: *Interpersonal Distance as Measure of Relationship in Primary Family after Re-parenting Disadvantaged Youth.* Unpublished doctoral dissertation, University of Hawaii, 1974.

Boggs, M.: *Relationship Definition: The Influence of Selected Physical and Social Contexts on Interpersonal Distance.* Unpublished doctoral dissertation, University of Hawaii, 1974.

Cade, T.: *A Cross-cultural Study of Personal Space in the Family.* Unpublished doctoral dissertation, University of Hawaii, 1972.

Engebretson, D.: *Cross-cultural Variations in Territoriality: A Base-line Determination of Interactional Distance Between Shared Culture Dyads.* Unpublished doctoral dissertation, University of Hawaii, 1969.

Fullmer, D. W.: *Counseling: Group Theory and System.* New York, Intext, 1971.

Haley, J. (Ed.): *Changing Families: A Family Therapy Reader.* New York, Grune, 1971.

Hall, E. T.: *The Silent Language.* New York, Premier Books, 1959.

Hodgson, G.: Do schools make a difference? *The Atlantic, 231(3):*35-46, 1973.

Miller, H.: *The Smile at the Foot of the Ladder.* Kansas City, Hallmark, 1948.

Watzlawick, P., Beavin, J. H., and Jackson, D.: *Pragmatics of Human Communication.* New York, Norton, 1967.

X

GROUP COUNSELING AND DEVELOPMENT PROCESSES

WARREN C. BONNEY

INTEREST IN THE FUNCTIONING of small groups has become one of the most significant social phenomenon in post-World War II America. This interest has intensified and broadened even more greatly in the past ten years. The trend appears to stem from the rapidly accelerating complexity with consequent need for group management of the social structure. Large organizational and institutional efforts are dependent on basic small group factions for leadership and direction. The small enduring group appears to be the basic functional element in modern society. In order for these groups to function well, cooperative effort is essential, which in turn demands some degree of identification of the members with the group.

The danger or threat of the trends described above to a progressing democratic society appears obvious. If people cannot express and act on an individually evolved idea or belief without first ensuring correspondence to the norms of their groups, their creative productions, and to a lesser degree, their creative potential would be severely limited and eventually eliminated. The trend of increased social complexity and urbanization may also affect the individual at a deeper and more significant level. For many individuals in this culture, their sense of self-identity relies almost solely on their various group identifications. It would be difficult for many people to survive psychologically without these external definitions of self.

To rebel against or stand aloof from the trend towards social and individual control through group decisions may be individually noble but socially unproductive, if not destructive. The inescapable but difficult solution is the fostering of a sense of individuality, initiative, and creativity within the group setting.

313

The choice of slavish adherence to group norms or rebellion against them is, like most other dichotomous choices, unnecessary. People can be helped to realize their greatest creative potential within cooperative, cohesive groups. From experiences with counseling and psychotherapy groups, *ad hoc* laboratory groups, rifle squads, planning committees, and research teams, many individuals have come to believe that the most profound expression of individuality can be achieved through membership in a creative, interdependent group.

Much of the aim of group approaches such as counseling, psychotherapy, guidance, T-groups, church groups, and others is to assist individuals to function effectively in groups without loss of personal freedom. The primary concern of this chapter is an exploration of the development and processes of counseling groups; however, it will often be helpful to refer to other types of groups to elucidate further the dynamics investigated as well as the social significance of derived principles and theories. The counseling or therapy group, because of its exaggerated cohesiveness and intensity of emotional interaction, provides a kind of action laboratory for the study of the dynamics of other more specifically task-oriented cohesive groups. Similar dynamics occur in other groups but are more subtle and are less easily identifiable.

Counselors in schools and colleges work mostly with essentially normal people who range in age from adolescents to young adults. These individuals come to counselors, on a referral basis or self-referral basis in most cases, because of some sort of difficulty in interpersonal relations, often involving their membership, or lack of it, in groups. Some of these concerns might include (1) inability to make friends, (2) lack of popularity, (3) failure to find acceptance by the "right crowd," (4) a discomfort with the effect on individual development as a result of group identifications, (5) a rebellion against broader peer conformity pressures, and (6) difficulty with older people, particularly in authority positions. One of the more frequently identified causes for early nonacademic dropouts in large universities is the sense of alienation felt by many of the residents of high-rise dormitories. These as well as other concerns seem most appropriate for a group counseling or group guidance approach.

Counselors who decide to use group processes in dealing with any of the above cited concerns would first need to decide upon an overall goal or direction. They could adopt the adjustment approach, and through group discussion, help the members realize that there really is not much one can do about the environment; the intelligent thing to do is accept and adjust to it. This approach usually involves the practicing of social skills and working through of interpersonal problems through role playing, sociodrama, lectures, and discussions of socially approved behaviors. The result, when successful, is a highly conforming social automaton. One would expect the recipient of this method to have considerable difficulty in maintaining his or her adjustment in a rapidly changing society.

The counselor could also adopt the openness approach. Techniques are abandoned. The counselor stimulates the members to relate to each other at a deep emotional level with total openness and honesty of feeling and attitude. The situation is highly permissive, almost uncontrolled. The members are encouraged to express freely their innermost impulses and thoughts. Confrontation is common, presumably followed by acceptance. In some extreme examples, the situation takes on the appearance of an emotional orgy. One can scarcely argue the virtue of honesty and openness, but the general application of the behavior learned in such a group seems highly limited. This social system is simply not geared to this type of behavior, and the individual who attempts it outside the counseling group may and frequently does suffer severe rejection.

A third choice would obviously fall somewhere between the two extremes just described, in terms of group structure and content of discussion. The point of compromise would depend on at least four important factors: the composition of group membership, the goal or intent of the counseling, the skill of the counselor, and the setting in which the counseling occurs. These factors will be referred to again at various points in this chapter.

THEORETICAL RATIONALE

The point of view toward group counseling presented in this chapter is better understood not as a compromise but rather, a combination of the two extremes just described. A degree of management and control of the dynamics of the group is maintained towards social reality and at the same time individuality and creative (rather than explosive) expression is encouraged and rewarded. The management of the group's dynamic development is not held secret from the members. They understand the role of the counselor in this respect and it becomes an accepted part of the structure and norms of the group. As the group progresses toward maturity, everyone accepts responsibility for group management. This is not in itself an original conceptualization of group processes. The uniqueness of this approach lies in the use of developmental stage model as a basic guideline of the progress of the group and the direction of its movement. The level of functioning of the group during any given period should also help the counselor to determine his or her most appropriate modes of responses as well as provide clues as to the expected and/or desired succeeding developmental direction. The system may also be used as a means of identifying deviations from natural development and the reasons for these deviations.

Counselor's Role

As stated above, the counselor's major goal in the system described here is to assist the group toward a mature level of functioning. This experience is therapeutic in itself. Through the emotional support and courage derived from other group members and the counselor, plus direct meaningful interpersonal experiences, the group members achieve the capacity to resolve much of their personal and relationship problems on their own. Deep insight may not be necessary.

This kind of group maturity cannot be achieved and maintained with stability except by progressing through certain growth sequences or developmental stages. Just as a child is not a "little adult," neither can a group be considered mature at its inception regardless of the maturity level of its individual members. Also, like a child, a group may fixate at any level of maturity short of creative interdependent functioning.

Although the primary function of the counselor is the management of the dynamics of the group, he or she must also respond to individual concerns and conflicts and neurotic entanglements between and among group members. At times an individual may express concerns or problems which are beyond the therapeutic maturity level of the group. At such times, the counselor may respond at length to the concerned individual or individuals almost as if the other members of the group were not present. The group members soon learn to use these occasions as modeling-type learning experiences. They perceive the importance of listening intently to all the client is expressing, and the significance of responding to his or her feelings with sufficient empathy to encourage further and deeper exploration. They also learn that content responses are intended to assist the client in clarifying the nature of his or her problem rather than attempting to solve it. These are obviously solid counseling principles. The importance in group counseling is that if the counselor even occasionally responds to individual group members in this manner, the other members soon perceive the impact it has and begin to react to each other in similar fashion. After the episode is completed or postponed, the material involved, the counselor's behavior, and the group's reaction to it can be brought back to group-centered discussion resulting in further maturational progress.

It seems evident, then, that the group counselor needs to be proficient in two major areas of knowledge and skill. He or she needs knowledge of the basic principles of counseling and the effective use of them, and he or she needs a thorough understanding of the dynamics of cohesive groups and the skillful management of them.

The importance to society of creative efforts within small groups should be clear. Group counseling has the potential for contributing significantly to this goal both through action and research. Counseling groups are usually formed to help individuals with personal problems, but they could easily be extended to include social goals as well. One would hope and even expect that the experiences gained in group counseling would extend to other groups to which the participants belong. A creative group experience should not be limited to troubled people; anyone could profit from it. Many organizations, such as NTL, work with normal and often highly successful people.

Considerable speculation and research has been directed toward an understanding of why some counseling groups reach a mature and creative level of functioning while others do not. Many efforts have been made to identify the significant factors leading to success and the methods employed to achieve it. Factors that have been studied include the characteristics of the counselor, the characteristics of the participants in terms of personality types and backgrounds, and the dynamics of the total group in its development. It is the contention of this writer that the dynamics of a group are the overriding factors determining success or failure. Other factors, of course, are related to this. Counseling groups succeed mostly because of the natural dynamics of small groups more than because of the skill of the therapist or leader or the particular techniques employed. Sometimes a group succeeds in spite of the therapist.

The most fundamental dynamics of counseling groups will be discussed in the following paragraphs. These dynamics are *group norms, cohesiveness, conformity, maturity levels,* and *stages of development.*

Group Norms

The concept of *group norm* is basic and essential to the understanding of the functioning of people in groups. The term *norm* when used in reference to groups is somewhat different from its definition when used in other contexts. The term when used in reference to test scores is directly associated with the normal distribution curve. In this context the norm of a group of scores of people who have been tested represents an average or mode of performance and behavior as derived from the scores of the test. The generalized term of *normal behavior* as used in psychology refers to the observable average. The important point in both of these two instances of testing and observable behavior is that these are estimates based upon what people generally do. The term *group norm* as used in the literature in group psychology and group dynamics is a definition or description of expectations rather than averages. The norms of a group are not solely determined after the fact as would be true of the other two examples cited. They represent the expectations, aspirations, and hopes of the group as well as the recognition of the group's limitations. Group norm could be more properly thought of as a set of rules and standards rather than of observed averages.

The reality of group norms as expected standards of behavior can hardly be questioned. It appears to exist in any group that could be called cohesive and enduring even over short periods of time regardless of the nature of the group and where it occurs. The delinquent gang, the neighborhood gang, the executive committee, and the counseling group are all influenced and to a greater or lesser degree are dominated by the norms of the group. A more formalized definition of a group norm can be stated as *the limits of allowable behaviors of individual members of the group which also include variable rewards and punishments when the behavior exceeds the allowable limits.* Put in simpler terms, the group norm defines what a member can or cannot get away with and still remain an acceptable member of the group. When an individual within the group behaves in a way that is not according to the established and agreed upon group norm, but does so in a way that is constructive and enhancing to the group, he or she is rewarded by the granting of power and influence over future decision. When an individual deviates from the group norm in a nonconstructive manner, he or she will receive punishments through subtle and overt rejections, with the final punishment being expulsion from the group. Instances of the dynamic of the group norm are apparent to everyone from his or her personal experiences. A few examples of punishment will be cited, then the nature of group rewards will be described.

A teacher who violates the norms of a faculty group in a public school by "palling around with the students" or "carrying tales to the principal" will probably receive a cool reception in the teacher's lounge; i.e., the conversation ceases or is changed, several teachers may get up and leave, or sometimes all of them leave.

*   *   *

In offices and shops the most common norm violator is the "apple polisher" who seeks special attention from the executives or foremen. Punishments take the form of withholding gossip from the individual, making it difficult for the individual to do his or her work well, and finally "the freeze-out" in which the person's very existence is ignored.

*   *   *

Punishment for the violation of the norms of a counseling group usually takes the forms of cutting the person off when he or she tries to speak, failing to respond to his/her comments, and sometimes physically turning away from him. If the unacceptable behavior continues, he or she will eventually be confronted with it. The counselor may allow the group to exercise these punishments because he or she does not like the behavior either. A more constructive action for the counselor would be to confront the group with the dynamic early in the process and attempt to help the violator.

Rewards are given to individuals in the group by other members when their behavior fits the group norms. If the individual's behavior enhances and more firmly establishes a group norm, he or she will be rewarded even more explicitly through positive comments regarding his or her contribution and other forms of approval. If a person behaves in this manner frequently enough, he or she may even be allowed to alter the norms of the group.

Cohesiveness and Conformity

The concept of cohesiveness has already been referred to and will be again, many times. It is almost impossible to discuss the dynamics of small groups without reference to cohesiveness. In group counseling the cohesiveness of the group is an essential element in the process of individual change. It is most important that this concept be thoroughly understood, since it is so elusive but yet so important. Cohesiveness is very difficult to validate experimentally, but it is very evident in realistic situations. One can know and immediately feel the difference between an involvement in a cohesive group and one that is not cohesive.

Cohesiveness may be defined superficially as identification of all members with the group resulting in a sense of unity. Based upon a multitude of experimental studies, Cartwright and Zander (1968) identify three major variables that contribute to group cohesiveness. These are "(a) attraction to the group, including resistance to leaving it; (b) motivation of the members to participate in group activities; and (c) coordination of efforts of the members." The most important aspect of cohesiveness appears to be the acceptance of common goals and the willingness to work cooperatively toward the accomplishment of those goals, whatever they may be. The identification of degrees of cohesiveness is most readily accomplished with small groups (five to twenty people), but the concept also applies to larger social units, even whole societies. Individuals are now dramatically, and at times tragically, faced with the lack of cohesiveness in modern American society. There are many differing sets of goals and many differing ways of achieving them. When a small group loses its commonality of purpose, it is in danger of dissolution, and so is a nation. Fortunately, the larger the social unit the more able it is to tolerate differing goals and opinions. Conflict and dissension may be present but not disastrous; however, the divergence of aims and beliefs may become so great that the social system cannot encompass it. With a small group the tolerance level of divergence of goals is quite low. Differences in attitudes and beliefs may even be therapeutically useful but not differences of opinion about the major purpose of the group's existence.

One intuitively "feels" the degree of cohesiveness of a counseling group, or other small groups; at least he/she thinks he/she does. One could also be very wrong. There are ways of obtaining more objective indications of a group's cohesiveness. A number of sociometric devices (Bonney and Happleman, 1962) can be employed as useful determinants. Some of these would include a comparison of choices within the group and outside of it on some issue pertinent to the counseling group; another could be the extent of mutuality of choices, and also the overall degree of interpersonal acceptance. Many other sociometric approaches more specific to the interests of the counselor could be utilized. Measures of desire to remain in the group and resistance to leaving it have been employed. Resistance to outside attack is a strong indicator of group cohesiveness. There are many other measures of social interaction that the counselor can use to fit his or her specific interests. The need to employ objective measures of cohesiveness are greater when there are overt or subtle pressures upon the group members to remain in the group despite their wishes. When there are no external pressures, the extent of cohesiveness is usually apparent.

Another very significant dimension of cohesiveness may be clarified by a very simple example. A collection of people waiting at a street corner for a signal light to change in order to cross the street should be referred to as an aggregate but not a group. They have physical proximity and a similar goal, but they do not need each other for the achievement of their individual (though similar) goals. Dependency upon each other for the achievement of individual as well as group goals is an essential element for cohesiveness in a counseling group. In group counseling the common goals become the development of a therapeutic atmosphere in which each individual can experience the freedom to openly explore himself/herself with the confidence that he or she will have the support and understanding of the other members of the group. Until the group believes this goal to be attainable, therapeutic change is not likely to occur. The first task of the group counselor is to assist the group toward a sense of cohesiveness.

Concomitant to the dynamic of group cohesiveness is the dynamic of conformity to group norms. Cohesiveness is best established when a group reaches consensus on its definitions of social reality. Social reality means the beliefs that people hold about what is true and correct concerning human behavior and particularly about relationships among people. The more cohesive a group becomes the greater is the in-group pressure to come to a consensus concerning certain vital aspects of social reality. The group works hard toward achieving a unanimous agreement as to what is correct and true about those behaviors which are intimately involved in the functioning of the group. Because the counseling group must sustain itself without the assistance of outside forces, the in-group pressures to reach uniformity of agreement on certain issues becomes very intense and demanding. Without these agreements the group cannot sustain itself. However, a group can become so self-conforming that it loses its potential for creative functioning. The participants in a counseling group can easily become more involved in meeting the expectations of the group norm than in seriously exploring their inner feelings. Conformity pressures may also be brought into the group from the larger peer culture. The counselor may misinterpret norm-conformity behavior as sincere self-exploration. The counselor should always be alert and knowledgeable enough to recognize the difference.

Group cohesiveness and conformity to group pressures cannot be dealt with separately. Cohesiveness is essential to the efficient functioning of a group, but this condition inevitably brings with it the danger of overconformity to group norms and the consequent stifling of creative productions. If conforming behaviors can be recognized and openly dealt with for what they are, the danger to creative functioning can be avoided.

Cohesiveness and conformity are fundamental concepts for the understanding of any group. The understanding of these concepts are especially important for the counselor who is working with a group of young people whose values and attitudes are expressed in a manner that is unfamiliar to him or her. The understanding of basic dynamics applicable for all groups become the essential repertoire for effective counselor functioning. The counselor of a group of disadvantaged youth must work to accomplish group cohesiveness, but at the same time, he or she must be constantly alert to conformity pressures which may mediate against the development of a therapeutic climate.

Levels of Group Maturity

Group maturity means that all members of the group are working cooperatively toward the agreed upon goals of the group. Put another way, group members are specifically task-oriented. All members of the group feel and express concern for each member within the group. If one person deviates from or detracts from the group effort, that person will be reminded of this and assisted, in one manner or another, to understand the deviation and rejoin the mainstream of the group work. Mutual respect is evident at all times. No one's contribution is ignored or rejected no matter how simple or inappropriate it may first appear. The person who makes such a contribution is helped to develop it into something significant or helped to realize that the idea should be abandoned.

When an individual presents an idea or behaves in a manner that is creative or different from the group norms in a constructive way, this person is encouraged and supported. Any group may occasionally lose sight of its goals and regress to even a chaotic level of functioning. A group that has reached a high level of maturity will recognize what has happened, identify the problem, and resolve it.

There exists in society a great variety of small groups serving many different needs and functions. These natural groups represent many differing levels on a group maturity continuum; most of them fall far short of the definition of group maturity given above. Insight into the maturational development of a counseling group may be enhanced and clarified by an understanding of the more static maturational levels of these natural groups.

A few examples of groups at differing maturity levels should make the further use of the term more explicit. The cohesiveness of a group may be based almost solely on interpersonal attraction or affection and sustained by a rather superficial common interest. Examples would be a housewives' neighborhood coffee klatch, a men's beer-drinking group at the local tavern, and in most instances, college fraternities and sororities. Groups of this sort tend to disintegrate readily under duress or separation. The maturity level of such group identifications is almost infantile since it is so egocentric.

A second maturational level of group functioning might be best typified by a preadolescent gang or club. Rather severe initiations are characteristic; rituals soon develop; and a secret language or symbolism evolves. Loyalty to the group becomes the paramount virtue. The group exists almost purely for the sake of identification with a group and the motivational value is a sense of exclusiveness.

The similarities between preadolescent boys' gangs and adult fraternal and civic organizations is striking, particularly in terms of ritual, symbolism, initiation, and secrecy, all of which enhance a sense of exclusiveness and self-identity. The major difference is that, with the adult groups, a socially valued reason for existence, such as charitable or rehabilitative work, is usually considered necessary. Here, loyalty to the group and the importance of acceptance by the group will usually override purely self-centered motivations.

Athletic teams, particularly those which require a high degree of cooperation and mutual support such as basketball teams, move another step up the maturity continuum in terms of group functioning. Adolescent delinquent gangs possess nearly all the qualities of a maturely functional group except for the constrictions placed upon them by the nature of their antisocial goals. (The reader should keep clearly in mind that the emphasis here is on the maturity of group functioning, not the maturity or the social value of the group's goals.) Planning committees, church groups, volunteer charity groups, local mental health societies, and many others of comparable intent may be functioning at any level on the group-maturity continuum regardless of their socially mature and noble goals.

The effective combat unit and the successful counseling or therapy group appear as the ultimate in functional, creative, mature groups. These groups must attain a high level of maturity or they cannot achieve their proposed or imposed goals. Other groups, such as committees or organizational units, can produce acceptably with something less than full cooperative effort. The counseling or therapy group and the combat unit may not even survive as groups unless they are able to achieve a full sense of interdependency.

As the reader may have derived from the preceding description of types of creative groups on a maturity continuum, cohesiveness may be attained on two major dimensions: interpersonal attraction and interpersonal respect. The balance between the two will determine the maturity of the group. Interpersonal respect would include respect for task-relevant skills, attention to expressions of individual ideas and feelings, and the right to individual and differing opinions. If interpersonal respect is sufficiently well developed, interpersonal attraction is probably prerequisite for the development of respect. If cohesiveness is based almost solely on interpersonal attraction, it will inhibit task-relevant activities and thereby restrict the movement toward the preestablished goals of the group.

A GENERALIZED MODEL OF SMALL GROUP DEVELOPMENT

A theoretical model is only an approximate representation of reality. In the behavioral sciences, the deviations from the model are usually more frequent than the replicas. A theoretical model of the sequential development of small groups can only be a very loose, generalized representation, for which there are many variations and exceptions. The variations and exceptions are themselves the most significant clues to the understanding of the dynamics of a particular group. The model proposed here should be regarded as a point of departure rather than a point to be proven.

Establishment Stage

When a group first forms, it has the same problem (multiplied by the complexity of the number of individuals involved) as a dyad in establishing a working relationship of whatever sort. The first stage, the Establishment Stage, may be divided into two overlapping aspects: exploration and socialization. During the exploratory or initial stage of the group, the members attempt to estimate each others' interpersonal impact and characteristic relationship modes. They further attempt to determine the kinds of roles they may play in this situation and still remain psychologically safe. Put another way, each individual estimates the emotional needs he or she may satisfy in interaction with the others without being rejected or overly exposed. The leader is often severely tested by the group in order to determine his or her orientation to the task and his or her leadership competencies. If the leader fails to meet this challenge, he or she may be rejected and psychologically isolated for the remainder of the group's existence or until such time as he/she proves his/her worth.

The chaotic nature of the initial phase of the group results in expressions of insecurity and leader dependency. Resistance and hostility toward the leader and conflict among group members are also expected outgrowths of the basic insecurity of procedural direction and uncertainty concerning the capacity of the group to achieve its proposed aims. The behavioral forms of these exploratory efforts are superficial social interchange (talk about the weather, current events, and job-related topics, intellectualizing the task, humor, apparently out-of-field behavior unrelated to the task, and general horseplay). All of this talk has a purpose and appears to be essential for group formation. If the group leader fails to recognize the significance and need for this kind of behavior, he or she may well lose the group before it starts.

Phasing into the second aspect of the Establishment Stage, socialization, is characterized early by the distribution of "idiosyncratic credits" (Hollander, 1964), norm setting and consequent conformity pressures, and finally the first evidence of cohesiveness. The cohesiveness achieved at this point appears as a warm, congenial, social atmosphere which may be, to some extent, camouflaged by superficial task efforts. Interpersonal attraction is often at its height at this stage, but somewhat falsely so. The cohesiveness represents the warm glow of achievement at having successfully managed the first hurdle in the formation of a psychological group. The members know now that they can cope with each other and function at some level of significance. Some groups never move beyond this point and accomplish little that is meaningful as a group or for individual members.

Hollander's concept of "idiosyncratic credits" is the process by which the group, consciously and unconsciously, assigns power and influence, in varying degrees, to each member of the group. It represents the extent to which each member will be allowed to deviate from the group norms. Some group members may be granted extensive idiosyncratic credits while others receive little or none.

The leader's behavior during the Establishment Stage is in some ways similar to the behavior of the members of the group. The leader, too, attempts to estimate the developing roles and positions of the members of the group, and what can be expected of them in relation to himself or herself. At the same time, the group is working very hard both subtly and directly to anticipate and formulate the role of the leader. The leader must be very alert to his or her role assignments by the group. He or she needs to accept the right and need of the group to express their concerns and demands, and should respond to them with reflections and limited or relatively superficial interpretations. This will naturally lead to some loose definition as to his or her perception of his/her role in the group. At this point, the leader may very likely be asked about his or her qualifications for the task. His or her answers should be direct and honest but very brief and concise. Through these kinds of interchanges, the leader will have fulfilled the group's need to test his or her competency.

The leader should assume an active though not highly directive part in the formation of the group's norms. Ideally, the setting of norms should emanate from the group itself; however, if certain issues considered vital by the leader, such as confidentiality, are not broached, the leader should suggest to the group that these issues be given some serious consideration. The eventual acceptance of a group norm should still be left to the consensus of the group and not forced by the leader, particularly in the early stages of the group's development. If a group-determined norm is unworkable, it will soon become evident to them and subsequently altered. The leader may influence openly or subtly, to a limited extent, the types of norms developed. The extent will depend upon his or her acceptance as a leader.

The following protocol of an audiotaped group session is presented as an example of the dynamics of the Establishment Stage. The group is composed of young adults. Norm setting, with particular reference to confidentiality, is the focus of the group's attention. The protocol is an excerpt from the third session.

Establishment Stage Protocol—Norm-setting, Confidentiality

D.: Last Monday, when I went home, I went home and I said to my wife, "Well, we had our group tonight." And she said, "Oh, you had your group." (laughter) Anyway, I decided I couldn't tell her a thing about it; I couldn't tell her a darn thing, even things I wouldn't consider breaking confidence—like mentioning names— not even incidences. It might be the beginning of starting to tell about somebody. Yet, there is the need to want to share things. You know, with my wife. Who else can you talk to? I didn't tell her anything. I'm wondering how the rest of the group felt about this. What can we say and what can we not say? What are our rules for not breaking confidentiality?

Th.: Well, uh, well, first have any of the rest of you had a similar reaction?

E.: I did. I think maybe because we had a good group session. By the time I drove an hour I had overcome some of this. (group laughter) I had the same feeling of wanting to share it with someone else.

J.: I didn't want to share it with my husband; I wanted to share it with someone in the group.

D.: I could risk this in individual therapy because I'm just talking about myself then; but when I tell about a group, it's not my province to tell. But yet there's a need to want to talk about it to somebody.

Th.: Would you like more clarification about how we ought to deal with this—where the limits are?

R.: I think it becomes a question of who. I've come to the conclusion it's better not to say anything, except with other members of this group. I feel when the session is over, everybody just kinda stands around, like they want to continue. Anybody else feel this way?

G. and J.: Yeah. Yeah.

R.: Is this wrong to discuss with someone else within the group?

Th.: This is encouraged by some group therapists, but this could be difficult for some of you to do, like if you have a husband or a wife, you may be expected to come home—could lead to difficulty.

P.: As far as D.'s concerned, this might have particular significance for you if you want to have a closer communication with your wife—talking about these things might give you a chance to air some of your own feelings.

D.: Yeah, yeah, that's right. I usually tell her just about everything, but I came up to this point where. . . . Gee, this is nothing spectacular; you're not going to tell on all these people. But I thought, "Why should this be different?"

Th.: I don't suppose anybody in this group would object to your telling your wife. I doubt if anyone here would object to your telling her anything that happened here—in last week's meeting, but there may come a time when things would occur here that they would not want you to tell even to your wife.

D.: Sure, they don't know her or who she is!

Th.: Or who she might blab to.

D.: Right!

Th.: Well, I think you will do some of it; people usually do tell some things. I think within a few weeks you will have developed a sensitivity to what's all right to talk about and what isn't. But to expect you to be absolutely closed-mouthed about this and never mention it to a soul is kind of silly because you probably will. One thing that might help you, D., particularly if this is something that has relevance to your marriage—I know people have done this and I have done this—to say to your wife or someone pretty close to you, "Something came up in our group discussion tonight that I think might be of interest to you and me." And then not repeat what was in the group discussion, but take off on the topic, "We had a good discussion of marital relations between two people who are both professionals and some of the problems that might arise from this. Let's continue it; I'd like to talk with you about it." And then you're not repeating anything; you're just bringing up the topic which is the point you are trying to make anyway.

D.: Right!

Th.: Not that you want to repeat what's been said.

D.: Right!

Th.: Or if you say, "I had an insight in the group tonight. I found a new way of looking at some things and I would like to talk to you about it." Then you are talking about your insight, not anything the group said. That's all right; that's good, if it stimulates you to do things like that. That's one of the things we would hope to get out of this.

Th.: Does that seem acceptable to everyone—as a way to deal with it?

Group: (nodding of heads—seemed unanimous).

B.: I agree. It's a very difficult thing to build up this emotion in the group and then suddenly drop it.

Th.: I think you're right, and you probably shouldn't. But you can, I think, develop ways to release it without feeling you have broken confidence.

Transition Stage

With a group of mature individuals or a group of individuals in serious need of problem resolution, the social stage of cohesiveness soon wears thin. The realization comes through the instigation of one or more group members or from pressure from the leader that the group is not seriously pursuing the goals for which it was originally formed. If the group as a totality accepts this recognition, it enters into what has been termed the Transition Stage. If the majority of the group members are not ready for this recognizance, the group will likely revert to its original chaotic state and soon disintegrate, if circumstances allow it to do so.

Transition has its usual implication here of a critical period of movement from one developmental stage to another. The group feels a sense of embarrassment at having pretended task-relevant behaviors for which they had little commitment coupled with a sudden lack of confidence that they can actually accomplish the original group aims. If the group has maturity potential, it will reevaluate its purpose, reform its norms, and determine to try again at a deeper and more intentional level.

The counselor's behavior during the Transition Stage is of vital importance to the continuation of the group. The nature of this stage has been described as a state of incongruity (Bonney and Foley, 1963). The members of the group (especially adults) have learned that it is socially unacceptable, if not dangerous, to discuss deeply personal problems in a group, particularly a group of strangers or mere acquaintances; yet this is the reason for the formation of the counseling group and the presumed intention of every member in it. The reluctance to discuss personal concerns is referred to by some writers as a "basic social fear" of group rejection (Bach, 1954). The counselor can relieve the conflict and the anxiety associated with it by accepting and agreeing that withholding personal concerns in normal social groups is not only understandable but probably wise. The counselor then redefines the counseling group as normatively different and therefore appropriate for the discussion of personal concerns. The very nature of the norms they have established and are still in process of establishing protect them from the dangers inherent in the normative structure of more usual social and work groups. The counselor's acceptance of the conflict and his or her clarification of the purpose of the counseling group stimulates the group members to more serious norm development and group commitment.

The following protocol, taken from the sixth session of an all-female group, is included here to illustrate the Transition Stage. The problem discussed is typical of the concerns of the Transition Stage. The group seriously questions its capacity or willingness to be truly helpful and resolves to accept the challenge.

Transition Stage Protocol

> E.: I think we just felt concern talking about your problems when you weren't here. I didn't feel that we talked of anything much—mainly because two of us were missing.
>
> D.: My main concern was that we hadn't helped P. when she had asked us for help.
>
> G.: That's what we discussed, why we hadn't helped and just how we could go about it.
>
> P.: I guess that's how I felt afterward. What is that old Indian saying? "Don't judge me until you have walked a mile in my moccasins!"
>
> E.: I've had problems similar to yours, but I still didn't feel I could tell you what you should do. As far as the group is concerned, I

don't feel we have come along far enough to tell each other what they should do.

D.: I think the thing that surprises me the most was E. thinking that I was mature. I thought I was falling down on my part and E. saw it altogether differently.

P.: This is the one thing that concerns me, too. I get the impressions from Mrs. C. (therapist) that we should just let go! And I think that E.'s holding back looks like a sign of maturity. (directed to therapist) Well, I think that you feel that we hold back too much!

Th.: I think the point I would like to make is that this is different from any other kind of group. We can only understand each other and therefore help each other by talking openly.

D.: I feel that we turn away from each other's problems, because we are embarrassed or we don't really feel that it's real or whatever. What we need to realize is that whatever we do say is significant in some way.

Th.: P. wasn't particularly asking you for advice; she was asking you for understanding. Just by the mere fact that you stay with a person and listen indicates that you are concerned. And this is the way that you are going to be able to work with each other.

E.: Oh, good! I'm glad you said that. Now, I don't have to solve her problem. (laughter)

D.: Just listen carefully and try to understand.

E.: It also makes a difference how we state our problems. If I say it as a joke, the group will laugh at it.

Experimentation Stage

Having successfully passed the Transition Stage, the group enters the Experimentation Stage in which the first serious attempt as a group is made at goal-related work. These first attempts are often highly tentative, sometimes blundering, and fraught with interpersonal conflict and frustration. The difficulties encountered at this stage of development are mostly due to one or more members who were not quite ready for the transition or who did not completely understand the new norms of the group. If the conflicts or the frustrations become severe enough, the group will have to engage itself in a second transition or Retransition Stage.

Many groups fail to mature beyond the Experimentation Stage and never become creative groups. Some individuals lag behind or actually impede progress while a few do most of the group work. The typical committee tends to function in this manner. If the goal is sufficiently well defined and specific, the group product can still be quite acceptable. However, if the goals are not easily specified, such as in a counseling group, or are extremely threatening and difficult for some members, such as in a combat unit, a sense of frustration will continue and satisfaction with the group will be minimal.

Early efforts by individual members at serious self-exploration are often hesitant and confused and they may need considerable assistance from the counselor in organizing their thoughts and expressing their feelings more clearly. These early efforts should be strongly reinforced by the counselor but he or she should also be very cautious that he or she does not push the client too fast. The client may reveal more than he or she intended or can later tolerate, and the other group members may be threatened by it and withdraw from further participation. The interpersonal conflicts and frustrations should be allowed to work themselves through. If this working through is not at least partially accomplished within a reasonable length of time, then the Retransition Stage becomes necessary. The counselor responses to these conflicts and frustrations should be simple reflection and clarification, and possibly some interpretation.

The following protocols are taken from two different adolescent groups and present two of the more common developmental difficulties during the Experimentation Stage. Both examples represent the tentative, approach-avoidance nature of this stage.

The first excerpt is an example of a group ready to accept and, in fact, pressing the client for depth exploration; the client is unwilling to pursue it. The second excerpt is an example of a male client willing to explore himself in depth, but with a group that is unwilling to permit it.

Experimentation Stage Protocol—First Group (College Freshmen), Eighth Session

(At the end of the previous session, R. (Robert) had stated he thought he should talk about his father. The counselor has invited him to do so.)

R.: Well, I can't really see how my dad could have influenced me. I wasn't brought up by him. I didn't get any of my ideas from him. The only thing I've learned from him is the type person I don't want to be. Really, no reason to talk about him.

Co.: You really feel you have no feelings about your father now.

R.: Except I wish he were different.

E.: You feel cheated?

R.: No, I'm glad he left.

Co.: But, every time you mention your father, you have always appeared upset. It seems like it might be important.

R.: OK, I'm ashamed of him.

Co.: You haven't been able quite to bring up anything really personal.

R.: I think I could if I really wanted to. (The counselor withdrew and turned to another client.)

It is not uncommon, in this stage, for clients to announce their intentions to explore a personal concern, then become quite inhibited and withdrawing once they have started. In this instance, the client may also have been resisting the efforts of the counselor to draw him out.

Second Group—High School Seniors, Sixth Session

Co.: Does anyone feel like starting today?

B.: Yes, I want to talk about my fear of trying new things. I make myself try things and I usually do all right, but I'm so afraid beforehand. Like last summer, I was a camp counselor and I did OK, but I was miserable for weeks before it started.

Co.: What's so different about that? Doesn't everybody feel that way?

F.: Sure, I've felt that way lots of times.

B.: I know other people feel that way, but I feel like I'm more so.

Co.: Seems like what you're saying is that this fear is controlling your life.

B.: Yeah! It prevents me from looking into things or being open-minded.

Co.: Prevents you from knowing what you can be.

P.: Uh, Huh!

B.: Yeah!

F.: But, after you've shown some ability in something, it doesn't bother you anymore. I would feel that way too, and you can do things I can't do.

B.: Yeah, but there are some things I really get so afraid of I just don't try.

P.: But still you do a lot of things even though you are nervous about it.

B.: Well, yeah!

The client, B. (Bob), was attempting to explore his feelings of anxiety and timidity at a greater depth than the other group members were willing to accept. They tried to reassure him that he didn't really have a problem. During the session, the group finally understood what he was trying to do and supported him.

Retransition Stage

During the Retransition, the group members reexamine their position and attempt to identify the sources of their difficulty in achieving their assumed potential. Emotional commitment and genuine concern of all members is soon identified as the missing and necessary condition. Direct individual confrontation is a typical means of attempting resolution. Interactions are highly charged emotionally and often accusatory and defensive. Regression to former stages of resistive behaviors is typical. The group members seriously face the possibility that they may not be capable of achieving the task of fully cooperative, creative functioning. If the interpersonal conflicts are resolved and full commitment obtained, the group moves into the Operational Stage of development.

Operational Stage

In the Operational Stage, all group members function at a task level and evince respect and support for the efforts of all other members to behave similarly. Each member's contributions are given full attention and are considered seriously in respect to the overall aims or goals of the group. If a group member's contribution falls short of expectation, the others confront him or her with this and attempt to help the member achieve a higher level of functioning. From here, the group phases into the final or Creative Stage of full interdependency. Even here, interpersonal conflict is not uncommon, and occasional regressions to earlier developmental stages are to be expected. However, resolution of difficulties is almost assured, even though the process may be traumatic and stormy.

The following brief excerpt from the eighteenth session of an adult group represents the kind of serious, searching efforts of the Operational Stage.

Operational Stage Protocol—Self-exploratory

M.: Then this caused me to begin to think, "How did I look at myself?" I look at myself, first of all, as mother, second of all as . . . um . . . I guess as good old M., but never as a woman.

Th.: And felt you had to deny that in order to function in these other ways?

M.: No, I don't think I denied it. I just didn't believe it.

J.: Kinda afraid to, too. . . .

M.: Might be, but I don't think I really believed it. I'm not sure I believe it yet. (Several somewhat irrelevant interchanges among the group members followed this comment.)

M.: I don't have a feeling of hopelessness now as I had before. I feel I can be a valuable person, I guess, without having to be valuable in things I do—be valuable for what I am. I'm still trying to talk myself into it, but I'm intent on it. I'm working at it. (At this point the group members understood and became quite accepting and supportive of M's efforts to reach out for something more in life.)

Creative Stage

During the Creative Stage, the counselor responds almost solely to group-centered dynamics. The group members have learned to deal with each other in a therapeutic, open manner with little or no reservation or unnecessary protectiveness. Because of lack of experience and their own highly emotional involvement in the process, they are usually unable to resolve and sometimes even recognize a total group dynamic which pervades everything they attempt to do and inhibits efforts to deal with each other as individuals. The counselor must now identify the nature of the dynamic for the group, trace its origin, and help them resolve it. An example of a total group dynamic might be an unrecognized or unconscious reaction to the previous group meeting. The group just cannot seem to get going, but the members do not know why.

In this ultimate or creative, self-actualizing stage of the group's development, dependency upon the leader is negligible.

The leader is used now primarily as a resource person or for emergencies of gross confusion or very severe interpersonal conflict. A full sense of interpersonal responsibility and group commitment has developed which allows for and rewards idiosyncratic behavior. To break the norm constructively has become the norm. In this atmosphere, one can learn to become a responsible individualist while functioning fully as a member of a cohesive, task-oriented group.

FACTORS AFFECTING DEVIATIONS FROM THE DEVELOPMENTAL MODEL

The major factors which are likely to affect deviations from the model are the combination of personalities within the group, the goals of the group (guidance-discussion, focused counseling, open counseling, depth therapy), conditions and events outside the group, and unexpected and unpredictable events within the group. These factors are stated in terms of counseling groups, but a very similar list worded differently would apply to other small cohesive groups as well.

A student counselor, under supervision with the threat of a grade, would probably try to accomplish too much and too fast to the detriment of the group's progress. One would expect the student counselor to have greatest difficulty at the first Transition Stage.

The total possible time that a group can spend together most probably influences how long the group will remain at one stage of functioning. The end of a semester or school year or the deadline for a committee report are examples of this type of influence. The physical setting and the meeting time can have some influence. A meeting time just prior to some very different kind of demanding situation, such as an academic class, will limit the returns from both experiences. Highly unique factors could arise which might exert some minor deviating influence. Occasionally an unusual occurrence can have a major impact, such as the death or psychotic breakdown of a group member.

The major forces toward progression or regression arise from the interpersonal dynamics within the group and the individual motivation of each member for group-centered goal achievement. This latter concept has been referred to, in reference to the training of rifle squads, as Team Task Motivation (TTM) (George, 1962). TTM is, to some extent, developed according to the summation of task-relevant or goal-relevant skills of the group members, but more basically, it appears to be dependent on the attitude toward group participation which the individuals brought with them from their early past experiences, most likely rooted in the nature of the family relationships during their early childhood and their position in the family constellation. Group-centered motivation could probably be fairly well estimated through a carefully structured interview prior to the formation of the group.

The interpersonal dynamics of the group refers to the mutual pairings, the cliques, and the personality clashes that inevitably develop in any cohesive group. The extent to which these interpersonal encounters can be managed for the enhancement of group effort rather than its delimitation will determine the success of the group experience and the course of its movement from one developmental stage to another. The successful management of these interpersonal dynamics is related to the extent to which they are neurotically based and to the skill of the group leader. These two major aspects of the group's development, individual attitude toward group participation and interpersonal dynamics within the group, are closely interactive. It is often difficult, and sometimes impossible, to separate them observably.

Earlier in this chapter, the suggestion was made that deviations from the model presented here could provide interesting clues to understanding the nature of a particular group and the prediction of the group's future progress. One can also often use the deviations of the group from the expected pattern as leads for developing more effective managing techniques. For instance, if the group progresses too rapidly, skipping certain developmental experiences, the leader might anticipate severe transition problems later. Goal preparation and anticipatory experiences prior to the formation of a group appear to alter the expected pattern and produce some unique management problems (Foley and Bonney, 1966). An example familiar to all group counselors is the psychologically sophisticated, therapy-wise group member who starts too fast and at a depth which threatens the other group members and impedes progress. In a similar manner, an "old Army pro" assigned to a relatively inexperienced squad can wreak havoc with the leader's control and the general morale, or the veteran may, under favorable conditions, prove to be an invaluable asset to the development of the group, playing the role of a secondary resource person. The same could be true of the sophisticated member of the counseling group.

There are other factors which may alter the developmental pattern. Familiarity of all group members with one another prior to the group formation will usually facilitate movement up to and through the Transition Stage. Familiarity among some members but not all will often make progress difficult and sometimes impossible. The relationship of group members to the leader outside the group is usually a hindrance rather than a help. The intent and skill of the leader is of vital importance. It is certainly not unheard of for leaders of many types of groups to seek a leadership role in order to satisfy their own neurotic needs for dominance and control rather than goal achievement or individual development. The inept leader, no matter how appropriately motivated, may also impede group progress. The highly skilled and goal-oriented leader can often overcome or resolve relationships with individuals which would tend to mitigate against progress of the group.

Many individual gains are possible through participation in an evolving, creative group experience. The usual lists of personal improvements as a consequence of involvement in cohesive groups seem valid and evident. Some of these benefits would include the use of the group as a source of consensual validation of social and emotional reality, an increase in interpersonal skills, an extension of one's role behavior repertoire, a greater tolerance for differing opinions, and more appreciation for the value of cooperative effort. Beyond these usual claims, the mature group may also provide the participant with an increased sensitivity to individual, interpersonal, and group dynamics, and a new perception of the meaning and necessity for human interdependence. One might expect that an individual would develop a deeper appreciation of the horizons of human potential and the significance of interpersonal encounter as a means of realizing individual potential. Most important, one might hope that the participant would achieve a more profound understanding of the meaning of maturity through the development of a deeper sense of interpersonal responsibility.

SUMMARY

This chapter has dealt with group dynamics which appear to be universal. Whenever a group of people get together for some common purpose, the dynamics of norm setting, cohesiveness, and pressures toward conformity invariably develop. The counseling group is not an exception. The similarity of counseling groups with other types of groups does not deny that the counseling group is, in some ways, different and therefore demands special skills of the leader for goal achievement. This chapter has concerned itself with the *management* of a group.

In addition to group management, the counselor must also be capable of developing an effective counseling relationship with each individual member of the group. Group management is stressed here because it applies similarly to guidance groups, discussion groups, sensitivity groups, counseling groups, and therapy groups and because it seems to be the aspect of group work that counselors know least about. If the natural dynamics of the group can be managed toward the creation of a helping, therapeutic climate, the communication of facilitative attitudes and comments becomes relatively easy whether they are of an in-depth therapeutic nature or are simply advice and information.

An experience in a cohesive, creative group can be personally valuable and rewarding in itself, regardless of the intent of the group. The major concern of the group counselor should be assisting the group toward increasingly mature functioning and allow the experience itself to be the primary therapeutic effect.

Too frequently the counselor interferes with the natural developmental process of the group with his or her need to demonstrate his/her insight into individual dynamics. The dynamics of the developmental processes of a group are much more predictable than the dynamics of individuals, and are therefore much more easily managed. If the prime focus of the counselor is on group development rather than individual therapy within the group, the emotional depth of the interactions and the content of the discussions are not so significant; it is the group experience itself that is important.

REFERENCES

Bach, G.: *Intensive Group Psychotherapy*. New York, Ronald, 1954.

Bonney, M. E., and Hampleman, R. S.: *Personal-Social Evaluation Techniques*. Washington, D.C., The Center for Applied Research in Evaluation, Inc., 1962.

Bonney, W. C., and Foley, W. J.: The transition stage in group counseling in terms of congruity theory. *Journal of Counseling Psychology, 10:*136-138, 1963.

Cartwright, D., and Zander, A.: *Group Dynamics, Research and Theory*. New York, Har-Row, 1968.

Foley, W. J., and Bonney, W. C.: A developmental model for counseling groups. *Personnel and Guidance Journal, 44:*576-580, 1966.

George, C. E.: *Some Determinants of Small Group Effectiveness*. Research memorandum, Ft. Benning, Human Resources Research Organization, 1962.

Hollander, E. P.: *Leaders, Groups and Influence*. New York, Oxford U Pr, 1964.

NAME INDEX

A

Acheson, E., v, x, 144
Ackerman, N. W., 148, 160, 163, 179
Adler, A., 11, 12, 247-248, 259, 270, 272
Adler, K., 166, 179
Allen, R. D., 3-4, 5, 9, 10, 16, 21
Allport, G. W., 161, 179
Allred, G. H., 273, 282
Alper, T. G., 66, 85
Alschuler, A. S., 100, 102, 104, 143, 144
Altman, I., 54, 84, 88
American College Personnel Association Task Force on Group Procedures, 32
American Group Psychotherapy Association, 32, 176
American Medical Association's Council on Mental Health, 27, 32, 34
American Personnel and Guidance Association, 32, 139, 143, 176, 278, 305
American Psychiatric Association, 32
American Psychological Association, 31, 32, 139, 143, 305
American Society of Adlerian Psychology, 270
Ames, L. B., 38, 87, 148, 180
Amster, F., 83, 105, 143
Anderson, A. R., 55, 85
Ansbacher, H. L., 11, 21, 166, 179, 259, 282
Ansbacher, R. R., 11, 21, 259, 282
Arnold, D., 20
Aronson, E., 238, 244
Asbury, F. R., 87
Association for Specialists in Group Work (ASGW), 20
Atkin, 161
Ausubel, D. P., 148, 179

Axline, V. M., 90, 100, 131, 142, 143
Ayer, F. L., 149, 179

B

Bach, G. R., 46, 56, 58, 85, 156, 157, 161, 162, 164, 179, 332, 342
Back, K., 43, 87
Bales, R. F., 55, 57, 86, 99
Balzer, F. J., 87
Bandura, A., 83, 222, 233, 244
Barclay, J. R., 105, 143, 186, 214
Bartell, W. R., 172, 179
Bartelt, W., 273, 282
Barten, H. H., 166, 179
Bass, B. M., 56, 85
Bates, E., 287, 312
Beach, A. I., 225, 244
Beavin, J. H., 304, 312
Beck, D. F., 62, 85, 152, 153, 160, 179
Beebe, J., 46, 87
Bell, G. B., 55, 85
Bender, D., 100, 145
Benne, 58
Bennett, M. E., 9, 16, 21
Berenson, B. G., 40, 41, 50, 83, 86
Bergin, A. E., 170, 179
Bernard, H., 17
Berne, E., 44, 45, 86
Berzon, B., 32
Bessell, H., 102, 143
Between Parent and Child, 253
Beyer, L. M., 95, 461
A Bibliography of Adlerian Psychology, 270
Birdwhistell, R. L., 142
Birnbaum, M., 32
Blake, R. R., 55, 56, 86
Blakeman, J. D., 69, 70, 83, 86
Blocher, D. H., 38, 83, 86
Boggs, M., 287, 311, 312
Bonner, H., 14, 21

343

SUBJECT INDEX

A

Action techniques, ix, 64-65
Action therapy, 272
Activity group counseling, 68
  study of, experimental and control, 68-70
    criterion instrument in, 68, 69
    findings of, 69, 70
Activity-interview group counseling, *see* Group counseling, developmental
Adlerian group counseling, *see* Group counseling, Adlerian
Adlerian "open-door" treatment procedure, 11
Adolescence, 148
  period of, characterization of, 148-149
Adolescents, 148
  needs of, 148-152
    adult assistance in, 151-152
    characterization of, 148-149
    dependence and, 150-151
    rebellion and, 151
    summary of, 150
  problems of, 147-148
    description of, 148-149
Adolescent group counseling, x, xi, 147-178
  adolescent needs as goals for, 150
  adolescent problems and, 147-148
  approach to, eclectic, xi
  counselor qualifications for, 172-176
    counseling groups and, 174
    group counseling course, 174
    group dynamics laboratory, 174
    licensing process, 175-176
    practicum, 173-174, 175
    training problems and, 173
    training program, 173-175
  forces in, therapeutic, 152

  foundations of, theoretical, 152-158
    acceptance, 153
    attractiveness, 152
    belonging, 152-153
    commitment, 155
    communication, open, 156
    congruence, 156-157
    expectations, 154-155
    responsibility, 155-156
    security, 153-154
    tension, 157-158
  frequency, length, and duration of, 166
  goals of, client, 158-160
    counselor role in, 159-160
    intake interview for, 158-159
    setting of, initiation of, 158
  group setting for, 164
    space and equipment in, 164-165
  group size in, 165-166
    decision of, 166
    ideal, 165, 166
    increased, 165-166
    transference reactions and, 165
  initiation of, 167-170
    client selection for, 167-168
    counselor presentation for, 167
    discussions in, 169-170
    intake interviews for, 168
    introduction of group members in, 168
  interview group counseling in, 75, 79
  limitations of, 177-178
  psychodrama in, x
  readings in, selected, 178
  research in, 170-172
    focus of, 170
    improvement in, 171
    questions in, 170
    results of, 171-172
    techniques of, 170-171

351